Ultimate Catastrophe

How MtGox Lost Half a Billion Dollars and Nearly Killed Bitcoin

Mark Hunter

TULIP
—PUBLISHING—

Copyright © 2023 Mark Hunter

All rights reserved.

No portion of this book may be reproduced in any form without written permission from the publisher or author, except as permitted by UK copyright law.

ISBN: 9781068475580

Tulip Publishing,
27 Sutton Grange Close,
Harrogate,
England,
HG3 2UR

Second edition 2025

Also by the Author

Faketoshi - Fraud, Lies and the Battle for Bitcoin's Soul

For the creditors

About the Author

Mark Hunter is an author and ghostwriter with twenty years of experience in the literary world. He has ghostwritten for a very eclectic range of clients, from members of the Kuwaiti royal family to self-made millionaires, and has worked as a writing workshop leader in British theatres.

Mark became interested in the cryptocurrency world in 2017 and has been writing for blockchain projects and crypto sites ever since. He is the co-creator, writer, and co-host of the podcast series *Dr Bitcoin – The Man Who Wasn't Satoshi Nakamoto* and co-author of the resulting series of books, *Faketoshi - Fraud, Lies and the Battle for Bitcoin's Soul*.

Mark lives in Harrogate, England, with his wife and two children.

Contents

MtGox Loss Timeline viii
Author Notes ix
Introduction xiii
Chapter 1 – MtGox 15
Chapter 2 – MagicalTux 18
Chapter 3 – 1Feex 27
Chapter 4 – Compromised 33
Chapter 5 – The Google of Bitcoin 47
Chapter 6 – Growing Pains 52
Chapter 7 – Seizure 60
Chapter 8 – Pressure 69
Chapter 9 – Missing 83
Chapter 10 – Collapse 97
Chapter 11 – Sorry 108
Chapter 12 – Willy 117
Chapter 13 – Private Investigations 123
Chapter 14 – Fallout 127
Chapter 15 – Answers 132
Chapter 16 – Arrest 139
Chapter 17 – The Russian 152
Chapter 18 – On Trial 164
Chapter 19 – The Tokyo Whale 172
Chapter 20 – A Greek Drama 180
Chapter 21 – Gox Rising 185
Chapter 22 – Coinlab 190
Chapter 23 – Verdict 195
Chapter 24 – Identified 202
Chapter 25 – End in Sight 208
Chapter 26 – Legacy 219
Chapter 27 – Blame 224
Acknowledgements 234
References 235

MtGox Loss Timeline

Date	Event	Loss	BTC Losses	USD Losses
Jan 2011	Liberty Reserve API hacked	$50,000		$50,000
Mar 2011	Hot wallet stolen	฿79,957	฿79,957	$50,000
May 2011	Wallet compromised (hacker bounty)	฿3,000	฿82,957	$50,000
Jun 2011	Admin account compromised	฿2,000	฿84,957	$50,000
Jul 2011	Bitomat bailout	฿17,000	฿101,957	$50,000
Sep 2011	Server hacked	฿77,500	฿179,457	$50,000
Oct 2011	Mark Karpelès transaction error	฿2,609	฿182,066	$50,000
Oct 2011- Jan 2014	Hot wallet compromised	฿647,000	฿829,066	$50,000
Oct 2011- Jan 2014	Incorrectly detected deposits	฿30,000	฿859,066	$50,000
May 2013- Aug 2013	US law enforcement seizures	$5m	฿859,066	$5.05m
May 2013- Aug 2013	Coinlab payment	$5m	฿859,066	$10.05m
2011-2013	Gox Bots	฿22,800 + $51.6m	฿881,866	$61.65m

Author Notes

There are a few things that need explaining with regard to Bitcoin and MtGox before we begin. These will be addressed here.

Bitcoin

Almost any book that features Bitcoin starts with a description of what Bitcoin is and how it works. This was perhaps necessary many years ago, particularly at the time of MtGox's collapse in 2014 when Bitcoin was still seen as a kind of mysterious Internet money. Since then, however, times have changed. Billions of people worldwide have now heard about Bitcoin and know enough about it to not consider it a currency from Mars. They may not know the finer points, but they know what it does, or at least what it is supposed to do. As a result of this shift in understanding, it is my assumption that the people reading this book will have enough knowledge of Bitcoin, or at least interest in it, to understand the part it plays in the MtGox saga, which, in all honesty, is a minor one. This is a book about human failings such as dishonesty, ignorance and what happens when we fail to communicate. It's a book about how not to deal with a crisis and how many of us could have ended up in the position in which Mark Karpelès found himself in February 2014.

Bitcoin's meteoric rise between 2011 and 2014 was almost totally unanticipated, and MtGox just happened to be in the right place at the right time to capitalise on it – for a while at least. Were we able to cast the major players in this story back in time to the California gold rush or the Pennsylvania oil boom, we'd be telling the same story. For this reason, I have decided to eschew an explanation of Bitcoin and how it works, for, in truth, its role is relatively minor. Assets may change, but people don't.

Nomenclature

Naturally, this book uses the word 'Bitcoin' throughout, but there are different meanings attached to Bitcoin depending on how it is spelt:

- 'Bitcoin' – the system, overarching concept or brand
- 'bitcoin/s' – the coins/currency transmitted on the system

There is no concrete agreement on the plural of 'bitcoin', but given that Bitcoin's creator, Satoshi Nakamoto, used the term 'bitcoins' to refer to multiple coins, I shall do the same. When other cryptocurrencies are discussed alongside Bitcoin, its ticker (BTC) will be used. All references to dollars refer to American (US) dollars unless specified otherwise.

MtGox

When it comes to 'MtGox', multiple alternative spellings have been afforded to it over the years (e.g. Mt Gox, Mt.Gox, Mt. Gox). The only official word on this comes from a 2018 Reddit post from Mark Karpelès:

> *The official naming of the company is:*
>
> 株式会社*MTGOX*
>
> *But it can also be written 'MtGox Co., Ltd.' according to the company legal files as can be seen on all English translations on the mtgox.com site.*

For this reason, I have adopted the spelling 'MtGox' throughout.

When it comes to pronunciation, the commonly accepted version is 'Mount Gox', an inference drawn from the image of a mountain in the company logo and the connotation of strength and resilience that this supposedly imbues. In its heyday, some jokingly pronounced the name 'Em Tee Gox', which was far too close to 'empty Gox' for comfort, given the reason for its collapse. Mark Karpelès himself typically refers to 'Mount Gox' in interviews, and this is the generally accepted pronunciation.

Quotes

Many of the quotes in this book are posts from social media platforms and online forums. The nature of these posts means that spelling and grammar will be erratic. It is standard practice to use '[sic]' to indicate when a word has been copied in its original, misspelt form, but given the sheer volume of quotes used in this book, this would be impractical. As such, all quotes have been faithfully reproduced except where corrections are required to ensure comprehension.

Figures

The multiple hacks and financial misdemeanours surrounding MtGox have left a trail of six- and seven-figure losses that have changed over time as new research has come to light. For this reason, there may appear to be discrepancies throughout the book over individual and cumulative losses. This is inescapable, but consistency has been sought wherever possible, and any major discrepancies have been explained.

Introduction

It doesn't matter if you use the strongest bank vault in the world if you leave the keys out.

Kim Nilsson, MtGox investigator

The collapse of the Bitcoin exchange MtGox in February 2014 made headlines all around the world. The implosion of the poster child for the new financial frontier of Bitcoin was the culmination of years' worth of hacks, mistakes, bad decisions and fraud, all of which saw over 880,000 bitcoins and $61.5 million in cash reserves either stolen, given away or lost by MtGox in just three years. At the time of its demise, this loss was valued at around half a billion dollars. Today, the value of that loss exceeds $80 billion.

While the outside world was shocked that MtGox had lost so much money, those who had witnessed its slow death over the preceding months were less surprised. There had been rumblings that something was wrong at MtGox for almost a year before it went under, rumblings that had turned into warnings of a full-scale avalanche. The problem for those with funds on the exchange, however, was that they were stuck in the avalanche's path with no way out. Less than 3% of MtGox's million-plus customers made a claim when MtGox entered bankruptcy proceedings, and yet the total valuation attributed to these claims still reached $414 million. This group of 24,750 creditors had to endure a decade-long wait for payouts that at times seemed destined never to arrive, watching on as the value of Bitcoin rose more than 5,000% in the intervening years. Eventually, in early July 2024, these long-suffering customers began to be reunited with their holdings, although they had already steeled themselves to the fact that they could expect only a fraction back.

The story of exactly how MtGox lost half a billion dollars of its customers' money has been revealed in stages in the years since it collapsed, with the full story never yet told. A combination of debilitating hacks, poor coding, bad business decisions, rank amateurism and the actions of underhanded US officials caused MtGox to experience death by a thousand cuts until it finally expired on 28 February 2014. It wasn't until 2017 that the world finally found out how MtGox had been brought to its knees, and it took until 2023 for anyone behind the multiple hacks to be named. The search for truth has gone on as long as the creditors' search for recompense, and it is still going on.

One man has been at the centre of the MtGox storm ever since the first bitcoin was swiped from the exchange in March 2011: Mark Karpelès. The Frenchman, CEO of the company from early 2011 until he stepped down in March 2014 in the wake of its implosion, was immediately cast as the villain; some blamed the huge losses on his incompetent management, while others believed he was responsible for a record-breaking theft. While his customers have been engaged in a decade-long battle to get their bitcoins back, Karpelès has fought to clear his name. Many are still unwilling, despite the passage of time, to accept his version of events: that he had no idea of the scale of the loss and that his only crime was running the company badly. Karpelès has not kept quiet about his time running MtGox and has admitted some of his failings. As we will see, however, there are some crucial secrets that remain untold to this day.

The collapse of MtGox was the event that brought the exciting new world of Bitcoin, with its promise of a self-stored currency free from interference by banks and governments, back down to earth with a crash. It was the pin that burst the balloon, a balloon that has inflated and burst again repeatedly in the years since, but never to the same extent or with the same ideological fervour.

The rise and fall of MtGox isn't a story about Bitcoin or cryptocurrencies. It's a story about how the combination of criminal opportunism and stunning incompetence led to a multi-year theft that may one day be valued in the hundreds of billions of dollars. It's a cautionary tale about the dangers of covering up the truth and of what happens when these cover-ups are stretched to breaking point. It's a story of what happens when you feel the water lapping at your neck… and go off to design a café instead.

Mark Hunter

Harrogate, November 2023

Chapter 1 – MtGox

The story of MtGox doesn't start with Bitcoin. It starts, instead, with a card game. Magic: The Gathering, which launched in 1993, is a fantasy-themed collectable card game that has gone from being a Dungeons and Dragons-style niche pastime to an online phenomenon with thirty-five million players worldwide. It has dedicated YouTube channels that regularly pull in hundreds of thousands of viewers for each video. As an example of this astonishing growth, a rare, autographed Magic: The Gathering playing card sold in January 2021 for over half a million dollars.

Back in 2007, Magic: The Gathering was just starting to find its feet in the online world. Thirty-two-year-old programmer and entrepreneur Jed McCaleb, living in New York after dropping out of the University of California, Berkeley, had spent the past six years riding the peer-to-peer file-sharing wave with his platform eDonkey, which at its peak had four million users. eDonkey was effectively shut down by the Recording Industry Association of America (RIAA) in 2006 during what became known to many as the Napster Wars, a time when record companies sued file-sharing companies instead of capitalising on the coming MP3 boom. As a result of its transgressions, eDonkey was forced to pay a $30 million settlement fee to the RIAA and was prohibited from distributing its software.

By this time, McCaleb had moved his family to Costa Rica, primarily for the surfing, when he came across Magic: The Gathering. As he found his way around the game, one thing struck McCaleb: there was nowhere to trade cards online. He decided to do something about this, and in January 2007, he registered the domain 'mtgox.com' (Magic: The Gathering Online Exchange). McCaleb set about building an online exchange for Magic: The Gathering cards on mtgox.com but quickly got bored and moved on to other things. One fellow Magic: The Gathering player was gaming enthusiast and California State

University graduate, Jesse Powell, who was eager to trade cards on the new MtGox exchange and was disappointed when MtGox never made it further than a static web page. Powell would come to play a big part in the MtGox story, and the exchange, in turn, would come to play an even bigger part in his.

While McCaleb was letting his plans for the MtGox card exchange lapse, and Powell was founding the Verge Gallery & Studio Project in Sacramento, someone somewhere going by the pseudonym Satoshi Nakamoto was busy inventing Bitcoin. Jed McCaleb says that he first heard about Bitcoin on the social news website Slashdot in the summer of 2010, some eighteen months after the protocol went live. McCaleb found the concept of sending and receiving money peer-to-peer 'super powerful and awesome', and he wanted to get involved straight away. At this time, the chief Bitcoin communication forum, BitcoinTalk, had just a couple of hundred members, and the only recognised way to trade bitcoins was in person. Individuals wanting to buy or sell would arrange a deal on BitcoinTalk with someone in their neighbourhood, then meet up and make the exchange, with the transaction completed via digital wallets on phones or, more commonly, laptops. This may sound insanely dangerous now, but back then, Bitcoin had no value, so there was no real risk of being robbed, at least not for your bitcoins. This is in stark contrast to today, where tens of billions of dollars worth of bitcoins are traded on the world's exchanges on a daily basis, and in-person trades are almost unheard of.

McCaleb realised that this physical trading situation was problematic for several reasons, leading him to wonder why bitcoins couldn't be traded online, like stocks and shares. After all, having to trade an Internet-based currency in person was almost offensive to its very concept. McCaleb fired up his laptop, logged into mtgox.com and started converting it to a Bitcoin exchange, repurposing the matching system he had intended to use for his cards. After a few weeks' work, it was ready, and the exchange that McCaleb started for 'a lark', but that would turn into a multi-million dollar behemoth, was born. Contrary to popular belief, MtGox was not the first online Bitcoin exchange; Bitcoin Market had launched in February 2010, five months earlier, with its first trade taking place in March of that year. Indeed, when McCaleb announced MtGox on BitcoinTalk on 18 July, one of the first responses was, 'Why would I use MtGox instead of BitCoin Market?' McCaleb responded, '[MtGox] is always online, automated, the site is faster and on dedicated hosting and I think the interface is nicer.' But then he would say that.

The first trades on MtGox were conducted for just six cents per bitcoin, but McCaleb ran into instant problems when users wanted to get their cash off the platform. This would be a problem that would haunt MtGox for many years, and it has not gone away in the decade since; even today, the majority of banks and payment processors want nothing to do with cryptocurrency exchanges, and users face having cash withdrawal options pulled at short notice. The situation in 2010 was only different because most banks had no idea what Bitcoin was. MtGox launched with only PayPal support, which levied a 2.9% fee on all transactions, although other options, such as bank wires, were added later. Deposits through Liberty Reserve, an illegal Costa Rica-based pseudo-bank, would also be added in time. The issue for MtGox was that it had no bank accounts of its own through which to process transactions, with all the cash that flowed between MtGox and its customers coming through Jed McCaleb's personal accounts. McCaleb knew full well that this would inevitably result in him having his accounts shut down at some point, but he considered this a worthwhile sacrifice; he would use the borrowed time to attract users to the concept of an online Bitcoin exchange, earning money from the transaction fees as he built the user base and would deal with the bank account issues as they cropped up. This commingling of company funds with user funds would not stop with McCaleb and would come back to bite the exchange years down the line.

Early feedback on MtGox was positive, especially when McCaleb scrapped commission fees for PayPal transactions, but this honeymoon period didn't last long. After just three months of operation, PayPal banned McCaleb from sending money to and from MtGox, citing chargebacks and other types of fraud, and eventually hitting him with a lifetime ban. Still, McCaleb didn't mind; the user numbers were going slowly up, and there were always bank wires and Liberty Reserve to fall back on. Bitcoin deposits and withdrawals, of course, were uninterrupted, with no prying eyes watching over them at all.

With his exchange getting slowly into gear, McCaleb began trying to convert Bitcoin Market users to MtGox, being proactive with customer queries and feature requests and extolling the potential of his exchange over its rival. However, MtGox soon became a victim of its own success. Within weeks,

McCaleb was receiving wire transfers amounting to tens of thousands of dollars, and the responsibility of dealing with this amount of people's money, plus the workload of maintaining the exchange, was much more demanding than he had expected. Before long, McCaleb realised that there were three options open to him: go full-time, hire a team or get out. McCaleb toyed with the idea of raising money and building a team to run MtGox, but the thought of being a manager rather than a creator didn't appeal to him, especially when it came with the responsibility of hundreds of thousands of dollars of other people's cash and bitcoins. The day-to-day of running MtGox was not as 'intellectually interesting' a job as he was used to, and in late 2010, McCaleb began floating the idea that he was considering selling MtGox. One of those he sounded out was a French IT consultant who McCaleb had hired to do some work on MtGox's backend, an eccentric Japanophile with a love of apple quiche and no experience of running a cryptocurrency exchange whatsoever.

    His name was Mark Karpelès.

Chapter 2 – MagicalTux

Robert Marie Mark Karpelès was born on 1 June 1985 in Chenôve, France, to a geologist mother, Anne, and a father whose only reference is as the 'unknown' parent listed on Karpelès's birth certificate. He learnt how to read and count before primary school age, stunning his teacher at Dijon's Chevreul primary school in the process, before he was sent to the Collège Prieuré de Binson in the Champagne Valley. There, the shy and socially awkward boy was bullied by his classmates, an all-too-common treatment for the atypical at that age. Karpelès was frequently lambasted by his teachers and derided by his contemporaries for not being able to look them in the eye when conversing, a trait that is commonly associated with those on the autistic spectrum. This is far from the only such trait that Karpelès has displayed, both in public and privately to employees. Karpelès learnt to compensate by looking at the corner of people's eyes so that no one could tell he wasn't making direct eye contact. This, along with other strategies he developed over the following years, helped him 'pass myself off as human'. As a form of escape from the difficulties of the real world, Karpelès spent his free time devouring Japanese comics and getting into electronics and early computers, his first direct exposure having come around the age of five when Anne, a technophile herself, purchased a ZX Spectrum. A passion for video games and an early interest in computer coding soon developed, with the pair working together on a dinosaur-themed game.

By the age of seven, Karpelès had the intelligence of a twelve-year-old, but his inability to focus at school was causing problems. After the 'terrible student', in Anne's words, finished middle school, the pair moved to Paris, where Karpelès took and passed the Mensa entrance examination, such was his prodigious intelligence. In Paris, Karpelès was able to expand his passion for Japanese culture, which soon became an addiction, dragging his mother to the House of Culture of Japan most weekends. Karpelès showed his naivety when, in his first year of high school, he drew the attention of a criminal gang who blackmailed young people into handing over the credit cards and bank account details of family members, which they would use to buy hundreds of mobile phones that they would then sell at a low price. Anne says that Karpelès's activity in this arena caused both her and her mother's bank accounts to be wiped out before he was extricated from the gang's clutches. It was a sign, however, that the big city might not be the best fit for him.

Having no interest in pursuing further studies, Karpelès left home shortly after finishing school in 2003 and temporarily lived a nomadic lifestyle, fighting depression as he battled to find his place in the world. He got occasional work handing out flyers or working in Internet cafés and spent his nights sleeping rough in the stairwells of apartment blocks, having gained entry by memorising access codes entered by residents who were unaware they were being watched. Karpelès eventually found a more suitable job as a developer for his favourite online role-playing game, GraalOnline, after he emailed the game's management asking if he could help out. Freed from the awkwardness of face-to-face interactions, Karpelès felt much more at home behind the protective barrier of a computer screen and adopted the moniker MagicalTux, a name inspired by Tux, the penguin mascot of the Linux operating system.

Karpelès's mother and grandmother were still feeling the effects of his involvement with the gang, however, and wanting to relieve Anne of the burden of having him around, Karpelès moved out and rented a small studio flat around the corner. Soon after this, he landed himself a job as a software developer and network administrator for a small company called Linux Cyberjoueurs, although this first taste of proper employment ended badly. Karpelès didn't get on with his boss or the work, which he found menial for a man of his talents, and used a new blog under the MagicalTux name to complain about both, as well as explain his struggle with depression. In a bid to make his work life more interesting, Karpelès pushed his role further than his job description, developing and implementing a new security protocol, but then he took things too far; he began exfiltrating customer data to his own server and bought a domain name featuring the company name. The company director suspected a scam, but Karpelès quit before he could be investigated over it, having lasted two years in the role. Nevertheless, the company director filed a police complaint about Karpelès, alleging computer fraud. This resulted in a trial, which Karpelès did not attend, and a one-year suspended sentence for the Frenchman.

With this unpleasant experience under his belt, Karpelès moved to Israel to set up his own server company in 2005, but this was curtailed in August when the Israeli disengagement from Gaza sparked the Gaza–Israel conflict. Karpelès returned to France, where a friend's influence helped him land another developer role before he was hired by e-commerce platform Nexway in the same position in 2006. His MagicalTux blog, which had been flourishing in the past year thanks to his frequent posting, had earned him quite a following in the online computing community, a notoriety that didn't go unnoticed; in 2007, he was contacted by a filmmaker who was planning to document the cyber culture in France. Karpelès's appearance in *Nuit Du Geek* (Suck My Geek) represented his unveiling as MagicalTux and amplified his reputation still further with the community. In the film, Karpelès is seen discussing life as a cyber geek, working away on various computers and discussing his love of Japanese anime, showing off his trinkets and gadgets.

Karpelès's penchant for livening up his working life with a little under-the-counter skulduggery reappeared in his role with Nexway, where his boss, Gilles Ridel, noticed that the Frenchman was carrying out what to him appeared to be hacking activities on company time and machines. These were eventually curbed, but when interviewed for a 2022 documentary on Karpelès, Ridel explained how his employee had behaved:

> *We are in this world, it's kids moving forward. If you don't tap them on the fingertips they advance, they have no limits. That's Mark. If you don't tell him to stop, he advances. If you tell him to stop, he understands.*

As we will see, Mark Karpelès's inability to know when to stop would turn out to be instrumental in the collapse of MtGox.

Karpelès got wind of Nexway expanding to his beloved Japan and pushed to be the one to lead it, eventually being granted the opportunity. In June 2009, the delighted Karpelès realised a twenty-year dream and relocated to Tokyo on Nexway's dime. It was everything he had imagined, from the politeness of the people to the social and technological advances which had led to it becoming a technophile's Nirvana. At last, he was able to embrace the areas of his life that he had kept in the shadows for two decades. Karpelès had, perhaps unsurprisingly given that he had been reading Manga since his childhood, already learnt Japanese to a proficient standard, which allowed him to settle into life in Tokyo almost instantly.

It didn't take long for the new Mark Karpelès to branch out. In October, he founded Tibanne (named after the favourite of his pet cats but spelt with two 'n's), a company that offered server support, web and mobile applications and other IT services. This was followed by the web hosting company KalyHost, which he put under Tibanne's umbrella. His companies became popular, and he soon took on staff, although he still dealt with technical queries from customers himself due to his inability to trust others to do the work to the requisite standard, another failing that would be instrumental in the downfall of MtGox.

Karpelès time in Tokyo also brought about his introduction to Bitcoin; a KalyHost customer was having trouble getting a credit card and asked if he could pay for the services with bitcoins instead. Karpelès investigated the digital currency and was hooked at once. This led to KalyHost becoming one of the first, and possibly *the* first, Japanese companies to accept bitcoins as payment for goods or services. Karpelès ingratiated himself with the fledgling Bitcoin community, registering on BitcoinTalk in November 2010 (as MagicalTux, naturally), but by this time, he was already working for MtGox. In mid-2010, Karpelès's name had been mentioned to Jed McCaleb as someone who could help with MtGox's banking telecommunications, especially concerning API integration. McCaleb gave Karpelès the work, with the Frenchman proving himself competent at it. As their relationship developed, and as McCaleb began to search for a way out of MtGox, the founder began to see Karpelès as someone who might be tempted to take it off his hands. On 18 January 2011, McCaleb sent Karpelès an email:

Hi Mark,

Please keep all this confidential. I don't want to start a panic and I'm not sure I'll do it yet but I'm thinking I might try to sell mtgox. I just have these other projects I would like to devote more time to.

Would you be interested? It could be very little up front and just a payout based on revenue or something.

There is also an investment group that wants to fund mtgox. Probably around $150k. So you could most likely take it over with some cash.

Let me know,

Thanks,

Jed.

Karpelès replied that he was indeed interested, but he was strapped for cash, to which McCaleb responded with a proposal of a deal based purely on future revenues: a six-month 50% profit share, with McCaleb retaining a 12% share of the company. Karpelès was sorely tempted by the offer and didn't baulk at the fact that he wasn't being asked to put any money down for MtGox. He was also not put off when McCaleb said that full financial disclosure wasn't possible because he was still using his personal bank accounts for MtGox business, but Karpelès had been working on MtGox affairs for a few months and was getting a feel for how the business was being run. He also 'didn't want to risk losing [the offer] by wasting time' digging into the financial situation surrounding the exchange. After all, he was a techie, not a businessman.

The deal was thrashed out, with McCaleb insisting that some key terms be included in the contract the pair signed. These included the assertions that 'The Seller is uncertain if mtgox.com is compliant or not with any applicable US code or statute, or law of any country', and that 'The buyer agrees to indemnify Seller against any legal action that is taken against Buyer or Seller with regards to mtgox.com or anything acquired under this agreement'. This, Karpelès would later acknowledge, was his first, and perhaps gravest, mistake; he based his decision almost solely on the trust he had built up with McCaleb through their work together rather than sound business principles, as he relayed in a 2019 interview:

> *I'd been running a business alone without much budget, so there was no real due diligence except for confirming Jed's identity. Well, I used MtGox myself, so I knew it worked. So that was actually about it.*

Karpelès would later summarise the sale by saying that he ignored the 'huge red flags' and that he 'didn't expect [McCaleb] to screw me over' with the deal. Indeed, the way McCaleb went about sourcing his successor, the way the deal was structured and the clauses that were inserted into the contract all suggest a less-than-pure motive on McCaleb's part. A Reuters article from April 2014 cited people with knowledge of the deal as saying that McCaleb was 'nervous about regulatory scrutiny on bitcoin' and wanted rid of the site, and it is hard to shake the impression that McCaleb got exactly what he wanted from the deal and, to an extent, sold Karpelès nothing but a ticking time bomb. Of course, Karpelès made huge errors himself and was by no means forced to take over MtGox, but there is no doubt that the deal massively favoured McCaleb, who would enjoy the fruits of any gains that MtGox might make while absolving himself of all responsibility if things turned sour. The contract was signed on 3 February 2011, and the handover of MtGox from Jed McCaleb to Mark Karpelès began.

One thing that certainly wasn't mentioned in the contract was that Mark Karpelès was taking over a company that was already in debt. Jed McCaleb had noted that hackers had been 'probing' the site from day one, testing its security and seeing if they could mess with it in any way. Given that Bitcoin barely had a valuation in these early days, there was no financial motive for doing so, meaning it was a case of hackers simply exercising their skills. Various potential exploits were uncovered and patched in the first few months, but nothing serious was ever discovered. Nevertheless, there were 'weird things happening' all the time in those early years, according to McCaleb, which he was perpetually trying to combat.

The hack that put MtGox into debt occurred after just six months and concerned Liberty Reserve. The Costa Rican outfit used proprietary currencies in the form of Liberty Reserve Dollars to shift client funds around the world free from the gaze of financial regulators and police. A network of third-party currency processors deposited these funds into any bank account in the world, which Liberty Reserve's operators thought would help them fly beneath the regulatory radar. The anonymity provided to clients ensured that it became a haven for operators of the worst types of criminal activity. Back in October 2010, McCaleb had ditched PayPal as the main funding option for MtGox and had switched to Liberty Reserve, with a connection built into the backend of MtGox which allowed Liberty Reserve Dollars to be sent between the two platforms. However, McCaleb made some mistakes when adding the service, meaning that with a simple code patch, a user could get more money out of MtGox than they requested, a little like an ATM handing out twenties instead of tens. However, this wasn't the only flaw in McCaleb's integration of Liberty Reserve; users were also able to type in how much money they wanted to withdraw, but the code neglected to account for negative inputs. The upshot of this was that, in addition to getting more than they asked for, users were also able to withdraw money they didn't actually have in their accounts. $50,000 was stolen from MtGox between 20 and 23 January 2011 in this way before the exploit was found and the code patched. This was a warning shot across the bows for Karpelès, who knew he was taking over a company already $50,000 in the hole, but it was one he wouldn't heed.

On 6 March 2011, Jed McCaleb took to BitcoinTalk to inform the community of the change of ownership:

Hello Everyone.

I created mtgox on a lark after reading about bitcoins last summer. It has been. I'm still very confident that bitcoins have a bright future. But to really make mtgox what it has the potential to be would require more time than I have right now. So I've decided to pass the torch to someone better able to take the site to the next level.

MagicalTux has already contributed a lot to the bitcoin community and in many ways he will be better at running the site than I was. He has much more experience with web programming, system administration and integrating with banks and other payment processors than I do.

Karpelès replied to say that his priorities would be to provide 'a legal context around mtgox' as well as 'increases in security'. While some welcomed the new ownership, others weren't convinced:

Believe the new owner is in japan if he's the same guy running kalyhost. Which is not good considering [the] epic disaster.

This was in reference to the earthquake and tsunami that rocked Japan in March 2011 and which led to huge concerns over the safety of the Fukushima power plant, the collapse of which would have led to the evacuation of Tokyo and surrounding areas, directly impacting Karpelès and MtGox's operations. Mike Caldwell, the creator of the famous Casascius bitcoins, replied that he wasn't convinced about the security of MtGox regardless of its owner:

You know what, for what it's worth, I would leave money in MtGox if I weren't afraid of losing it there (getting shutdown, hackers, whatever)...I feel that if bitcoins were to drop a bunch, I'd wire something to MtGox and make a nice buy and then try to withdraw it quickly and stash it in an offline wallet. Maybe others would too. If it drops below 0.80, I doubt it'll stay there for long. If my faith meter in MtGox were much higher, the money would already be there in the form of outstanding buy orders.

Caldwell's words would prove to be very prophetic, but for now, MtGox had a new man in charge, and the exchange was preparing to help drive Bitcoin and itself to bigger and brighter horizons.

Chapter 3 – 1Feex

The transfer of MtGox from Jed McCaleb to Mark Karpelès was slated to be conducted in three stages, starting in February 2011. First, Karpelès would get access to the server and the hot wallets, then the cold wallets and finally the domain and registration. To put Bitcoin wallets into context, if we equate a Bitcoin exchange to a physical branch of a bank, a hot wallet is the money in the cashier's till that is used to handle everyday deposits and withdrawals, while a cold wallet is the money in the vault, only accessed when the tills need topping up. Hot wallets are connected to the Internet at all times, whereas cold wallets should be completely cut off, and access to them should be strictly controlled in order to minimise potential infiltration from hackers.

This dual-layer approach is one of the reasons why there is some debate over whether MtGox was solvent or not when Mark Karpelès took it over. Jed McCaleb, obviously, says that it wasn't ('there was somebody running it that had funds to keep it alive and pay people if they needed to') and believed that the business was on track to make a million dollars in a matter of weeks anyway. Mark Karpelès knew that the company was $50,000 in debt, but couldn't be sure of its true financial state because he had been unable to get a full financial breakdown of MtGox before taking over. The debate over MtGox's insolvency rests on one's definition of 'insolvent', which Cornell Law School describes thus:

> *The solvency diagnosis often varies depending on the solvency test that is applied; solvency under the one test does not imply solvency under another, and vice versa, because they measure different things. It is important to employ the appropriate definition of insolvency depending on the context because solvent firms may do things that insolvent firms cannot, such as pay dividends.*

One could argue, therefore – as McCaleb did – that MtGox was not technically insolvent when Karpelès took over because it was still able to pay its bills, its contractors and its staff. However, MtGox was far from a complex multinational company that paid dividends, and so using the simple balance sheet insolvency method (where the value of the assets is balanced against the value of the debts), MtGox was indeed technically insolvent at the point that Karpelès took over.

Whether it was technically insolvent or not, MtGox was certainly in trouble as Karpelès was taking the reins thanks to a second hack that took place in early March 2011. To this day, it's not clear how hackers managed to gain access to the MtGox servers during this handover period, but gain access they did. Jed McCaleb admitted in a 2019 interview that he may have overlooked some security patches on the servers, which were co-located, meaning that they were in two different geographic locations but linked over a network. However, he insisted that Karpelès had equal access at that point in the handover, leaving him open to culpability. Karpelès, conversely, says he *didn't* have access at that point in time. However it happened, the hackers got into the MtGox servers on or around 1 March and stole a copy of the hot wallet in the form of a single file called 'wallet.dat'. Back in these early days of Bitcoin, wallet files were unencrypted, meaning the hackers could whip the file off to their own computer, resurrect the wallet and withdraw all the coins in it, which they did, barring a few. The result was the loss of 79,957 bitcoins, representing around a third of the total customer deposits, with the other two-thirds still being in Jed McCaleb's possession. The coins were sent to an address beginning '1Feex', an address that has gone down in Bitcoin folklore for a couple of reasons that we'll come to very soon.

The theft went unnoticed for forty-eight hours, mainly down to the fact that there were just enough bitcoins to carry on operations, even though MtGox was running, as future investigator Kim Nilsson would later say, 'on fumes'. McCaleb discovered the theft on 3 March and told Karpelès about it through a Skype chat in which he revealed (in a rather understated way) that 'something bad happened' and that 'all the bitcoins is gone.' The pair discussed how to tackle the theft, with McCaleb saying something concerning the entire database that would turn out to be very prescient indeed:

Oh, one ugly thing would be if they grabbed the user table.

A shocked Karpelès replied, 'Passwords are not encrypted?' to which McCaleb replied that they were, but only with MD5 encryption, a form of encryption that had been cracked three years before MtGox even launched. Such was its age, it was no longer thought to be secure by anyone in the IT security business. The value of the 1Feex theft was only around $73,000 at the time, but the true cost to the exchange and Mark Karpelès himself would end up being far, far higher.

Karpelès wasn't sure whether to open up about the 1Feex hack, debating whether he could keep everything under wraps long enough to fill the hole, at which point the issue would be remedied. The alternative was admitting the theft now, which would invite a huge backlash and a possible exodus from the platform. He took the former option. In the years since the collapse, Karpelès has tried to excuse his decision to keep quiet about the 1Feex hack, but his reasoning is far from sound. One argument he has made is that he had signed a non-disclosure agreement (NDA), which he would have breached by bringing in outside help. However, the NDA was with his own company, so Karpelès was at perfect liberty to break it if he thought it necessary for the company's health. As for the worry about people deserting the exchange, this was, of course, a valid concern, but it would have blown over. As we will see, Karpelès's alternative actions contributed massively to the demise of the exchange, a far worse fate than a temporary drop in user numbers.

Eight weeks after the hack, the stolen 79,957 bitcoins were still a topic of conversation between Karpelès and McCaleb, with McCaleb pitching three potential solutions for making up the shortfall via email:

> *I can't tell how big an issue it will be to be short 80k bitcoins (*80,000 bitcoin) if the price goes to $100 or something. That is quite a bit to owe at that point but mtgox should have made a ton of bitcoins (Bitcoin) getting to there. There is also still the fact that the bitcoins (Bitcoin) balance will probably never fall below 80k. So maybe you don't really need to worry about it.*
>
> *There are 3 solutions I have thought of:*
>
> *- Slowly buy more bitcoins with the USD that Gox Bot has. Hopefully you would fill up the loss before the price got out of hand.*

- Buy a big chunk of bitcoins (really just moving the bitcoins debt to the USD side). If bitcoins goes up this is a huge win. Problem is there isn't enough bitcoins for sale on mtgox. Maybe you could find someone on the forum to do it.

- Get those crystal island people to invest. They have 200[000]+ bitcoins so they could fill in the gap.

Maybe you could just mine it?

The existence of a 'Gox Bot' is highly significant to the MtGox story, making it all the more intriguing that its operation as far back as April 2011 was only revealed two years after the exchange imploded. The Gox Bot was designed to do one thing: buy bitcoins on the sly, using company profits to purchase the coins from MtGox itself, thus repairing the hole left by the 1Feex hack. The concept would hang on the price of Bitcoin remaining low enough for the incoming USD to buy the requisite number of bitcoins over time. It seems from McCaleb's email that the Gox Bot had already been working away to repair the damage by this point, with Karpelès himself saying in 2018 that when he took over MtGox, the Gox Bot was already operational. Karpelès decided, fatefully, to continue to use the Gox Bot to buy back the missing bitcoins, deciding that it was his responsibility as MtGox owner to make up for the loss and calculating that he could plug the hole by 2013. He was, however, starting to wonder what on earth he had gotten himself involved in; running MtGox was nothing like what he had expected it would be, but he felt 'bound to this position', given that he couldn't leave the company in its present state for moral and legal reasons. Only once the debt was cleared could he even think of quitting MtGox.

On a side note, there is a strange story to tell regarding the 1Feex coins, which are, at the time of writing, still sitting in the address, untouched by the hackers ever since they were stolen. Already semi-famous following the collapse of MtGox, the coins enjoyed a new notoriety in 2020 when Australian computer security consultant Craig Wright, the creator of the Bitcoin fork BSV, made the astonishing claim that the coins were, in fact, his. Wright claimed that he bought the coins from a Russian currency exchange, WMIRK, in February 2011 and that the movement of the coins to the 1Feex address was simply the coins being deposited to him. Wright produced a purchase order to support his alleged acquisition, but it contained a litany of inconsistencies and basic errors that thoroughly undermined his case: the Bitcoin exchange rate was more than twenty times higher than the actual price at the time; the template on which the purchase order was based didn't go online until 2015; WMIRK didn't deal in bitcoins until 2013; and neither the entity that Wright says bought the coins nor the one that took over ownership of them were in existence on the dates they allegedly did so. The purchase order was used as evidence in a lawsuit Wright filed against sixteen blockchain developers in 2022, in which he alleged that a gang had broken into his home, infiltrated his home network and stolen the private key to the 1Feex address. This, he said, rendered him the victim of the biggest heist in world history at the time; the value of the bitcoins and the equal number of BCH and BSV coins created when those protocols forked in 2017 and 2018, respectively, amounted to more than a billion dollars. However, not only did the British police never ask for assistance from the public in identifying the gang, but they never made the 'hack' public at all. This is, perhaps, an indication of their level of faith in Wright's story, and indeed, Justice Mellor, the UK High Court judge who oversaw Wright's lawsuit, found his case to be 'totally without merit'. The entire story of Wright's alleged ownership and theft of the 1Feex coins is worthy of a Hollywood film and is laid out in its full glory across several episodes of the *Dr Bitcoin – The Man Who Wasn't Satoshi Nakamoto* podcast.

Back in the land of MtGox, to hide the loss of the 79,957 bitcoins and prevent anyone from potentially finding out about it, Mark Karpelès embarked on a process of locking everything down so that no one, not even the company's accountants, would be able to uncover the truth about the exchange's financial situation. His first employee, Ashley Barr (AKA Adam Turner), discovered this shortly after being hired in June 2011; Barr found a 'garden-walled' system to be in place, which meant running every decision past Karpelès and, crucially, not being allowed access to the company's financial infrastructure or performance data. This meant that the Gox Bot could work out of sight behind the wall, trying to recoup the stolen coins and allowing Karpelès to put the hack behind him and concentrate on growing the exchange. And grow it did, helped in no small measure by *Time* magazine, which featured Bitcoin in a piece for the first time on 16 April 2011. The resultant exposure saw user numbers rocket from 3,000 to an incredible 60,000 within a matter of weeks, although none of these users were aware that two hacks had already taken place and that MtGox was currently $50,000 and almost 80,000 bitcoins in debt.

So far.

Chapter 4 – Compromised

Three months down the road from the 1Feex hack, life at MtGox had calmed down somewhat. Jed McCaleb was now completely off the scene, having left to create his own cryptocurrency company, Ripple Labs, leaving Karpelès to build MtGox solo. This mainly involved 'fixing issues with Jed's code' because there were 'a lot of very basic mistakes or issues' that were perhaps forgivable with an exchange that served 'a handful of customers', but not for one with ambitions the size of MtGox's. In fact, the issues were so numerous that Karpelès would later admit that he shouldn't have run it as he had found it, although he tempered this admission by adding that many of the issues were initially undetectable and that there was 'no way for me to find all of this unless I spend a lot of time reading through all of the existing code.' This, many argued after MtGox's collapse, was exactly what Karpelès *should* have done: stripped it back to the bare bones and rebuilt it.

To make matters worse, Karpelès was trying to fix the fundamentals while dealing with the exponentially growing user base, thanks to the *Time* piece. Perhaps unsurprisingly, MtGox was struggling to cope with the sudden influx, but Karpelès didn't help matters by insisting that he personally verify accounts, a microcosm of the issues that would end up severely hampering the exchange over the coming years. Karpelès did, however, find time for oddities such as buying the rights to the Bitcoin trademark, a somewhat leftfield move that would prove to be idiosyncratic of its leader. By this point, MtGox had grown so big that Karpelès, much though he would have preferred, could not continue doing everything himself. He took on Barr, who would be the first person to experience life under the enigmatic Frenchman. Barr grew quickly frustrated by the lack of trust placed in him despite his important role as a recruiter, frequently finding it difficult to answer questions asked by candidates on certain elements of the company and either having to disguise his inability to do so or simply admitting that he didn't know. Things got worse when Karpelès informed Barr of his conviction over the computer fraud in France, which Barr says contributed to him disbelieving anything Karpelès told him after just a month at MtGox. Barr also claims that Karpelès asked him to take over as CEO in January 2012 and find new investors for the company, something that Barr said would be impossible if he didn't have access to the company's financials. Karpelès refused, which resulted in Barr and some other employees doing their best to work out an approximate balance sheet and cash flow from the figures they could lay their hands on. The results worried them:

> *The expenditures far exceeded every model we had for income. I confronted Mark about it, told him I couldn't take the role if he couldn't explain this gross incompetence in spending (he was also asking employees other than myself to find investors...something impossible without knowing the financial status of the company).*

Barr duly turned down the promotion and set about warning investors about the 'missing money', which resulted in them all backing out. Barr also says that these exploratory efforts yielded another shocking result: MtGox was still only using one bank account, a personal account owned by Mark Karpelès, representing the continuation of illegal commingling of company and personal funds. This, he says, was the 'nail in the coffin' for his faith in Karpelès and signalled the end of his time with the company; he left in May 2012, taking a 10,000 bitcoin severance payment with him. Barr's decision to warn potential MtGox investors of the issues he had discovered but refrain from warning customers drew heavy criticism following the collapse of MtGox, but his rationale for keeping quiet both during and after his time there was, he says, based on self-preservation:

> *I explained the situation to anyone who would listen, but I certainly would have voided my NDA, which would have meant I needed to pay back the amount of bitcoin I initially received, plus any damages to the company. Mark has excellent lawyers, I almost certainly would have lost, and that loss would have meant that I would have spent the rest of my life paying him back.*

The 10,000 bitcoin payout was, Barr says, simply the result of him demanding a year's salary as severance. He expected Karpelès to negotiate him down, but Karpelès simply asked if he could pay the bulk in bitcoins, which Barr accepted.

June 2011 saw MtGox move into a new office to house its expanding team, which soon included three more support staff members. Shortly after this, Karpelès married and fathered a child, but his focus remained on the baby he was already supposed to be looking after, a responsibility he was struggling with. This struggle was reflected in an incident that could and really should have killed MtGox three years before its eventual demise. One day in May 2011, Karpelès's home router failed, and to try and get it back online, he hooked it up to a computer. This computer was connected to a network drive that contained a portion of MtGox customers' bitcoins, which were being held there while Karpelès was carrying out his maintenance work. An opportunistic thief who clearly knew something about Karpelès and MtGox just happened to be online at the time and saw a private network with a shared drive. The drive had a Bitcoin wallet on it, which, upon opening, the hacker found contained 300,000 bitcoins. And so he took them.

Fortunately for Karpelès, the thief realised that there was no way he could cash out this huge sum without being caught, so he contacted the Frenchman to arrange a partial return. Once he had gotten over the shock of losing 300,000 bitcoins without noticing (not an entirely unfamiliar situation, as we will see), Karpelès and the hacker negotiated a 1% bounty. Panicking at just how severe the repercussions would be if the hacker didn't stick to his word, Karpelès refreshed his Bitcoin wallet every few seconds once the deal had been agreed, praying that the coins would come back. To his unutterable relief, 297,000 bitcoins did indeed arrive back into the wallet, and the Frenchman could breathe again. It was another cannonball across the bows, but it meant more debt for MtGox.

If Karpelès thought he was out of the woods, however, he was in for a shock. Just days after this incident, on 15 June, a Bitcoin blogger by the name of Buttcoin posted about a mysterious tip he'd been sent:

> *There is a pastebin post going around that was created by a group called Buttsec. They claim to have 'compromised' MTGOX and possibly other play money-to-real money sites.*

The post took Karpelès to a website for Buttsec, which made the following concerning claim:

> *MtGox users,*
>
> *Have you noticed some recent cases of large sums of Bitcoins being stolen? MtGox has been compromised. Word is there will surely be more users who are robbed of their Bitcoins.*
>
> *Bad news: MtGox is fucked.*

Indeed, MtGox users *had* noticed bitcoins going missing from their accounts, and they were kicking up a stink about it. In the days before the post was published, complaints had started trickling in of users logging into their accounts to find that they had been emptied. This trickle turned into a flow, with losses of up to 25,000 bitcoins reported by mid-2011. At the same time, Ashley Barr was receiving emails regarding a potential vulnerability, emails that Karpelès was ignoring because he thought them 'unworthy' to address. These were the tremors before the eruption, and Karpelès was not listening to them. Instead, on 18 June, he denied accusations of a wholesale security breach:

> *Ok, we've been seeing a 'lot' of cases [of theft] recently. So far I have 10 known cases of people whose coins were stolen (someone logged in on the account using their password, traded USD for bitcoins, withdrew all the bitcoins). Considering we have now over 60,000 accounts, this seems to be a problem coming mainly from users.*
>
> *Problem is many have been posting in various places (forums, reddit, twitter, irc, etc) causing a lot of fear among users when the problem is still fairly limited.*
>
> *Trust me, if we had a problem in Mt.Gox and it was actively exploited, we'd have way more than a dozen compromised accounts.*

Users were naturally affronted that Karpelès was blaming them for having weak passwords instead of looking inside MtGox for the issue, a theory that was tested the very next day when another message from the hacker appeared:

> *I have hacked into mtgox database. Got a huge number of logins password combos. mtgox has fixed the problem now. Too late, cause I've already got the data. Will sell the database for the right price.*

The potency of the hack was initially dismissed by MtGox customers, with some even mocking the hacker over his amateurish approach, but their hubris was soon undermined when the entire database was leaked online, including usernames, email addresses and passwords in an 'unsalted' manner. This was the 'ugly' thing that Jed McCaleb had referred to when he and Karpelès had been discussing the ramifications of the 1Feex hack earlier in the year. MtGox customer and future investigator Kim Nilsson described the importance of salting in a 2019 interview:

> *That is a technical term that basically just means that if a hacker gets into the system, or is able to copy your user's table, it's much simpler for them to start cracking passwords. 'Salting' passwords is basically a method where you make it much harder for hackers to crack those hashes. But in Jed's version it was just a simple MD5 hash with no salting and there's very strong reasons to believe that this user's table was compromised and taken out at some previous point in time.*

This 'previous point in time' was almost certainly the still secret 1Feex hack, and the fact that Karpelès had not upgraded the database protection from MD5 became a source of incredulity from knowledgeable Bitcoin users. It's highly likely that the user database, complete with passwords, was taken in the same hack that saw the 79,957 bitcoins stolen, and now the hacker was starting to use it. When presented with evidence that the database had been stolen, Karpelès doubled down:

> *Password are encrypted one way (+salt). Someone cannot be selling 'user + pass' (password) unless he has some way to revert this.*
>
> *In one expression: FUD*

In cryptocurrency vernacular, FUD means 'fear, uncertainty and doubt', or concerns raised with no evidence or basis in fact. Karpelès stuck to his guns that a database leak could not have been responsible for the thefts that were mounting across the platform, stating to one user that 'we assume no responsibility should your funds be stolen by someone using your own password'. The question of whether it was users or MtGox who was truly to blame for the losses was answered just hours later when, at 3 a.m. Tokyo time, Karpelès was woken by a phone call that informed him that the site had been overloaded and crashed by massive trading volume. Karpelès logged on and was shocked to find that the price of Bitcoin had cratered from $17.50 to $0.01 in a matter of hours, driven by massive sell volume on MtGox.

Realising that something was seriously wrong, Karpelès pulled the plug on the exchange to prevent it from coming back online and scrambled to find out how the price could have been crushed to such a spectacular extent. There was nothing regarding Bitcoin itself that could have led to people wanting to desperately cash out, so Karpelès and his team dug into the details of the sellers or, as it would turn out, the seller; one customer had gone on a five-figure selling spree and forced the price down. It wasn't immediately clear how the sole account holder responsible for the crash had gotten hold of so many bitcoins to fund his selling spree, but it was apparent that a feature of the exchange had prevented massive losses. All non-verified accounts had a daily $1,000 withdrawal limit in cash and bitcoins, which, in the case of this hack, limited the losses to just 2,000 bitcoins. As Karpelès acknowledged the following day, this withdrawal limit saved the exchange from an untimely end, although, of course, his customers didn't know that this was the second such incident in a matter of weeks.

Initial investigations into the hack revealed that the individual responsible had somehow gained access to the backend of the site and simply awarded themselves tens of thousands of bitcoins, which they had then sold for whatever price they could fetch, driving the value into the ground as a result. Karpelès quickly realised that because the bitcoins the user had awarded themselves weren't 'real', he could just rewind the transactions to the state before the hacker started selling. He couldn't get back the 2,000 bitcoins the hacker had taken off the exchange because they *were* real, but the rest were just numbers. However, this would also reverse the transactions of legitimate buyers who had taken the opportunity to scoop up cheap bitcoins, including those who had had orders sitting at lower levels for months, hoping for a day just like this. Ignoring their complaints, Karpelès emailed users and added a note to the MtGox site:

> *The bitcoin will be back to around 17.5$ per bitcoin after we rollback all trades that have happened after the huge Bitcoin sale that happened on June 20th near 3:00am JST (japanese standard time).*

The notice also offered an update on the allegations of a leaked database:

Leaked information includes username, email and hashed password, which does not allow anyone to get to the actual password, should it be complex enough. If you used a simple password you will not be able to login on Mt.Gox until you change your password to something more secure. If you used the same password on different places, it is recommended to change it as soon as possible.

Here, then, was an admission that the database had, in fact, been leaked after all, and users were not happy:

F$% THIS.*

You know I had alot of faith in Mtgox. Even when alot of dumb ass conspiracy theroys started to pop up. Now seeing my email and login info. Im done. Thats a 100% die hard support to 100% against using mt gox. I want my money and I want it now!

You were stupid and ill equipped, and you should admit defeat.

This is my take as well. The fact is that you were compromised. We've all seen absolute proof. When you decided you were going to move into real commodities of significant value, along with seeing dollar signs, you should have made SURE you were secure. This is on you. Most people will cut you a break, but you were lax on your security. You saw $ signs, got greedy, and didnt take necessary precautions.

One respondent on the Y Combinator forum opined with regard to the MD5 encryption used to protect the data, 'There should be capital punishment in software development for things like that.' Another respondent on Reddit added that 'salted or not, they should not be using MD5 at all. For a financial institution to use MD5 shows a complete lack of intelligence.' Karpelès tried to quell the angry mob by stating that he had begun criminal proceedings and was already working with the FBI to try and identify the hackers, aware that news of the hack and the resultant crash was already making global headlines. Users threatened lawsuits over the rolled-back trades, including the 650 people who had managed to scoop up bargain bitcoins that they were about to lose, but no lawsuits ever materialised.

With the bleeding staunched, attention turned to how the hackers had gotten in. The customer database was known to have been compromised, but even if the hacker had access to every single customer account, they shouldn't have been able to do anything more than steal the bitcoins already assigned to them. The kind of manipulation the hacker was able to enjoy suggested access to a higher level, perhaps up to that of administrator. Investigations of all those MtGox accounts with admin rights high enough to wreak such havoc resulted in a breakthrough: Jed McCaleb was still registered as an administrator, with full privileges over accounts and balances, some four months after he had stepped back from the project. Realising how bad this would look, MtGox publicly laid the blame at the feet of an account belonging to auditor Auden McKernan, but Karpelès later explained that this wasn't entirely true:

> *Jed keeping admin access for six months for auditing was part of the agreement, but also we had an indemnification clause meaning that we had to protect Jed no matter what, so we disclosed that as "an auditor" which wasn't false, but not true either.*

Regardless of whose account the hacker used to gain access, the revelation that the server had been compromised in this way only added to the accusations of incompetence. Of course, customers had no idea of the mistakes and losses that hadn't yet gotten out.

By now, the hack had made global news, with some outlets laying the blame at the door of hacking groups Anonymous and LulzSec, both of which denied any involvement. Nevertheless, the pressure was on Karpelès and his small team to get MtGox back up and running. They spent the next week reversing trades, certifying user balances, responding to irate customers and generally doing everything they could to get the exchange back online. Early Bitcoin adopter Roger Ver pitched up at the offices and offered to help out, soon roping in his friend Jesse Powell and other volunteers to lend a hand. The hastily assembled team set about trying to fix MtGox, but the number of people in the office 'made it very hard to concentrate' according to Karpelès, citing this as one of the reasons why MtGox took so long to get rebuilt. Ver and Powell have since offered alternative versions of the story, however, where they lay the blame for the difficult working conditions at Karpelès's door. Soon after the exchange collapsed in 2014, Powell recounted how, instead of staying at the office with the volunteers one weekend to work on the site, Karpelès went home on the Friday and didn't return until the following Monday. When Karpelès did come back, Powell said, he spent the bulk of that first day stuffing envelopes, although he took time out from this vital task to engage in a Q&A on Reddit, where he was peppered with demands to prove that the exchange was still solvent. Karpelès did this by transferring 424,242.42424242 bitcoins from one wallet to another in a nod to Douglas Adams' *Hitchhiker's Guide to the Galaxy* books, saying, 'Don't come after me claiming we have no coins'. Incidentally, this transaction, too, has been claimed by Craig Wright as one of his, telling the Australian Taxation Office during their investigation of his tax returns that it was a transfer between two addresses under his control.

Powell, Ver and the team rewrote much of the MtGox code from scratch, taking everything back to moments before the hack, almost as if it had never happened. McCaleb's account, which still had certain other administrative privileges attributed to it, was also finally downgraded. The hack pushed Karpelès into adopting a new bitcoin storage strategy, where he allegedly moved the bulk of the coins into offline 'cold' wallets. The story goes that Karpelès split the majority of the coins between numerous addresses, printed off the private keys to those addresses (essentially their access codes) and locked them away in multiple banks or safety deposit boxes around Tokyo. This ensured that nobody could access the bitcoins in those addresses unless they broke into the banks and stole the private keys, which supposedly allowed for redundancy; there was an outside chance that one location could be broken into, but not the six or seven that Karpelès allegedly used.

Karpelès's new system was intended to minimise the risk of what Jed McCaleb had called the 'ultimate catastrophe' of the cold wallets being emptied by hackers. Karpelès's idea is nice in theory, but it presents several critical problems when it comes to operating a Bitcoin exchange. Firstly, the only way to safely top up a hot wallet with a paper cold wallet is to go and get the paper wallet and execute a multi-step manual transaction on an ultra-secure network. This must be done every single time, which is, of course, entirely impractical for any Bitcoin exchange, no matter what its size or trading volume. No MtGox staff member has reported seeing Mark Karpelès nipping into town every lunchtime to bring back and scan paper wallets, and this is the only way this could have happened if it was being done properly. Karpelès has never offered proof that he stored the paper wallets in bank vaults or any other kind of secure storage location, and the sheer volume that he says he ended up with at the time of MtGox's collapse, which he puts in the region of 200-300 pieces of paper, is totally incompatible with this process. After all, there is no limit to how many bitcoins you can fit into a wallet, so why use so many and increase the risk of one getting hacked? We can, therefore, all but discount the idea that paper wallets in Toyko banks and safety deposit boxes, if there at all, were the only access Karpelès had to the cold wallets. This presents us with two other options for these cold wallets: either Karpelès kept a copy of the private keys at the MtGox office for quick top-ups, which entirely undermines the point of the bank vault/safety deposit box setup, or he developed a piece of software which took care of the balance transfers automatically. This, while being the most practical route, would have left the cold wallets vulnerable to exploitation by hackers.

There is another option to consider: the cold wallet storage claim is a fabrication created by Karpelès to absolve himself of blame. We know that until 2011, the bitcoins under MtGox's control were spread around dozens of different types of wallets – some online, some on paper and some on his computers or USB drives – with no records kept as to which was which. What if Karpelès, preoccupied with getting MtGox back online at this crucial time, took no steps whatsoever towards enhanced bitcoin storage and simply left things as they were? Ashley Barr, for one, only ever saw a hot wallet during his time there, never a cold wallet, and there are no first-hand accounts of anyone seeing a MtGox paper wallet. The same goes for Kim Nilsson, who worked with Karpelès for years after the hack; he found no records on the blockchain pertaining to offline cold wallets being used by MtGox. However, Nilsson also noted that telling the difference between a hot wallet and a cold wallet from blockchain records alone is down to one's interpretation of the data, such as the frequency and amount of individual withdrawals. We only have Karpelès's word that he employed cold wallets, which, as we have seen and will continue to see, is inconsistent at best.

Many believe that Mark Karpelès knew of MtGox's perilous position with regard to its bitcoin holdings ahead of time, which would indicate some kind of monitoring system that allowed him to watch the balances across the wallets.

Interestingly, he has referenced such a system in the past, such as a 2019 interview in which he said that by 2013, the 'cold wallet was working well' and that 'most of the system worked as expected', adding:

> At the time, those Bitcoin was supposed to be in the cold wallet. So I assumed this was working, because when I checked balances in the system which were growing, the hot wallet of course was not supposed to grow and it wasn't. That was the way things were supposed to be at the time.

This statement appears to undermine Karpelès's claims that he had no idea of the balances in the cold wallets until the exchange collapsed in 2014. It could be argued that he was led astray by 'phantom coins' that never arrived, but, as Kim Nilsson told me, this isn't possible:

> It's inconceivable that any designed cold storage system could confuse the thefts as cold storage deposits. In other words, if Mark didn't know about the problem it's because there was no information, not that there was incorrect information.

Karpelès offered a rationale behind the creation of a system that operated with no monitoring during an interview for a 2018 documentary, where he said that it was 'very possible' that he subconsciously created a blind system so that other employees would never find out that the company had tens of thousands fewer bitcoins than it should have had. This theory certainly fits with his perpetual refusal to allow anyone behind his 'walled garden', but it therefore presents the argument that Karpelès put self-preservation above the good of MtGox and its customers.

During this fractious period, MtGox's accountants urged Karpelès to take the opportunity to conduct a full audit of the exchange, including the hot wallets, cold wallets and cash balances, saying that it was the perfect time to get all the finances in line and reconciled. Karpelès, however, claimed that his new system made such an audit 'difficult and risky' because he would have to 'put the cold-storage bitcoins in a hot wallet', which would make them more vulnerable to 'cyber predators'. This, as Kim Nilsson pointed out in 2017, was simply not true:

> As far as Bitcoin engineering goes, that is nonsense. The very idea of using public key cryptography to secure bitcoin is that, no, you do not need to do

anything risky to verify a balance, you can look it up on the blockchain if you only have the public key, which is perfectly safe to have around.

The question we have to ask then is: why did Mark Karpelès believe that a 'difficult and risky' method was required if a simple public key scan would have done? There are two possible reasons for this: either Karpelès was lying to try and keep his accountants at bay, or he no longer had the public keys. The former is certainly plausible for obvious reasons, but the latter is possible too. In the early days of Bitcoin, there were misconceptions regarding the security of the cryptographic algorithms used in its design, including the possibility of being able to derive a private key from a public key. Some people speculated about potential weaknesses in the algorithms or undiscovered mathematical shortcuts that could enable such a computation to be made by bad actors, but there were never any practical examples of hacks carried out through this method. Nevertheless, Mark Karpelès could have destroyed the public keys to eradicate any possibility of such a hack, which would explain the difficulty of accessing the wallet balance. However, this doesn't explain his concern over the cold wallets becoming hot because there were well-known tools around at the time that allowed public keys to be securely extracted from private keys. This means that either Mark Karpelès wasn't aware of these tools, or he was indeed lying to ensure that he didn't have to go through an audit.

MtGox reopened for business on 26 June 2011, a week after the hack, with users divided as to whether Karpelès and MtGox could still be trusted. Debate raged on Bitcoin forums, with some leaving for other exchanges, but many remained faithful to MtGox because it still had the best trading volume and interface. On 30 June, MtGox released a lengthy update, penned by Powell and signed by Karpelès, which acted as a post-mortem as well as a mea culpa. The update revealed that an 'SQL injection vulnerability in the mtgox.com code' was the likely method of penetration, confirming that some of the passwords in the stolen database were 'unsalted'. It continued:

> *We speculate that the credentials of the compromised admin account responsible for the market crash were obtained from this database. The password would have been hashed but it may not have been strong enough to prevent cracking.*

> *Regrettably, we can confirm that our list of emails, usernames and hashed passwords has been released on the Internet. Our users and the public should know that these hashed passwords can be cracked, and many of our users' more simple passwords have been cracked.*

Here, at last, was an admission that the MtGox users had been right all along; it was the exchange that had been at fault, not them. Karpelès signed off this update with an admission:

> *The truth is that MtGox was unprepared for Bitcoin's explosive growth. Our dated system was built as a hobby when Bitcoins were worth pennies a piece. It was not built to be a Fort Knox capable of securely handling millions of dollars in transactions each day.*
>
> *We can attempt to blame the owner of the compromised account for the recent events but at the end of the day the responsibility to secure the site and protect our users rests with us. The admin account responsible had more permissions than necessary, and our security triggers were not as tight as they could have been.*
>
> *Going forward, we are certain that the launch of the new site will exceed the rightful expectations our users have of the service. We only hope that we can once again earn the trust of the Bitcoin community. In the meantime, we sincerely appreciate the patience all our users have shown.*

As for the 2,000 bitcoins stolen by the hacker, MtGox would cover that, Karpelès said, taking the total number of bitcoins lost by the exchange to 85,000, with the public and the MtGox employees, of course, unaware of the other 83,000. Ver, Powell and the other volunteers flew home, leaving Karpelès to resurrect his, and MtGox's, reputations.

The June 2011 hack would prove to be a turning point for those both inside and outside MtGox. For Karpelès, it was the first time that his shortcomings had been so publicly exposed; he had been savaged by his customers, his peers and the media, and he was feeling seriously out of his depth as a result. The Frenchman would later say that he was angry with Jed McCaleb at the time for the fact that McCaleb's old account had been the entry point for the hackers and noted how, as per the terms of his contract, he had a legal right to 'protect' the site's founder. McCaleb, for his part, had offered Karpelès advice on how to prevent a recurrence but found that doing so was like talking 'to a wall', suggesting that Karpelès was actively refusing to take lessons from the hack. For MtGox customers, the hack came as a double shock as they realised for the first time just how badly MtGox was being run and also how vulnerable their assets and, indeed, their identities were. When discussing the hack in a March 2013 interview, MtGox's Business Development manager Gonzague Gay-Bouchery was in no doubt where the blame lay:

> *Before you take over a business like MtGox you have to make sure that the code is bulletproof. This was actually not the case, and when Mount Gox was hacked Mark had to work for two consecutive weeks to completely rebuild [the exchange] from the ground up and make it secure.*

As we know, Karpelès wasn't exactly present for the full two weeks, so this claim paints him in a more flattering light than he deserves. What Karpelès did do in the wake of the hack was to implement new security principles in line with contemporary banking standards, something that was long overdue.

There is one final twist to this particular tale, as Jesse Powell explained in a blog post following MtGox's collapse in 2014:

> *...when I left, I thought—for the greater good—somebody oughta make another exchange pronto because this ship is going down in flames.*

That 'somebody', as it would turn out, would be Powell himself, who used his experience helping get MtGox back on its feet to found Payward, which launched competing crypto exchange Kraken in September 2013. In September 2023, while the world was just a few months away from the 10th anniversary of the collapse of MtGox, Powell and Kraken were celebrating a decade of hack-free operations.

Chapter 5 – The Google of Bitcoin

If MtGox was leading the way in the number of hacks on a Bitcoin exchange, Polish outfit Bitomat was about to take the gold medal in the stupidity stakes. By the end of July 2011, Bitomat had grown to become the third-biggest Bitcoin exchange by volume in the world, and its future under owner Bartek Szabat looked bright. On 26 July, Szabat, realising the exchange was reaching computational capacity, turned off the servers and installed a new memory block. Upon rebooting, he realised that in turning the servers off, he had terminated the virtual software on which the exchange was running. This, at a stroke, lost all Bitomat's data, including customer records, Bitcoin wallets and backups. In an instant, Bitomat was down 17,000 bitcoins, worth some $150,000 at the time. Szabat called Mark Karpelès and offered him Bitomat in return for his lost coins, intending to repay customers with the funds. Karpelès passed the phone to Ashley Barr, the only native English speaker on the team, but before Szabat could explain the situation, his wife ripped the phone from his hand and laid things out in black and white: she was pregnant, and her husband had just eviscerated their entire life savings and future prospects, with lawsuits inevitable. Barr hung up, and he and Karpelès discussed the merits of taking over Bitomat. Karpelès was keen for inroads into Europe, especially in the form of an exchange with European licences and banking partners already in place, and he calculated that it would take around three years to break even on the deal if Bitomat was bought with MtGox's profits. The expansion would also generate some badly needed positive PR for his company.

Karpelès decided to go ahead with the buyout, handing over the 17,000 bitcoins and taking ownership of Bitomat, which saw the Polish zloty currency added to the trading pairs on MtGox. The deal was concluded on 11 August, with Karpelès calling it a 'windfall for its users' and adding that 'for the first time ever on a Bitcoin exchange, users are now able to access a substantially larger market with their local currency, so we think it's a happy ending all around'. The acquisition went down well with the MtGox community, with one Reddit user calling it 'great news'. Indeed, the principle of buying out a competitor for a rock-bottom price was very sound, but with MtGox's history, including what wasn't known at the time, the question of whether Mark Karpelès was the right person to be running it was far from clear. While Karpelès may have gotten some good PR and access to Europe through the buyout, it was terrible for his bottom line, as Kim Nilsson explained to me:

> *In effect, once Bitomat's customers gratefully withdrew the funds they thought they had lost, they were actually pushing MtGox further into insolvency and it came out of existing MtGox customers' pockets.*

Bitomat customers may have walked a two-week emotional tightrope following the collapse of the company, but in receiving a 100% payout, they would end up faring much better than the customers of the outfit that had just rescued them. With a swish and a click of his mouse, Mark Karpelès loaded another 17,000 bitcoins onto MtGox's debt and possibly saved Szabat's marriage.

The question of whether Karpelès had learnt his lesson following the June 2011 hack was answered just twelve weeks after it when the MtGox server was once again compromised. On this occasion, a hacker was able to create and verify a new account, which they credited with some 77,500 of the company's bitcoins and withdrew the lot, deleting almost all traces of their activities as they went. This took the number of stolen coins alone to over 162,000, but once again, this hack went completely unnoticed and would remain so until it was detected by Kim Nilsson in 2015. Days after this hack, on 23 September, Bitcoin developers launched private key encryption, which meant that if a repeat of the 1Feex hack were to happen, the hackers would need the decryption password in order to spin up a replica of the hot wallet and move the coins out. Karpelès switched MtGox's hot wallet out for an encrypted version, unaware that invaders had already broken in, stolen the gold and made their escape before he had secured the castle.

The 77,500-bitcoin hack may have gone undetected, but a public example of Karpelès's mismanagement would soon sully his already debased reputation. On 29 October 2011, a user on BitcoinTalk started a thread entitled, 'Someone fucked up and lost ALOT of money'. This was accompanied by a snippet of code which showed that 2,609 bitcoins had been sent to a non-existent Bitcoin address thanks to a simple error in the code, where a '00' had been used instead of '14'. This 00 represented a crematorium into which the bitcoins had just been sent. It didn't take long to find out who was responsible; Mark Karpelès confessed on MtGox's Internet Relay Chat that it was he who had sent the bitcoins into the ether, saying it was the result of a faulty transaction script he had created:

> *All failed withdrawals were reissued. I just spent all of my bitcoins earnings in a week. It's a problem, but not the worst we've ever encountered.*

This was certainly true, although his customers didn't quite know *how* true. Nor, as it would transpire, did Mark Karpelès.

If 2011 had been an annus horribilis for Mark Karpelès and MtGox, 2012 would turn out to be its annus mirabilis. A company overview published at the start of the year claimed that, despite its various missteps, the exchange could boast an astonishing 92.8% market share, with over $20 million in turnover in 2011. However, its operational costs surprised some, including Jed McCaleb, who emailed Karpelès to express his shock, asking, 'Are you guys really spending $788k a year! What on earth are you doing?' Karpelès responded by denying that the costs were as high as McCaleb had made out, but admitted that they probably would be once all the legal matters were taken care of and MtGox was a fully licensed entity that was no longer at risk of a 'police raid'. McCaleb argued that while he knew Karpelès to be 'a smart guy and a good programmer', he needed to 'find someone that is a competent manager' for the company to scale effectively. McCaleb added that he had spoken to staff at MtGox, who had all pointed to Karpelès as the 'bottleneck for everything' and added that Karpelès was 'really holding the company back'. He then reiterated that his entreaties would probably fall on deaf ears because 'the other issue is you don't listen to anyone', asking Karpelès if he had noticed how many people in the company were upset with him and then asked him the very pointed question: 'Do you think you are doing a good job?' Karpelès dodged this question but said that someone else would likely be installed as director once all the licensing issues were resolved. He also ignored McCaleb's comment about workforce morale, arguing that MtGox was 'globally moving in the right direction'. On the surface, he wasn't wrong, with the business flourishing as Bitcoin gained wider notoriety in 2012 thanks to its explosion in price to $30 the year before.

This increased notoriety had a huge impact on MtGox, with traffic going through the roof. This led to Karpelès expanding the team to dozens of employees, moving the company into an office building in Shibuya, Tokyo, formerly occupied by Google (this also got McCaleb's goat, with the founder accusing Karpelès of unnecessarily renting the most expensive office space in the city). MtGox went from operating in a single office to taking five floors of the building, with the teams now divided up across the floors. This expansion reinforced Karpelès's vision for the company and his belief in Bitcoin, an enthusiasm that rubbed off on many employees who began to get very excited about MtGox's position at the forefront of the blockchain revolution. The customer base was surging, the team was growing, and they had just moved to an impressive new office that had undergone a hugely expensive refurb. Karpelès was also being interviewed by Japanese media outlets on a regular basis, while employees who had only ever flown economy were suddenly flying business class to overseas meetings. The implementation of encrypted wallets had also helped halt the string of hacks on the exchange, a change in fortunes that coincided with other exchanges themselves falling victim. Suddenly, MtGox seemed the safest option, which played a huge part in the sudden influx of users. The whole thing had the air of a high-performing startup ready to take the world by storm; according to former MtGox employee Thomas Glucksmann, the team believed they were on the way to becoming 'the Google of Bitcoin'.

Among the masses taking an interest in Bitcoin were, crucially, US lawmakers and financial regulators. In June 2011, Senator Chuck Schumer demonstrated on national television how it was possible to buy illicit drugs online from a website called Silk Road. This website, Schumer said, used something called Bitcoin to ensure that transactions were kept private and called on the authorities to shut down the marketplace and look into Bitcoin itself. Investigators were initially baffled as to where to start, knowing next to nothing about Bitcoin or how it worked, but they soon found out that many of the bitcoins going to and from Silk Road went through MtGox. Karpelès, realising the potential danger of this link and the heat it would bring, wrote to the US Drug Enforcement Agency (DEA) shortly after Schumer's appearance and offered to comply with any investigation into Silk Road, saying he was trying to build a law-abiding Bitcoin exchange and would help where he could. Indeed, Ashley Barr says that Karpelès was 'pretty against narcotics and anarchism to begin with', only ever talking about Silk Road in a 'negative light'. He also never mentioned or endorsed any contact with its creators or operators, who were unknown at that point. MtGox began to track suspicious transactions, especially those moving large sums, closed accounts Karpelès suspected of being linked to Silk Road and cooperated with requests by law enforcement agencies in a manner that did not infringe the privacy of MtGox users. Had his users known about such cooperation, however, the exchange would have lost its customer base overnight.

It didn't take DEA agents long to realise that the operator of Silk Road was someone going by the pseudonym Dread Pirate Roberts, and by the summer of 2012, the lead investigator in the case, Jared Der-Yeghiayan, had zeroed in on a 'good target' for the moniker: Mark Karpelès. Der-Yeghiayan thought it likely that, should Karpelès's emails be combed through, they would find evidence of him operating the world's first Bitcoin drugs store as well as the world's biggest Bitcoin exchange. Not everyone shared his beliefs, but the Silk Road task force continued looking into him. As the Silk Road investigation progressed, Der-Yeghiayan came to believe that Karpelès and the MtGox team were not doing all they could to help, even though, in truth, there wasn't a great deal that Karpelès *could* do, given that there was no such thing as automated Bitcoin tracing software at the time. Nevertheless, this put a target on Karpelès's back and, by extension, that of MtGox, too.

In late 2012, Karpelès's presence as a major player in the Bitcoin world was confirmed when he was named as a co-founder of the Bitcoin Foundation alongside other such luminaries as Gavin Andresen, Jon Matonis, Charlie Shrem and Peter Vessenes, the latter of whom would end up playing a huge part in the MtGox story in later years. This ensured that 2012 ended on a high for Karpelès, who seemed to finally be getting a grip on running MtGox, which was by now the biggest and best-known Bitcoin exchange in the world by some margin.

Finally, things were looking up.

Chapter 6 – Growing Pains

As 2013 dawned, there was little indication that this would be the year in which the snowball of catastrophe would begin rolling down the hill for MtGox and Mark Karpelès. Expansion plans were going great guns, with the team working on a number of avenues to grow the business, including the world's first Bitcoin debit card, a mobile app for the Japanese market and a major rebrand that, according to Thomas Glucksmann, 'would have taken the firm to a different league'. Gonzague Gay-Bouchery was also excited about the exchange's future, as he told an interviewer in March that year:

If everything goes according to plan, maybe at the end of this month or early-middle of next month, you may have something really amazing coming up. After that – maybe June – another crazy amazing thing.

He was to be proved right, but not in the way he imagined.

Spurred by interest from US authorities, MtGox was also looking for ways to become compliant in its key regions, with Hong Kong, the EU and Australia targeted alongside the US. Identity verification had been mandatory for some time, but this hadn't put users off, with MtGox clocking up 400,000 accounts by April 2013. One of the growing criticisms during this period was the length of time it took to get verified, with some new customers complaining that it took them weeks to get clearance to use the site, but MtGox was drawing up plans to launch a new service that would reduce this to just one day. Its growth had attracted the attention of VC firms wanting a piece of the profitable pie, too, attention the company hoped to turn into investments that, once MtGox was on its various regulatory paths, would help with international expansion. In a sign of how big its eyes were, MtGox even planned to advertise its services at the 2013 G8 summit in Northern Ireland.

2013 saw MtGox taking on more and more staff, with around forty eventually employed in a variety of roles, although Karpelès was, once again, still doing much of the work himself, micromanaging to the point of distraction. He was the only person with access to the backend of the website, which ensured that no one could go digging around and find something he didn't want them to, but it also meant that he had to personally implement every software change. This inevitably led to a backlog of updates and critical security patches, putting the site and customers' bitcoins at risk. Despite this, Gay-Bouchery still had the confidence to say in that March interview that security was 'paramount' for MtGox, adding that 'a stable and safe exchange is very important, so people will trust us for that'. Karpelès couldn't possibly keep tabs on everything that was going on with MtGox as it grew in tandem with Bitcoin's price, but he did his darndest. This desire to know all the details of all the facets of the company almost certainly blinded him to the wider picture of where the exchange was headed if it didn't meet the increasing demands being placed upon it. He was head of every department but refused to properly delegate to his underlings, admitting after its collapse that he found computers and servers much easier to manage than human beings.

Karpelès's micromanagement was, in some respects, understandable. While on the surface, things were going well, behind the scenes, he was a worried man. Firstly, the huge number of bitcoins the site was holding for customers was keeping him awake at night, which should have told him something about his storage solutions. He was also well aware that the exchange was still tens of thousands of bitcoins in debt to itself, and there was no way he was going to meet his initial target of a 2013 repayment. This was partly because of his spending elsewhere but also because Bitcoin had enjoyed a spike from $14 to $230 in the space of a few weeks at the start of 2013, making it more expensive to buy back the missing coins.

On the plus side, all this growth was, naturally, having a tremendous impact on the company's income. MtGox was making money hand over fist, taking a cut of the 150,000 bitcoins per day being traded on the site, among other fees it levied, and Karpelès was taking full advantage by paying himself a handsome salary that allowed him to live the high life. He moved into a $10,000 per month penthouse apartment in Megouro, an exclusive area of Tokyo, which he furnished with a $40,000 bed among other luxuries and even had a room set aside for his precious cats, which had a view of the city that most Tokyo inhabitants would never experience. He spent his money on the latest toys and gadgets, which he would bring to work and play with in meetings, splashing out on other pointless extravagances for the office, such as a $5,000 robot that 'sits in the corner' (Ashley Barr) and an electric massage chair. His largesse was in stark contrast to the lifestyles of his staff, half of whom were being paid less than $2,000 per month and were routinely denied pay rises.

According to Barr, Karpelès's lavish spending had, in fact, taken root the year before; in an August 2015 piece for *Bitcoin Magazine,* Barr recounted how Karpelès mentioned to him that he was considering buying a Lamborghini, leading to Barr having to point out that a CEO turning up in a supercar while denying his staff pay rises wouldn't do much for morale. Karpelès acquiesced, but it is clear just how ill-suited he was to the delicate nature of man management. Staff were also worried about Karpelès's frivolous use of company money on office toys, parties, travel and other extravagances, with even the MtGox accountants left in the dark over its financial standing thanks to Karpelès's refusal to hand over all the records to them. Karpelès was also attracting ire because of his management style, if it could be described as such; he went out of his way to avoid pressing issues over the exchange's creaking infrastructure, inability to scale and concerns over his use of company funds and would instead deal with issues that should have been beneath him, such as fixing staff laptops and researching thousands of dollars' worth of novelties and trinkets to make the office more fun. MtGox's growth, combined with Bitcoin's increased notoriety, led to further interest from outside investors, but Karpelès resisted every approach. There are two schools of thought as to why he may have been hesitant to welcome such investment: the first is that MtGox was doing so well that he didn't need any outside help and the responsibility that would have come with it, and the other is that he didn't want to open up the company's books to anyone.

With MtGox experiencing such rapid growth and with nobody other than Karpelès allowed anywhere near the company's finances and Bitcoin wallets, the MtGox team began to voice their concerns about what would happen to MtGox if something happened to Mark Karpelès. With 90% of the exchange's bitcoins allegedly held in cold storage at any one time, if Karpelès was hit by a Tokyo tram, how could the exchange operate? Karpelès's response to this issue baffled employees to the point of laughter: he had left a trail of hints that a specific friend could follow to find and unlock the cold wallets. When Ashley Barr asked the friend in question, the friend had no idea what he was talking about. Even Mark Karpelès's apologists cannot deny that his actions at this time were, at the very least, reckless, and it was becoming clear to those on the inside that far from nurturing the golden goose Karpelès had inherited, he was instead leading it perilously close to the slaughterhouse.

It wasn't just Karpelès's distracted nature that was threatening to derail the MtGox gravy train. As the first half of 2013 ticked by, the growing pains that the exchange was experiencing and that Karpelès was ignoring were starting to morph into foundational cracks. These were reflected in the performance of the site, with the platform's front-end lagging and downtime increasing. This peaked in April when multiple users complained of website errors, trading lag and an inability to access their accounts, issues that were caused, MtGox said, by 'a major DDoS attack' which left it 'scrambling to fine-tune the system every few hours to make sure that things don't go beyond a few 502 error pages and trading lag'. It added that 'there is pretty much nothing that can be done', claiming that even the New York Stock Exchange could be laid low by DDoS attacks. Not everyone was buying this, however, with one respondent on Reddit calling MtGox and Karpelès out:

> *As somebody who's been involved in the architecture, development and operation of distributed transaction-processing systems for some fairly high end companies, this is a load of shit.*

Another blamed the architecture of the MtGox system for the meltdown:

> *This is not a DDoS problem, those happen in larger scales to other websites you use all the time. This is a problem with their system being tightly coupled. The shameful thing is they had 2 years to prepare for this.*

Gonzague Gay-Bouchery told tech website Computerworld that the exchange was in the middle of a total rebuild of its architecture, which would separate the 'tight coupling' of its trading platform and front-end. Gay-Bouchery added that he hoped the new system would be in place by the end of the year, warning that 'It takes a lot of time to make something bulletproof. We cannot release something half-baked.' This might be prudent in one sense, but it led to the exchange being, in the words of Kim Nilsson, 'held together with duct tape and 'we'll fix that one day' thinking'.

Things would only get worse for MtGox as April progressed, and Bitcoin's price continued to rise, as did its popularity. The fragility of the MtGox system was highlighted on 10 April when Bitcoin experienced a massive twenty-four-hour price rally, sending users flooding to the site to try and cash in. Inevitably, the site crashed, with suggestions of another DDoS attack immediately doing the rounds. MtGox denied this, saying instead that the exchange was a 'victim of our own success!', suggesting instead that it was the 'rather astonishing' amount of new registrations and the sharp increase in trades that had rocked the boat so much it had tipped over. It now had 20,000 new accounts being created every day, the exchange said, and had taken on more than a dozen new members of staff to handle the influx of registrations and verifications. MtGox added that it might have to close the exchange 'for two hours in the next 12 to 24hrs to add several new servers to our system'. This it did, going offline for three days while frustrated customers watched the price of Bitcoin reverse, unable to sell. During the halt, MtGox made efforts to stabilise the exchange and implemented measures such as rolling back trades to a certain point before the crash occurred.

MtGox came back online with an improved trading engine which garnered praise from some, but the good times weren't to last. On 21 April, it was hit by more DDoS attacks, which caused it to again temporarily cease functioning, prompting several suggestions on forums that users leave MtGox for one of the other exchanges that had started popping up in recent months. According to Vitalik Buterin, who was just months away from releasing the whitepaper for his own blockchain, Ethereum, one of the reasons why the April 2013 Bitcoin crash was so bad was because of MtGox's 'poor preparation' for such an event and how it dealt with it afterwards:

> *The sheer volume of bitcoins traded on the exchange, combined with the prime importance of exchanges to the Bitcoin economy, gives MtGox the power to, whether through malice, incompetence or simple human error, significantly manipulate the Bitcoin price in either direction unilaterally.*

He also, presciently, addressed its technical failings:

> *Despite this advance warning, and despite the massive amount of resources that the company had at its disposal following three months of rapidly*

increasing profits from trade commissions, the exchange did nothing to improve its systems – until it was already too late.

Indeed, MtGox's massive resources had gone, in part, on hiring some very talented developers, but with a Mark Karpelès-shaped blockage in the way, they were permanently hamstrung. Even if they had been given free rein, however, it would still have been the equivalent of applying sticking plasters to the hull of a sinking submarine.

In the wake of these attacks, and in a sign of just how much mainstream interest Bitcoin had garnered following its mammoth price run, Reuters asked Karpelès for an interview to be filmed in the MtGox office. In a move that must have delighted the reporter, Karpelès chose to answer questions perched awkwardly on a huge blue exercise ball, explaining that the site still had thousands of people signing up for accounts every day, which merely added to the 20,000 in the queue for account verification already. The system was having to cope with the pressures resulting from this queue at the same time as being upgraded and while fending off persistent DDoS attacks. One viewer of this interview felt moved enough by what they saw to write a blog post about it, opining that it was 'a little concerning how unsophisticated [MtGox's] internal tools to monitor traffic seem to be'. During the interview, Karpelès said that the exchange had 'estimated' cash inflows of $5-20 million every day, with between $300,000 and $1 million going out. The huge variation and the fact that Karpelès was only able to estimate these figures also drew concerns from MtGox customers, in addition to the overall air of unprofessionalism that surrounded him during the interview. After all, this was the first time that many had seen in the flesh the man who was looking after their money, and he seemed to many to be much more suited to a job in the IT department of MtGox rather than being the guy in charge of it.

One of the reasons why less than $1 million per month was going out of MtGox was because of an issue with US dollar withdrawals. American users represented the biggest demographic on MtGox by some margin, echoing the wider trend within the Bitcoin space, with USD involved in 75% of all transactions across the exchange by early 2013. This, therefore, was the most important currency to keep liquid, but this had been a far from easy process. MtGox had already cycled through a number of payment providers to facilitate its USD deposits and withdrawals since Karpelès had taken over, including

OKPay, Paxum and Liberty Reserve. Most providers were still unsure of Bitcoin and therefore steered clear of MtGox or dumped it when they twigged, a situation that only worsened as Silk Road and its use of Bitcoin became publicised more and more. The combination of this narrowing of USD payment options, massive growth in the popularity of Bitcoin and technical inefficiencies on the exchange led to MtGox limiting the number of USD withdrawals it could process at any one time. This, in turn, led to a backlog of pending withdrawal requests building up during the first third of 2013, with irate customers jamming the support line's email inbox and phone lines, increasing the pressure on the already overworked and under-resourced support team.

Internally, Karpelès was feeling the strain of managing MtGox's ballooning growth and the pressure of personally managing the demands being placed upon it by customers, hackers and the growing threat of action by authorities. He was, however, masking it brilliantly by appearing to not give a shit. According to various employees, Karpelès seemed oddly detached from the extremely serious issues that they could all see marching over the hill like an approaching army, distracting himself with meaningless or irrelevant tasks. Stories abound about what Karpelès did to distract himself from MtGox's issues at this time: he spent hours a day watching *Breaking Bad* or his beloved Japanese anime in his office; he played videogames with developers; he drew up plans for Shade 3D, a software company he bought in 2013; and he designed and physically made MtGox-specific versions of security devices called YubiKeys. He even spent an entire day installing a hammock in his office. When Thomas Glucksmann first visited the company in early 2013, he assumed that the man he encountered fixing the smart door locks in the office was in the maintenance or IT department. It would take him until his employment to realise that this man was, in fact, the CEO, Mark Karpelès.

All of these trifles paled into insignificance, however, when compared to the Bitcoin Café. Karpelès planned to use the office space below the MtGox suite to open a Bitcoin-themed café where people could use the cryptocurrency to buy, among other dishes, his signature tarte aux pommes (apple quiche), which he would cook himself. Karpelès spent $35,000 on a pastry oven to create the perfect tarte aux pommes before realising (or being made to realise) that doing the cooking himself might not be the best use of his time. To remedy this, he hired a specialist pastry chef, but this only freed up time for him to source the café's coffee beans. It quickly became clear why this was so important: you can't just go putting Nescafé into a $23,000 coffee machine. In addition to the food and beverages, Karpelès also personally involved himself in the payment side, programming the Bitcoin terminals, which he eventually hoped to sell to retailers en masse. Brock Pierce, a former child actor famous for playing a young Gordon Bombay in the *Mighty Ducks* films who had transitioned into a tech entrepreneur and early Bitcoin adopter, summed up the issues with Karpelès's actions in a 2019 interview:

> *One of the problems is Mark Karpelès was running a bakery at the time, and I think he was spending 6–8 hours a day focused on making Danish and croissants, and this is as Mt. Gox was at its highest points. This is as Bitcoin was running up. So instead of securing those customer funds and making sure that the business was being well run, he was more interested in his baking skills.*

It must be noted that Karpelès was in the middle of a war of words with Pierce at this time over the ownership of MtGox, so Pierce's comments have to be taken in that context.

It wasn't just MtGox that was feeling the strain while Karpelès was performing coffee taste tests: his marriage, too, was on the rocks. His wife and son had not moved into his Tokyo apartment with him thanks to Karpelès's purchase of a villa in Tokyo's suburbs; Karpelès would stay in the penthouse in the week and then head to the villa for the weekend. However, he soon began to spend the weekends at his apartment, too, where rumours of an appetite for alternative female company began to do the rounds. Cracks began to appear in Karpelès's marriage as a result, and the pair divorced later in 2013.

However much Mark Karpelès truly knew, or allowed himself to know, about the state of MtGox at this time, he was about to find what years of improper management, bottlenecks and poor planning would ultimately lead to.

Chapter 7 – Seizure

One of the more interesting things about Mark Karpelès's purchase of MtGox in February 2011 is that, according to legend, he very nearly missed out. Peter Vessenes, the Illinoisan Bitcoin advocate and founding member of the Bitcoin Foundation alongside Mark Karpelès, met Jed McCaleb in late 2010 when McCaleb was first starting to realise that running MtGox might be more hassle than it was worth. Vessenes flew out to meet McCaleb in Costa Rica, paying 1,500 bitcoins for his flight, where the two discussed the prospect of Vessenes taking over MtGox. They could not agree on a deal, however, and Vessenes flew home. Shortly after Karpelès took over MtGox a few weeks later, he heard from Vessenes:

> *I got an email from Peter, telling me that he actually owns half of Mt. Gox and should have been paid half of whatever Jed was paid. So I forwarded this to Jed and Jed responded to Peter and me just saying, 'What the fuck', basically.*

Vessenes soon ceased his demands and fell out of Karpelès's life, only to dramatically re-enter it in 2012. Karpelès had just been informed that by transmitting USD to American citizens without the relevant licenses, he had been operating the site illegally, and with Silk Road pushing Bitcoin into the mainstream, US authorities were starting to look hard at regulating Bitcoin and the entities that dealt with it. Karpelès had found that the situation in the US was becoming 'increasingly difficult' by this point, and in an attempt to gain clarity on what to do, he approached three different lawyers, getting three different opinions in return. The first said that because MtGox was based in Japan, it had no need to obtain a US license, which was wrong, but the second two gave him much better advice: one said he needed to register as a money services business, while the other, MtGox's own lawyer, said that the exchange needed to be recognized as a more comprehensive money transmitter business. The latter was a much more onerous undertaking, given that states in the US all had variations of this law. This meant complying independently with all the states MtGox wanted to serve, a process that could cost up to $15 million, too much for MtGox at the time.

Enter, Peter Vessenes. Vessenes founded the Bitcoin development company Coinlab in Seattle in 2011 thanks to funding from, among others, Roger Ver, and had been keenly watching MtGox's progress. Still aware of its potential, in early 2012, he contacted Karpelès again and offered to buy the company, but Karpelès refused. The conversation then turned to the thorny issue of MtGox's US license. Coinlab offered, in Karpelès's words, to 'handle the legal situation in the US by representing MtGox, and be the MtGox USA front.' The offer was an attractive one: MtGox would receive 40% of all fee revenue for all existing US and Canada-based customers, which would be migrated to Coinlab, and 90% of all fee revenue for new US and Canada-based customers that signed up after the initial three-month transition period. The deal suited both parties, with Vessenes finally getting his hands on some prime Bitcoin real estate and Karpelès knowing that he would no longer have to deal with US regulations. In November 2012, the contracts were signed and, armed with five million dollars in development money and a March 2013 deadline, Coinlab got to work.

Initially, Coinlab looked like it was doing all the right things. It began speaking to licensed banks that would handle the cash flows to and from MtGox for US customers and settled on Silicon Valley Bank, an entity with a history, perhaps unsurprisingly given its name and location, of helping tech startups. Ironically, Silicon Valley Bank would itself go bust years into the MtGox bankruptcy process, with poor risk management and a downturn in the tech industry among several factors that led to its collapse in 2023, owing investors tens of billions of dollars. Coinlab registered as a money services business in late February 2013, the one that MtGox's lawyers believed wasn't comprehensive enough to cover the exchange's services, and the MtGox/Coinlab deal was made public shortly afterwards. Vessenes told the BBC that when his team looked at the best way to bring Bitcoin trading to the US in a legal capacity, 'it seemed clear that MtGox had by far the best security record in the Bitcoin exchange landscape'. He added:

> *After I personally came to Japan and audited their fraud and security procedures, I understood why – they are light years ahead of other exchanges at this stuff – the fraud and security experience (some of it hard-won) they bring to the table is incredibly impressive.*

Such positive assertions would have no doubt raised eyebrows to ceiling level among those with even the briefest knowledge of MtGox's rocky history, but perhaps Vessenes' claims were proof that MtGox had finally turned a corner.

With just two weeks to go until the transition deadline, Vessenes was still talking up the potential of MtGox's US operation, telling Forbes that Coinlab would provide 'a specialized user interface to the MtGox platform and facilitate larger transaction sizes for better liquidity, maybe even adding forex trading APIs and FIX protocol support'. Coinlab planned to migrate about 100 customers at the start of March and 5,000 customers on 15 March, with all remaining accounts going live on 29 March. Everything looked to be proceeding as planned, but on 18 March, the Department of the Treasury's Financial Crimes Enforcement Network (FinCEN) jammed a spanner in the works when it published new guidelines on digital currencies. These new rules stipulated that digital currencies were bound by the same laws as any other form of money, meaning that entities that received or exchanged them had to have the same licences as those that dealt with fiat currencies. This was in stark contrast to the Japanese authorities, who simply ignored MtGox, even though the same rules over fiat payments were applied there. This ruling changed the game overnight for MtGox and Coinlab and meant, more importantly, that US law enforcement agencies could now go after anyone they suspected of noncompliance.

Mark Karpelès, naturally concerned by this development, spoke to Coinlab, which reassured him that as a registered money services business, it was fully in line with FinCEN's new guidelines. MtGox lawyers maintained, however, that Coinlab needed to register as a money transmitter business and held back on transferring the next swathe of user accounts and bitcoins until it had. Coinlab, in return, accused MtGox of stalling on the deal. With only four days to go before the expiry of the transition period, the issue needed to be resolved as a matter of priority. Around the same time, Vessenes allegedly received a phone call from the enforcement division of the US Securities and Exchange Commission (SEC), which said it was planning legal action against MtGox and wanted him to testify against the exchange. As Vessenes told Bloomberg in a

2021 interview, 'As soon as we heard Gox was in an SEC enforcement, I was pretty sure we were done.' 22 March came and went with no resolution on the matter, despite $12.8 million in customer deposits already having been passed over to Coinlab. MtGox's legal team would later argue that Coinlab personnel made 'vague statements, without a schedule, a deadline or a plan to finance' an application to register as a money transmitter business, and so it pulled the plug on the deal. Coinlab did eventually apply to become a money transmitter business just weeks later, but it was too late. The deal was dead.

Coinlab didn't take MtGox's cancellation lying down, and on 2 May, it sued the exchange for breach of contract, claiming loss of earnings and the costs of obtaining the requisite licences, plus the work done on the site before Karpelès walked away. MtGox, it said, had triggered a liquidation clause worth $50 million by scrapping the deal in the manner that it had, with unpaid fees putting the final tab at $75 million. Karpelès denied the claims, and MtGox countersued, arguing that the breakdown of the partnership was Coinlab's fault due to its failure to get the proper licenses, with Karpelès summarising that Coinlab had 'provided no sort of work, instead undermining MtGox's compliance with US laws by falsely representing they were fully compliant'. MtGox also said that of the $12.8 million its customers had already deposited in Coinlab bank accounts, $5.3 million had yet to be returned. A trial date was set for March 2014, and MtGox was left in a worse position than before, now operating in breach of US laws concerning dollars *and* bitcoins. Worse was to come for Karpelès and MtGox, however, and in very short order.

Signs that MtGox's lack of compliance was inconveniencing customers had been brewing for some time. In February 2013, just as Coinlab and MtGox were about to put pen to paper on their deal, some users of mobile payment service Dwolla, a popular payment platform for American MtGox users, noticed that their accounts had suddenly become restricted, with withdrawals from MtGox being cancelled. The reason for this was Dwolla's implementation of new anti-money laundering requirements, and to make matters worse, the withdrawn funds never made it back to MtGox either; they stayed with Dwolla and were effectively being held by the US government. More and more users began to experience issues with USD withdrawals, with MtGox saying it was simply down to congestion and asking users to cancel their requests and try again. Behind the scenes, however, staff were struggling with the increasing number of complaints, and Karpelès's constant denials that it was anything more than congestion caused by the popularity of Bitcoin were wearing thin. The situation came to a head on 14 May when US customers trying to withdraw cash were greeted by a worrying message:

> *Due to recent court orders received from the Department of Homeland Security and U.S. District Court for the District of Maryland, Dwolla is no longer legally able to service Mutum Sigillum LLC's account.*

Quite what Mutum Sigillum was, nobody had any idea, but they found out pretty quickly thanks to a seizure warrant that instantly made headlines: the Department of Homeland Security (DHS) had frozen $2.91 million in the Dwolla account belonging to Mutum Sigillum, which it said was the US intermediary that MtGox had been using to handle US customers' deposits and withdrawals. The DHS alleged that when Karpelès had opened a Wells Fargo account for Mutum Sigillum in May 2011, he had pledged that the company would not exchange currencies for customers nor act as a money transmitter, both of which it was, in fact, doing. However, in July 2015, Karpelès hit back at this rationale in a blog post:

> *...the affidavit says I filled a MSB form and explicitly said that Mutum Sigillum LLC was not a Money Services Business. It should be known [I] registered and opened this bank account remotely. All the required documents were sent to me by email, and I sent them back all duly filled and signed. As such I have a copy of ALL the documents I filled, and I can say for sure that the affidavit statement 'Karpeles answered these questions...is false.*

The DHS didn't stop with Dwolla; it also raided the Wells Fargo account where the Dwolla deposits were sent and grabbed another $2.1 million. This meant that not only had MtGox lost its US payment processor, but it had also lost $5 million in liquidity, which it desperately needed to facilitate withdrawals. Unsurprisingly, many predicted that this was the end for MtGox in the US, wondering how it could possibly survive without being able to process payments now that no payment processors or banks would touch it. MtGox admitted that it had been blindsided by the action, saying that it had 'read on the Internet that the United States Department of Homeland Security had a court order and/or warrant issued from the United States District Court in Maryland which it served upon the Dwolla mobile payment service with respect to accounts used for trading with MtGox'. It added that it had not yet received a copy of the warrant and promised to investigate and issue 'further reports when additional information becomes known'.

While the news was undoubtedly a shock for Karpelès, it wasn't for someone who had been emailing him recently. On 8 April, while he was trying to think up new ways to make MtGox compliant with the new FinCEN rules, Karpelès received a LinkedIn invitation from one Carl Force, who proclaimed to be a DEA agent, asking to connect with him. Suspicious and knowing that the DEA was looking into Silk Road, Karpelès replied to ask if there was anything he could help with. Force replied two days later to ask if Karpelès could 'back me on a deal with 250 bitcoin. A sale.' Not liking where this was headed and assuming it might even be a joke, Karpelès ignored the request. On 7 May, just a week before the Dwolla and Wells Fargo seizures, Force was back:

> *I saw the news yesterday that you won't be partnering with Coinlab. Sorry to hear that. If you are still looking for a US and Canada representative, please keep me in mind. Thank you very much.*

Karpelès declined the offer, assuming there was something fishy about DEA agents offering to front MtGox in the US. Just hours after the $5 million seizure, however, Karpelès received another email from Force:

> *Told you should have partnered with me!*

This was clearly no coincidence, but Karpelès was too busy dealing with the fallout of the seizure to worry about Force's potential involvement. Force, however, would ensure that he wouldn't stay out of the Frenchman's thoughts for long.

The moment the news of the seizure became public, MtGox was plagued with calls and emails from US customers who were worried that their funds would be trapped. This episode instituted what Thomas Glucksmann called a 'major shift in focus and mentality' for the team; the long-term plans were all but swept from the table in favour of the sole task of getting new banking partners. From this moment on, MtGox was in firefighting mode, something from which it would never escape. Glucksmann and others hit the phones, calling every national and international bank they could think of to explain what MtGox was, what its plans were and whether it could be considered for an account. Time and time again, however, they were rebuffed, with no banks willing to deal with anything related to MtGox or Bitcoin.

With no progress being made in the month after Dwolla was forced to sever ties, MtGox took the nuclear option and halted USD withdrawals altogether. The result was an explosion of negative press and near hysteria from users. The official line from the company, which Glucksmann on reflection calls a 'bullshit, heavily lawyer-edited press release', ignored the banking issues that everyone knew the exchange was suffering from:

> *Over the past weeks Mt. Gox has experienced rising volumes of deposits and withdrawals from established and upcoming markets interested in Bitcoin. This increased volume has made it difficult for our bank to process the transactions smoothly and within a timely manner, which has created unnecessary delays for our global customers. This is especially so for those in the United States who are requesting wire transfer withdrawals from their accounts.*

The lack of a press office at this time only made things worse for Karpelès and MtGox, with the veneer presented by the company easily stripped away and the information vacuum filled with rumours of insolvency and accusations of mismanagement, a situation which dismayed those working hard every day to try and find a solution. The company was being peppered with requests for comment by media outlets, and, as the only person at the company who could speak or write English to any reasonable standard, Glucksmann soon became the lightning rod. Initially wary of speaking to the press, Glucksmann soon realised that the damaging conspiracy theories had to be countered, and so he responded to an email from *WIRED* to say that the issues had 'nothing to do with the U.S. Banks' and that they were instead related to 'processing the sheer volume through our banks in Japan'. This was a mistake for two reasons: firstly, he got a stern rebuke from the company's lawyers for speaking out, where he was warned not to do so again; and secondly, his name was now out there as a de facto spokesperson for MtGox. This led to a barrage of emails and phone calls from other media outlets, some of which resorted to harassing Glucksmann in order to get him to open up, but he held back.

The negativity being heaped on MtGox was also being reflected onto Bitcoin, given that MtGox was its chief exponent at the time, something that the fledgling cryptocurrency could ill-afford. To protect Bitcoin's reputation, Karpelès decided that the exchange shouldn't exhibit at that year's Bitcoin conference in San Jose, leading to the rather incongruous sight of the world's biggest Bitcoin exchange not exhibiting at the world's biggest Bitcoin conference. The Bitcoin price didn't escape unscathed either, falling from $108 on the day that withdrawals were suspended to just $66 within a few days.

With withdrawals paused and accusations raining down on them from all sides, the MtGox team began, as Glucksmann says, 'hustling like mad to find solutions to the fiat withdrawal issue'. With third parties either not willing to work with MtGox or not able to operate at the scale MtGox needed, Karpelès decided to take matters into his own hands. Within weeks, MtGox had set up a corporation in Delaware under its own name and registered it as a money services business. This, in the words of Vitalik Buterin, allowed MtGox to 'carry out money services business activities in sixty US territories including all fifty states, granting the company federal permission to carry out their Bitcoin exchange activities in all of those regions'. However, as Buterin also noted, MtGox still needed to register as a money transmitter business in forty-eight states if it wanted to conduct all areas of its business in the country.

With the US entity in place, withdrawals were reopened in early July, and life returned to normal... except it didn't. Withdrawals through the new system were glacially slow and, therefore, began quickly to back up once more. MtGox denied that its new system was to blame, instead pointing the finger at external factors, with Glucksmann once again breaking ranks to tell *The Wall Street Journal* that MtGox was now required to work with 'real world banks at bank speed', adding, 'We have no problems with liquidity and we never have.'

If the PR to this point had been shoddy, what happened next was simply disastrous. Roger Ver, who lived across the road from MtGox and who had helped get the exchange back on its feet after the database leak, posted an intensely uncomfortable video from the MtGox office in an attempt to reassure customers that all was fine. The video, which resembled a hostage telling the world that he was being well treated, had the opposite effect to the one intended, with many claiming that Ver had been financially induced to post it. Ver would eventually retract his comments in the video, saying he didn't have all the facts to hand at the time, while Mark Karpelès later apologised to Ver because 'this video you made to help us ended [up] causing so much trouble'.

Things got worse for MtGox before they had the chance to get better. Teikoku Data Bank, Japan's largest and most respected credit-rating agency, reviewed the company in July 2013 and gave it a grade of D4, the worst possible rating a company could receive. One of the reasons given for this atrocious score was the lack of qualified accounting staff at the company, something that would have surprised no one working there, save perhaps for the four beleaguered accountants themselves. July also saw something of a tipping point for MtGox and a sign that the repeated attacks and missteps were taking their toll. On 22 July, fellow Bitcoin exchange Bitstamp, which had been founded in 2011, overtook MtGox in daily bitcoin trading volume, with 8,294.02 bitcoins traded compared to 8,215.9 on MtGox. Having dominated the Bitcoin landscape since 2012, the event represented a seismic shift in customer habits, with Tuur Demeester, then editor at market analysis website MacroTrends, saying that Bitcoin traders were now 'afraid of having their funds frozen at Mt. Gox'. All was not lost, however; MtGox still retained 52% of all Bitcoin transactions across exchanges compared to Bitstamp's 18%, showing it was still the dominant force in that respect. How long it would remain this way depended on MtGox being able to get its USD withdrawals system up and running again, obtain the correct licenses and sort out its performance issues.

Chapter 8 – Pressure

Mark Karpelès could have been forgiven for thinking that the first half of 2013 was about as bad as it could get for himself and MtGox, but he was in for a shock. A press release of 4 July announcing the resumption of cash withdrawals was met with complaints from users that they were still taking as long as before, with callers to the support line informed that it would be several weeks until their cash was with them. Before long, the exchange was refusing to give timeframes altogether, although concerns over its insolvency were countered by the fact that non-USD withdrawals were going through without a hitch. This was great for the 10% of its users who required these services, but not for the other 90%.

As the summer moved into autumn in Tokyo, the wheels of the MtGox car, which had been wobbling for several months, began to fall off one by one. The issue of cash withdrawals also began to affect deposits, resulting in a swathe of newly angered customers and a sudden throttling of fresh dollars coming into MtGox. Karpelès had explained in an August update that MtGox's bank took up to ten days to credit a deposit, and up to that point, MtGox had been pre-crediting customers. However, more and more deposits were now failing, leaving MtGox increasingly out of pocket. Customers were stunned that MtGox had been pre-crediting users to this extent, taking on the risk of non-payment every time it did so. Karpelès added that the exchange was 'in the process of forming relationships with new partners, banks, and taking other steps' to resolve the issue. However, this only applied to deposits; the update entirely failed to address the bigger problem of withdrawals.

The complaints over withdrawals and deposits merely increased in the second half of 2013, with messageboards plagued by frustrated users looking for advice or solace as they sought desperately to get their funds off the exchange. Delays of more than three months were common, and MtGox found itself the butt of many a joke in the crypto space. However, trustworthy alternatives to

MtGox were still limited, and many customers persisted with the exchange simply because they thought it was better to stick with the devil they knew. In September 2013, *Bitcoin Magazine* drew attention to the methods employed by MtGox, claiming it wasn't being fair to new users:

> *Mt. Gox has unfortunately been opaque regarding these delays. Neither the current delays on USD withdrawals nor the ability to request a quicker 'manual' withdrawal for a 5 [dollar] fee (though only one of these per day may be allowed) is publicised on their site. Thus a new user of bitcoin might well hear that one can sell them on Mt. Gox, look at relative prices, and proceed to sell there, only to find out many weeks later that their USD are effectively stuck in Mt. Gox.*

The term 'Ponzi scheme' began to do the rounds, with angry customers and worried observers claiming that the incessant delays were a sign that the exchange was insolvent and might be relying on fresh deposits to fund withdrawals. Two of those fortunate enough to get out of Dodge at this time were the Winklevoss twins, Cameron and Tyler, early Bitcoin adopters and future crypto exchange operators who managed to get their bumper Facebook payout out of MtGox before things got too hot.

The avalanche of complaints continued, with the support staff overwhelmed with calls, emails and tweets on a daily basis. Things were made worse by the fact that none of the support staff spoke English as a native language, and almost all the complaints coming in were from English speakers. MtGox employees from other departments were roped in to help man the support line, but were unused to dealing with customers, so they simply passed the phones off to each other until they landed with someone who could actually help or at least say the right thing to get the caller off the line. Thomas Glucksmann often found himself drafted in to handle the most irate callers, something that soon grew wearisome and distracted from his job of trying to secure banking partners and global operating licenses. Recognising there was an issue, Mark Karpelès tried to ease the burden on the beleaguered support staff by contracting a company to provide first-line customer support, but their Indian call centre ended up causing more problems than it solved, with most of the calls being routed back to the Tokyo office anyway. MtGox would eventually get its customer service and press relations issues sorted, but this wasn't until the end of 2013, by which time the horse had already bolted.

Despite the increasing pressures from all directions, morale at MtGox was, by and large, still positive. Many continued to be proud of what the company was trying to achieve and had faith that it would dig itself out of its present crisis, so they were willing to help tackle the chimeric challenges. The expansion plans were still being worked on alongside the push for new banking solutions, with a 'keep calm and carry on' attitude adopted by the staff, most of whom felt frustrated that they couldn't tell the outside world how hard they were working to resolve the situation and how everything was reliant on the famously institutionalised banking industry. What couldn't be ignored, however, was the role of Mark Karpelès in all this. Already a bottleneck as far as company progress went, the Frenchman was also becoming a bottleneck for information, becoming much more secretive and giving away very little to even his most trusted members of staff. The MtGox recreation room, which occupied a whole floor and included a balcony with an enchanting view of Tokyo, had turned from a place of happy conversation to the focal point for gossip, rumour and, increasingly, concern over the impact of the damaging withdrawal issues. Employees relied on snippets of information from co-workers in different departments to get an idea of what was really going on, with Karpelès's motives being openly questioned more and more as the crisis worsened. Many were agog that the CEO was persisting with the Bitcoin Café, even holding meetings with catering consultants rather than with the MtGox product teams, right when the banking issues were threatening not just the existence of the café but the whole MtGox enterprise itself. This situation was summed up by Thomas Glucksmann:

> *Sometimes we weren't privy to anything because Mark would keep it to himself, or he would only tell the lawyers and we would have to find out from someone else. It was strange having that cloud over what was really happening...not having the full picture was very frustrating.*

Karpelès's need to control every aspect of MtGox had become even more troubling by this point, mainly because it meant his load was always full, and he couldn't sign off key things. The site had only introduced a test environment in late 2013, which is where software changes are tried out before going live to see if they negatively affect anything. Prior to this, all code changes had gone out live, with developers nervous that they might crash the exchange with some poor code or an unseen bug, to which Ashley Barr referred, saying, 'Mark was a maverick, making live updates to the exchange (some went well, others didn't).' Karpelès was still adamant that he had to sign off code changes before they went live, meaning that bug fixes and security patches were left lying dormant for weeks while developers waited for him to sign them off. These internal issues were compounded by the poor communication between the exchange and its customers at this crucial time, which included generic auto-responses to queries and complaints over email and on social media. This multitude of issues was dragging the reputations of MtGox, Karpelès and, by extension, Bitcoin through the mud and putting increasing pressure on the support staff, who spent their days getting nothing but abuse from increasingly irate customers. The only thing that MtGox could do to silence its growing base of critics was to re-implement withdrawals, which, it said, it was working on.

Glucksmann saw a definite change in Karpelès as 2013 wore on, noting that he was 'obviously stressed', which reflected itself in subtle but telling ways:

> *When I first encountered Mark in early 2013, he was a cheerful bloke, quiet but always seemed to be excited about the growth of the firm and the projects going on. But when the withdrawal issues started he was distracted all the time and seemed to me to become a bit more detached. For example, he insisted that meetings be scheduled (rather than previously accepting open-door instant message based communication) and often when you spoke to him in his office he was always doing something else, so I felt I never got his full attention.*

Given this cocktail of issues, it is no surprise that some in and around MtGox formulated a plan to move Karpelès out of a position of such all-consuming power and interference. The plan was constructed by a cabal of key stakeholders who believed that the company could be taken to the next level by a seasoned CEO who would take over day-to-day issues, installing directors to oversee the various departments and leaving Karpelès to move into a chairmanship position with an overall vision for the company. With an experienced CEO at the helm (a 'safe pair of hands' in the words of Glucksmann) and a defined managerial structure, MtGox would be in a position to reclaim its place as the world's top Bitcoin exchange and stay there. However, this idea would have to be presented carefully; Karpelès had ultimate control over every aspect of the exchange and was answerable to no one, so if he got a whiff of their true intentions, it could spell disaster. However, by playing the 'for the good of the exchange' card, the group was sure that Karpelès would see the wisdom of their idea. He didn't. Karpelès flat-out rejected any notion of him leaving his role as overseer-in-chief, torpedoing any hopes the group had of removing the various bottlenecks. Once again, whispers of financial impropriety filtered through the corridors as those behind the aborted plan discussed the reasons behind his inflexible attitude.

It wasn't just MtGox that was getting it in the neck at this troubled time. Mizuho Bank, which handled MtGox's business at a branch in Tokyo, was also being deluged with complaints from customers over withdrawal delays. Mizuho had been alarmed by the $5 million DHS seizure and had had several meetings with Karpelès, pressuring MtGox to close its account. However, Karpelès would not entertain that thought, and for a good reason: without Mizuho, MtGox would cease being able to honour cash withdrawals full stop, given that no other banks would touch them following the DHS action. Mizuho, which was looking for legal avenues through which to close MtGox's account, did everything in its power to convince MtGox to sever the partnership, including limiting the exchange to ten international bank wires at a cumulative value of $1 million per day. Eventually, it would prohibit all transactions not conducted in Japanese yen, which, for a company with a 90% American user base, presented a massive problem. MtGox tried various workarounds but eventually landed on just one surefire withdrawal method: every few days, a team of around ten people would collect the day's withdrawals in cash from various branches of Mizuho bank, place the money into bags and take them to branches of Japan Post Bank where they would manually wire customers' withdrawals one by one in dollar format, filling out forms by hand for each one. Hardly the future of finance, but a necessary evil until something else was worked out.

The saying 'necessity is the mother of invention' has never been more appropriately applied than to the MtGox product team at this time, which was being forced to think outside the box when it came to solutions to the USD withdrawal issue. The team soon struck on the idea of buying out services that already had the requisite licenses in place rather than trying to obtain a license for MtGox itself. One candidate in Ireland was identified, and some exploratory work was carried out with a view to an acquisition, but this and other potential avenues turned into dead ends. Part of the problem, as was becoming clear to everyone but the man himself, was the Mark Karpelès bottleneck. Through his micromanagement, the Frenchman had too many demands on his time to sign off or even read crucial documents needed to move the various processes forward, leading to them all stalling. What made things worse for the team in charge of resolving the banking issue was that its other partners said they were only willing to continue serving MtGox if the exchange didn't publicise its issues with getting a US banking partner, fearful that it would draw negative attention onto them. MtGox was now being prevented from external communication through two channels, right when communication was critical.

In November 2013, *WIRED* magazine travelled to Tokyo to try to speak to Karpelès about the mounting criticism. Its reporters were told that Karpelès and his lieutenant Gonzague Gay-Bouchery were out of town, with the receptionist eventually asking Thomas Glucksmann if he could come down to speak to the reporters. Even if he hadn't been warned off speaking to the press by MtGox's lawyers weeks before, ironically after speaking to *WIRED*, Glucksmann wouldn't have done so anyway: he says that the *WIRED* reporters were 'by far the worst' in terms of their harassment, so there was no way he was going to risk another reprimand for their sake. This turned out to be one of Glucksmann's final such acts for MtGox. Having tried for months to resolve the banking issue and been rebuffed at every turn, he was now running out of faith that the exchange could survive. This, plus the added stress of being the lightning rod for both the press and irate English-speaking customers, led him to seek an exit; he handed in his notice in early December and left the company in the new year. Two weeks after he departed Japan for another job, a former colleague at MtGox (Glucksmann won't say who) contacted him to advise him to remove all mentions of MtGox from his CV and online profiles but didn't explain why. Nevertheless, Glucksmann took the advice and watched as MtGox imploded the following day.

Having got nowhere with their attempts in the MtGox offices, *WIRED* eventually managed to speak to Roger Ver, who laughed off suggestions that his 'hostage' video was a front, saying that he hadn't been coerced into making it and that he had done so because he wanted to help the company out. Ver reassured *WIRED* that MtGox's issues were purely related to its banking partners:

> *Right before my eyes, Mark logged into his bank account at the biggest bank in Japan and showed me the account balances in their accounts. That's not proof that MtGox is solvent or not. But it's definitely proof that...whatever is causing all their wire transfer delays, it is not a lack of money in the bank.*

Mark Karpelès had another excuse for why things were taking so long on the withdrawal front, replying to a Twitter user a few days after the *WIRED* piece was published to say, 'Nothing much will happen on that front while the US govt is shutdown.' The perplexed user asked what a government shutdown had to do with private banks, but got no reply. The cash withdrawal issue was also impacting the price of Bitcoin on the site, with sellers asking for a higher price due to the difficulties in getting cash off the site once sold. This became known as the 'MtGox premium'.

While customers were understandably upset about their cash withdrawals, they still had the option of withdrawing their bitcoins and cashing them out elsewhere. Or so they thought. MtGox users had, in fact, been experiencing bitcoin withdrawal issues as far back as April 2013, with some alleging that bitcoins were leaving their accounts as expected but not showing up on the Bitcoin blockchain until hours, sometimes days, later. These issues prompted more calls from observers that the exchange might be bankrupt and operating as a Ponzi scheme:

> *Rumor has it their hot wallet is empty. BTC withdrawals might go through if someone has deposited BTC into the hot wallet so you can withdraw that.*

Other customers reported that MtGox was blaming 'network congestion' and an out-of-sync blockchain at their end for the delays. Initially, these new concerns were buried by the tumult over the dollar withdrawal issues, but as the bitcoin delays increased in both duration and volume, the theory that MtGox was bankrupt began to take hold, leading to panic: suddenly, a huge swathe of users feared they had no way of getting their funds off the platform in any format.

The issue of bitcoin withdrawals was much more concerning for Karpelès; he could blame the banks all he wanted for delays in dollar withdrawals, but bitcoin withdrawals were entirely his issue. Given that there was no third party involved, there was no reason why MtGox should be having problems sending bitcoins out. This was particularly problematic for customers because the price of Bitcoin was once again rocketing at the time, tipping $1,000 for the first time in December 2013, and holders were keen to either cash out or send their coins somewhere safer now they were suddenly worth much more. MtGox began to blame the bitcoin withdrawal delays on the ever-present technical difficulties and limitations within MtGox's infrastructure, saying that the exchange's systems were struggling to cope with the number of withdrawal requests and the continued scalability issues. This was despite the brand new system that Gay-Bouchery had promised back in April, which should theoretically have been helping to ease the burden.

The one thing MtGox really didn't want at this point was a bank run, but on 5 December, the Chinese government initiated one when it announced that it was banning its banks from handling money from Bitcoin-related entities. Chinese MtGox customers raced to withdraw their coins and cash them out before the deadline, leading to even more pressure on the exchange. Battered by a growing storm of criticism, and with MtGox losing both market share and customers on a weekly basis, Mark Karpelès was offered the chance to calm the waters somewhat thanks to a deal signed with UK-registered payment processor Mayzus Financial Services and its MoneyPolo platform. Karpelès promised that MoneyPolo would 'enable our customers outside of the United States to deposit quickly and without long processing times', which managed to resolve precisely none of the core issues affecting the exchange at the time, although he claimed that it was 'working hard to improve the withdrawal process' for American users. To celebrate the deal and its millionth customer, MtGox announced a 25% fee discount on all transactions made on the exchange between 20 December 2013 and 20 January 2014. Predictably, the offer was roundly mocked, with many stating that the discount didn't negate the MtGox premium and that there was no point in trading on a site that one couldn't get funds off anyway. The promotion failed to attract new users, and MtGox ended 2013 with just a 14% market share, having started it with 70%.

If dollar withdrawals had been the top gripe of 2013, bitcoin withdrawals had taken over by the start of 2014. More and more customers were complaining that their withdrawals were being debited from their accounts but not appearing on the blockchain, with delays of up to a week not uncommon. Users took to comparing excuses from the MtGox support desk as gallows humour took hold. By February, the complaints were getting to ridiculous levels, with thousands of threads on BitcoinTalk and Reddit dedicated to the issue. Some even penned 'Dear John' letters to the exchange as they bid it adieu:

> I remember you when you were ugly, slow and without a fancy logo. I remember you when I had to go to weird sites and fill in shady forms to even get my money there. You got that figured out in the end. I got some of my money stolen in 2011, but I still supported you. I rooted for you with the Dwolla bullshit. And with the more recent US account and withdrawal troubles, I still thought that you will sort that out and come back glorious.
>
> I am by no means a heavy Bitcoin trader, but you were my favourite exchange, for a long time. But it's time to say goodbye, since you are evidently no longer working as a money-bitcoin exchange anymore. I tried to root for you, but I really can't. Goodbye.

These issues were picked up by members of the Bitcoin Foundation forum, of which Mark Karpelès was a board member and founder, one of whom posted his concerns:

> According to several discussions in places like reddit and BitcoinTalk.org, there is a backlog of broken bitcoin transactions totaling in the tens of thousands of bitcoins. I personally have been waiting for over a week on five bitcoins withdrawals, totaling to quite a large sum, that never made it to the blockchain due to double spending. The probability that technical difficulties explain these delays appears to be vanishingly small, making insolvency appear to be more and more of a concern.

Swedish information technology entrepreneur and founder of the Swedish Pirate Party, Rick Falkvinge, also highlighted the issue on 4 February in a piece for his website where he put the figure of 'lost' bitcoins at $38 million. Falkvinge had analysed MtGox's data on failed transactions (withdrawals that hadn't been received by the customer) and had found that the number had been steadily increasing since 25 January. As of 4 February, the figure stood at a whopping 41,390 bitcoins. MtGox responded just an hour after his post to say that the problem was being worked on and that it applied 'primarily to larger transactions'. If this was an attempt to reassure customers, it didn't work, with many, including Falkvinge, pointing out that the size of a Bitcoin transaction has no bearing on the length of time it should take to go through. The explanation that many affected users and those watching on naturally gravitated to was a less palatable but increasingly plausible one: MtGox was bankrupt.

As the hoards gathered in larger and larger numbers at its virtual gates, Karpelès and the MtGox team were working on what they thought was the core issue behind the bitcoin withdrawal problems. At the start of February, the operator of a crypto exchange (thought to be Bitstamp) logged into the MtGox chat box to say that the exchange's bitcoin holdings were at risk through hackers targeting something called 'transactional malleability'. This vulnerability allowed a hacker to intercept a customer withdrawal and trick the system into thinking it hadn't gone through. The customer would request a withdrawal from MtGox to a Bitcoin address, with MtGox creating a corresponding transaction and publishing it to the Bitcoin network. Due to the way MtGox tracked confirmation of these transactions, its systems could be fooled into believing the transaction had failed, even though it was later confirmed by the network. MtGox would then credit the amount back to the user's account, as well as sending the same amount to the hacker, effectively losing a second bitcoin for every one that was 'rejected'.

The problem for Karpelès was that transaction malleability wasn't a new development of which he may not have been aware. It was, in fact, a known bug in Bitcoin that had been discovered in 2011 and which required a fairly simple piece of coding to mitigate it. However, Karpelès had chosen to code MtGox's wallet software in such a way that it didn't include any consideration of transaction malleability. It also seems that he didn't take it too seriously, given that it was left to the owner of a competing exchange to tell him he might be under attack. Karpelès and his team investigated the issue as a matter of priority but kept it under wraps while they did so, leaving customers to fill the void with naturally negative suppositions. Mike Hearn, one of Bitcoin's earliest developers and a MtGox user, replied to the Bitcoin Foundation forum thread to ask what Mark Karpelès was doing to address the issue:

> *It seems very likely to me that for some reason Mark K is not able to work on his codebase anymore, and isn't able to resolve bugs in a timely manner, leaving his support staff to try and clean up the mess by making horrible*

hacks like 'throw away and retry later'. The question in my mind then becomes – where is Mark and what is he doing?

A respondent to this message noted on 5 February, 'It is only a matter of time before this starts to really unfold.' If Mark Karpelès wanted to get a handle on the communications side of things, he was going about it the wrong way, taking random days off work right when his team needed guidance and, according to Thomas Glucksmann, making himself unavailable when he was in the office:

He didn't seem to accept the gravity of certain situations which makes me think that he did not understand what happened, that he was in another world, in his world.

By this time, MtGox customers were starting to go to extreme lengths to try and get their funds back or at least get some answers as to where they were. Fed up with phone calls and emails going unanswered, an Australian customer going by the pseudonym Coinsearcher took a sixteen-hour flight to Tokyo in order to protest outside the MtGox office and demand answers from anyone he could get hold of. Coinsearcher headed straight to the MtGox office after touching down, where he waited for four hours before finally being granted an audience with Gonzague Gay-Bouchery. Gay-Bouchery denied that the exchange was bankrupt and reaffirmed the issues with banks as the reason behind the cash withdrawal problems. As for the bitcoin withdrawals, which was what Coinsearcher really cared about, this was put down to an unspecified technical issue that was being worked on. Gay-Bouchery added that the negative news reports were down to anti-MtGox press outlets that had a 'vendetta' against the company and reaffirmed that the coins were safe.

Coinsearcher returned the following morning and waited for an hour and a half before Karpelès, 'carrying a large, and very fancy coffee in his hand that could have passed as a dessert', came along. The two had a conversation along the same lines as Coinsearcher had had with Gay-Bouchery the evening before, with Karpelès promising he would look into Coinsearcher's case. Some twenty minutes later, Gay-Bouchery arrived to give Coinsearcher the 'good news' that the issue of his pending withdrawal had been sorted. Coinsearcher relayed this disheartening development on the Reddit post documenting his trip:

After I got Wi-Fi connection back [at] the hotel I discovered my failed bitcoins withdrawal transactions had been cancelled and all my bitcoins were put back in the one place in the world I didn't want them: The MtGox website. Back to joining the queue of 40,000 other bitcoins.

The following day, 7 February, as Coinsearcher was on his way back to Australia, Mark Karpelès ensured that he would now *never* get his bitcoins. In an announcement on its website, Karpelès said that MtGox was finally doing the one thing everyone had feared but which had felt inevitable for weeks:

> *During our efforts to resolve the issue being encountered by some bitcoin withdrawals it was determined that the increase in withdrawal traffic is hindering our efforts on a technical level. As to get a better look at the process the system needs to be in a static state. In order for our team to resolve the withdrawal issue it is necessary to temporarily pause all withdrawal traffic to obtain a clear technical view of the current processes.*

MtGox apologised for the short notice and asked for patience as the team worked to resolve the unnamed problem, with many opining that this was the beginning of the end for the exchange. When one respondent on Reddit claimed that 'Gox is dead people', the exchange responded by saying, 'We just want to reiterate that this is not a 'stop' but a temporary pause so that we can implement a proper fix to the problem.' One observer read between the lines:

> *Let me translate this:*
>
> *We are insolvent and have been franticly trying to sell a stake in Mt.Gox to an investor for the last 3 months (white knight) to cover the shortfall. The wheels are now falling off the bus so until we raise some money, withdrawals have been suspended. If we do not raise any money, you will not see any of your cash. Thank you for supporting us over the years.*

The concerns over MtGox even made it as far as InfoWars, where host Alex Jones, previously an avowed Bitcoin supporter, warned that the US government was preparing to capitalise on the crash of MtGox for its own ends:

> *The government's going to use Bitcoin's fall down the road to discredit all cryptocurrencies and basically try to arrest a bunch of people involved. Maybe it'll end up not being bad, but my gut tells me: don't walk, run away from Bitcoin.*

What was clear from the deluge of comments and complaints that flooded social media platforms and the Bitcoin forums directly after this notice was published was that the 'large transactions' fudge had gone down like a tungsten parachute. The overwhelming consensus was that the exchange had somehow lost all its bitcoins, although more leftfield reasons began to spring up, too: some customers reported that MtGox support staff had blamed the delays on the arrest of BitInstant CEO Charlie Shrem, a friend of Mark Karpelès and fellow Bitcoin Foundation board member, the week prior. Others tried to steady the ship, with one saying that he had just spoken to Karpelès, who had reported that the issue was down to 'a technical glitch, not insolvency'.

Interestingly, Bitstamp was also hit with transaction malleability attacks around this time, but crucially, it reported that 'no funds have been lost and no funds are at risk' before managing to implement a 'simple solution' which allowed it to resume bitcoin withdrawals four days later. The story was far from simple at MtGox, however, where Karpelès and his team were searching for a fix to the transaction malleability bug. The most frustrating part about this for those carrying out the work was that it had been a known problem for three years, and yet Karpelès had demanded that the exchange be coded in his preferred way, leaving them playing catchup. They also knew, or at least heavily suspected, that the transaction malleability bug couldn't possibly account for the number of bitcoins that were reported as missing. As Cameron Winklevoss opined following the exchange's eventual collapse, 'While it is entirely possible that Mt.Gox was [a] victim of Transaction Malleability exploits, it is almost certainly a false explanation for its failure.'

The team worked over the weekend to tackle the bug and calculate the losses, with customers made to wait anxiously for any news. Of course, Karpelès being Karpelès, he chose to direct his attention to the coding of the patches rather than dealing with the fallout. Like Coinsearcher, customers who had submitted withdrawals prior to the cutoff saw their balances returned to their accounts, having never made it to the blockchain. They may not have known it at the time, but the last ship out of MtGox had already sailed. A press release issued on Monday, 10 February, revealed what the team had discovered and what next steps would need to be taken:

> *MtGox has detected unusual activity on its Bitcoin wallets and performed investigations during the past weeks. This confirmed the presence of transactions which need to be examined more closely.*

The exchange tried to reassure customers that it would resume withdrawals 'once the issue outlined above has been properly addressed in a manner that will best serve our customers', and promised more information soon. However, some observers felt that the damage had already been done, with a writer for the website Cryptolife suggesting that the exchange was operating illegally:

> *It's been long known that Gox is incapable of fulfilling all their USD debts ever since their main bank account was seized. On this front, they have been operating as a psuedo ponzi scheme, where new money would pay off old money. There's been a lot of debate lately whether or not Gox had the BTC on hand to pay off all their debts, and if you read between the lines, this press release confirms that they do not. Make no mistake about it: Mt Gox is likely insolvent in BTC as well.*

Worse was to come for MtGox as crypto news outlet *Coindesk* removed MtGox from its Bitcoin Price Index 'due to the exchange's persistent failure to meet the Index's standards', prompted by its decision to halt bitcoin withdrawals. This was hardly a hammer blow, but it was yet another sign that MtGox was rapidly losing respect in the Bitcoin world, something that became even clearer later that day when cult YouTube figure MadBitcoins put out what he called MtGox's 'Scheduled Press Releases' and suggested that the exchange was currently at phase two:

1. *Frozed accounts because of technical issues*
2. *Blame some old non relevant Bitcoin bug*
3. *Problem solved. Accounts will be released in 24h*
4. *Acclaim accounts were hacked and compromised*
5. *All bitcoins are gone!*
6. *Insolvent*
7. *Sorry*

Time would show this schedule to be scarily accurate.

Chapter 9 – Missing

On 12 February 2014, Edinburgh-based MtGox customer Kolin Burges woke up and realised he had to take action. Burges held some $320,000 worth of bitcoins on MtGox, and like so many others, his attempts to withdraw them were being repeatedly rejected. Inspired by Coinsearcher, Burges took a flight from London to Tokyo to challenge Karpelès in person about the missing coins, hoping to get both his bitcoins and answers. Burges arrived in Tokyo and met a fellow MtGox customer who had arranged media coverage for his intended exposè before heading to a Bitcoin meetup where he became acquainted with another MtGox user, Aaron, who was prepared to join Burges in his protest.

The following day, with *The Wall Street Journal* and *Coindesk* in tow, Burges went to the MtGox office and demanded to speak to Karpelès or someone in a position of power. The experience with Coinsearcher had seemingly led to MtGox tightening their policies, and Burges was informed that only those with appointments were allowed in. Burges requested an appointment with Karpelès, but his request was refused. Angered but not dissuaded, Burges decided he had only one option left. Early on the morning of the following day, Valentine's Day, he headed back to the MtGox office with the media outlets once again ready to film any encounter. A snowstorm had hit Tokyo overnight, and Burges stood outside the office as the white flurry spun around him, holding a now-famous placard asking, '*MTGOX – WHERE IS OUR MONEY*'.

Burges' resolve was repaid half an hour later when the t-shirted Karpelès, his famous dessert drink in one hand and a black umbrella in the other, rounded a corner and headed towards him. Burges blocked Karpelès's way into the office and asked him repeatedly why he hadn't got his bitcoins yet. Karpelès replied that he couldn't give Burges, or anyone, their bitcoins back due to a technical problem. Burges replied that this was 'simply not true' and then asked pointedly, 'So do you still have everyone's bitcoins?', at which point Karpelès abandoned his semi-helpful demeanour and shut down all questions, threatening to call the police and eventually barging his way past Burges into the building. When questioned by *Coindesk* reporter Jon Southurst, Burges summarised what he had just experienced:

> *I don't expect their company's going to last much longer. I think it's about to collapse, and I expect that no one's going to get their money back, but we'll see.*

Karpelès would later say that he 'shouldn't have been that cold to Kolin, but I didn't really know how to react to his confrontation', adding that he had 'a lot on my plate that day'. Burges maintained his protest following Karpelès's escape and was joined by Aaron a short while later. A third protester, a lawyer wearing a silver mask to protect his identity from his employer, joined them later that day after having read about the protest online. The masked protestor, who had added further intrigue to what was, as far as uninitiated observers were concerned, a rather bizarre situation, left after lunch, but Burges and Aaron remained there all day, explaining the reasons for their actions to the growing number of reporters and passersby.

Up in the MtGox office, Mark Karpelès was watching the protest and the traction it was gaining with a rising sense of panic. Not only was it drawing unwanted attention to MtGox's problems, it had come at the worst possible time; China's deadline of 14 February for its banks to stop handling money from Bitcoin exchanges had resulted in an unwelcome spike in bitcoin withdrawal requests. This had the effect of dumping thousands more cars onto an already jammed highway, with the swamped support staff facing a fresh deluge of calls and emails from irate Chinese customers on top of disgruntled Americans.

According to Karpelès, it was only at this late stage in proceedings that he was advised it might be a good idea to check the exchange's cold wallets to see if the bitcoins were actually there. The suggestion supposedly came from his lawyers rather than him, which, if true, adds another fairly hefty notch to the bedpost of terrible stewardship. There are plenty of observers who, for perfectly understandable reasons, don't believe that Karpelès can't have been aware of the state of the exchange's bitcoin holdings at this time or that he genuinely believed the transaction malleability bug was the only reason for the withdrawal issues. Prime among these was the suggestion that Karpelès should have known that the bug couldn't possibly have caused the multitude of errors or the withdrawal congestion that customers had been experiencing.

Given the borderline hysteria on Bitcoin forums and social media at the time, the suggestion that nobody at MtGox thought to check the cold wallets to make sure the funds were really there is inconceivable. No one at MtGox knew more about Bitcoin than Mark Karpelès, and so his employees trusted that he knew what he was doing and never questioned the company's bitcoin storage arrangements. Karpelès would happily demonstrate how a Bitcoin paper wallet worked to anyone who wanted to know, with his knowledge of the subject matter enough to assuage any doubts about the security of his customers' assets. It was this trust in Karpelès that likely prevented many from questioning him over the status of the cold wallets, even as the bitcoin withdrawals issues worsened, but it is equally as difficult to believe that no staff members raised the possibility of a deficit with him before February 2014 as it is to believe that he never thought to check the wallets himself. Of course, some withdrawals *were* getting through, so did Karpelès think that the exchange was operating perfectly well and that these people were just lucky that they weren't getting targeted by the transaction malleability hacker?

There are two further explanations to suggest why bitcoin withdrawals were being processed only sporadically: one is the improbable suggestion that MtGox staff were waiting for Karpelès to manually add cold wallet funds to the hot wallet before withdrawals could be processed, and the other is that MtGox was, as already suggested, unintentionally operating as a Ponzi scheme where external deposits were required for withdrawals to be possible. Regardless of whether the claims of withdrawal congestion, blockchain synchronisation, transaction malleability and all the other excuses handed out to users since August 2013 were genuine or just delaying tactics, the fact that Karpelès hadn't yet checked the cold wallets either speaks of gross mismanagement or a conscious reluctance to do so. This issue also raises huge concerns over the fact that MtGox was still accepting deposits at a time when its CEO might have known the company was bankrupt.

When it comes to how Karpelès actually scanned the wallets to check their contents, very little is known. He hasn't ever discussed this side of the MtGox collapse in any great detail, leaving, as we will see, more questions than answers. Karpelès says that, having been convinced to check the cold wallet balances, he embarked on the arduous task of driving around Tokyo collecting the paper wallets from the bank vaults and safety deposit boxes, supposedly the first time they had been accessed since being placed there years previously, estimating that there were some 300 pieces of paper to go through in total. As suggested earlier, this seems like overkill and once again raises the idea that he may have been storing bitcoins in more convenient locations. Reports vary as to whether Karpelès conducted the scanning process at home or in the MtGox offices, but it would not be a surprise if he used both locations to speed up the process, although this would in itself have raised security issues. The standard way of checking the balance of a paper Bitcoin wallet is by inputting the public key (the address) into an online blockchain explorer and reading off the screen, a process which takes all of ten seconds. Karpelès, on the other hand, says that he needed to trace MtGox transactions through the blockchain to identify the various cold wallet addresses in the first place, suggesting that he hadn't kept a list of wallet addresses after all. Several factors would have complicated this, not least the fact that documentation on certain wallets was missing or incomplete, while MtGox also employed a strategy called 'tumbling', whereby it mixed Bitcoin transactions in order to enhance customer privacy. The process became so laborious that Karpelès made a specific piece of software that extracted the public address from the private key on the wallet, allowing him to check the balances more quickly. He might have wished he hadn't bothered: every wallet he scanned was empty. What started out as a few missing bitcoins soon turned into a few hundred missing bitcoins, then a few thousand, and then tens of thousands. Karpelès says that he became scared to continue the scanning process for fear of what was becoming more and more evident, a feeling he described in a BBC radio program in 2018:

> *I would say it's probably very close to when you're falling from a building and you see the floor getting close. It felt like I was about to die.*

When the last wallet was finally scanned, the scale of the damage was brutally laid bare: every single one of MtGox's cold wallets was empty. Hundreds of thousands of bitcoins, perhaps as many as a million, had left the exchange via the back door. Someone had broken in completely undetected and emptied the vaults. The situation would have been dire enough had this been the company's money, but the overwhelming majority of the stolen coins belonged to MtGox's customers, and there were zero protections in place. Hundreds of millions of dollars had vanished, probably forever, and Karpelès knew that he would be held responsible. All MtGox had left in its kitty was 2,000 bitcoins in the withdrawal hot wallet, the equivalent of asking a car to run on a few drops of fuel. Of course, many believe that Karpelès was anything but shocked at this discovery, and some even doubt that this scanning process ever took place at all (no staff member has ever publicly stated that they witnessed such a process or heard anything of it at the time). There are, of course, extreme doubts about the existence of the cold wallets in the first place.

Whether his shock was genuine or not, Karpelès rushed to inform Gonzague Gay-Bouchery of the mammoth loss, and the pair hastily tried to work out what had happened and what they should do next. Gay-Bouchery made several phone calls and sent frantic emails, one of which was to former MtGox VIP customers, the Winklevoss twins, to whom he broke the news:

> [Gay-Bouchery] said that someone had been stealing from the company's online, or hot, wallet by changing the transaction identifiers [the malleability bug]. When the hot wallet was empty, Mark had unwittingly refilled it with coins from the cold, offline wallets, over and over again, until all the offline wallets were empty. The whole thing had been going on for months, or even years.

Here, we get the first concrete suggestion that Karpelès believed the hot wallet to have been the route by which the coins had been stolen, with Gay-Bouchery cementing (incorrectly) the transaction malleability bug as the attack vector. The email also sees Gay-Bouchery stating that Karpelès personally topped up the hot wallet with the contents of the cold wallets, the earliest known mention. As we have already discussed, however, this theory is impractical on several levels, and no one has publicly claimed to have witnessed Mark Karpelès doing this. We know that the only way the hot wallet-cold wallet system could have worked efficiently is for it to have been automated, totally undermining the purpose of a cold wallet (it should also be noted that Gay-Bouchery's source for this information was Karpelès himself rather than any first-hand experience of the events). Gonzague Gay-Bouchery has refused to discuss his time at MtGox since its collapse, and until he does, we will have to take educated guesses as to how much he knew of what was truly going on behind the scenes at this critical time. This interaction suggests one of two things, however: either he believed what Karpelès was telling him about the wallets, or he knew Karpelès was lying and was helping him cover up the truth.

It's not clear why Gay-Bouchery contacted the Winklevoss twins, of all people, with this highly sensitive information when they were no longer customers of MtGox, but presumably, they were one of a number of people he contacted with the same story that weekend, possibly to try and get ahead of any narrative from the press. How much was spin and how much he genuinely believed may never be known, but his story was an odd concoction of two almost certain mistruths.

Karpelès informed the company's lawyers of the massive loss and was told he needed to inform the Tokyo District Court at once. The court gave Karpelès until 24 February to find the missing coins or arrange a bailout and to not say anything publicly until then. This would prove difficult given that customers, staff and the media were breathing down his neck for answers. Karpelès had already given email interviews to *Forbes* and *The Wall Street Journal* that week, where he had apologised for the continued suspension of bitcoin withdrawals, saying that it simply wasn't safe to process them while the transaction malleability issue hadn't been resolved. This excuse was starting to wear thin, however, and things got worse when Karpelès blamed the Bitcoin Foundation for MtGox's inability to guard against the transaction malleability issue. Karpelès complained that it had been hard to 'keep pace' with all the changes being initiated by the foundation, of which he was still a board member, and said that the bug should have been rectified by the foundation when it was first discovered, rather than leaving it to exchanges to create their own workarounds. The Bitcoin Foundation's response was to say that transaction malleability wasn't a bug that could be eradicated in the code and that MtGox's complicated systems were the cause of the problem, pointing out that the exchanges that had successfully implemented workarounds had done so with little to no fuss. This included Bitstamp, whose patch had arrived that very week with no loss of bitcoins.

The Wall Street Journal also tried to pin Karpelès down on whether the exchange was solvent and if customers were protected in the event that it wasn't, with Karpelès responding that information regarding MtGox's solvency was 'confidential' and that the exchange was operating within Japanese law. Of course, as the world was to find out in a matter of days, the authorities had never given their blessing to MtGox's operation, and any semblance of customer protection was nothing but a myth. These interviews, accompanied by the efforts of Burges et al., ensured that MtGox's issues were becoming a global news story.

Karpelès's refusal to clarify the situation continued to have a hugely detrimental impact on the price of Bitcoin, both on MtGox and elsewhere. Desperation was leading to users selling their holdings at massively reduced rates, thinking that they had more chance of getting cash off the exchange than bitcoins, even if they were getting screwed by the exchange rate. Throughout February 2014, the price of Bitcoin on MtGox plummeted from $1,000 to under $100 per coin, which dragged it down to about $600 on other exchanges. There is evidence, however, of preferential treatment being shown to some clients around this time. In May 2014, an email surfaced which revealed that early Bitcoin investor Olivier Janssens had threatened to sue Karpelès if his funds, which equated to 12,410 bitcoins, weren't returned to him. The email, sent on 16 February 2014, presented Karpelès with an offer: if Karpelès sent 10,000 of Janssens' bitcoins to him within twenty-four hours, he would hold off with the lawsuit. Eight days later, a single sale of 10,000 bitcoins appeared on Bitstamp, with some believing that Karpelès had bought the bitcoins with the exchange's cash reserves and sent them to Janssens privately. Others believed that Janssens sold the coins to Bitcoin Builder, a platform that allowed the temporary sale of MtGox bitcoins. However he got rid of his coins, Janssens endeared himself even less to MtGox creditors when he later tried to make a claim for the 10,000 coins he had already sold, although this was rejected (a later claim for $385,117 was accepted). This wasn't the last tangle Karpelès would have with Janssens; in January 2015, the Belgian accused Karpelès of sending death threats to his own employees – a claim Karpelès denied. Questions also remain over the treatment afforded to the Winklevoss twins, with some creditors wondering how the brothers managed to get their massive holdings, thought to total some 100,000 coins, off MtGox when other users were unable to get just fractions of this amount off.

Much to Karpelès's dismay, Kolin Burges wasn't put off by the cold weather and the cold shoulder he had received from the CEO and returned to the MtGox office over the weekend with Aaron, even streaming the protest online for the world to see. This spurred more claims from the crypto community that MtGox was on borrowed time, with some suggesting that blaming the Bitcoin Foundation for its own issues had only served to alienate Karpelès further from the community. The day Burges' confrontation with Karpelès was posted to YouTube, a petition was posted on the website Change.org asking the Bitcoin Foundation to remove Karpelès from its board, claiming that he had 'continually proven himself to be incompetent, causing fear in the community and damaging the trust signals that Bitcoin relies on so as to be taken seriously.' This petition would go on to receive 1,733 votes of support before it was rendered irrelevant by later events. The same day, respected Bitcoin developer Andreas Antonopoulos told The Bitcoin Group YouTube channel that there was only one place to look when it came to identifying the problems at MtGox:

> The problems at MtGox are not problems with bugs, they're not problems with solvency, they're not problems with the team, they are problems that start with the leadership. Poor communication, deflecting blame, disorganised chaos, no software development process, and these things exhibit themselves every few months as a 'Goxing'. We're now in our fifth Goxing, and if you haven't learnt the lesson by now then history will deliver it again.

On Monday, 17 February, mere hours after Gonzague Gay-Bouchery had told the Winklevoss twins that MtGox's Bitcoin wallets were empty, an update appeared on the exchange's website as Karpelès was meeting with the Tokyo District Court to inform them of the exchange's bankruptcy:

> We apologise for the inconvenience caused by the recent suspension of external bitcoin transfers. Fortunately, as we announced on Saturday we have now implemented a solution that should enable withdrawals and mitigate any issues caused by transaction malleability.
>
> With this new system in place, MtGox should be able to resume withdrawals soon. At the beginning we will do so at a moderated pace and with new daily/monthly limits in place to prevent any problems with the new system and to take into account current market conditions.

The solution had arrived courtesy of Blockchain.info, but the team working on its implementation on MtGox apparently had no idea that there were no bitcoins left on MtGox to be withdrawn anyway. Mark Karpelès has denied being personally responsible for this communication, a necessary stance given his knowledge of MtGox's situation at the time. His claim that he was 'too focused on solving the largest issues (banks, governments, etc) to have time to deal with the issues happening inside the company' is a quite incredible one for several reasons, not least because he was often a hindrance more than a help when it came to resolving the banking issue. The suggestion that he was so laser-focused on certain issues that he didn't notice the company circling the drain shows either a total dereliction of the most basic duties of a CEO or the worst example ever attempted at absolving oneself of blame. For someone who was a confessed obsessive over every element of MtGox, it is inconceivable that Karpelès wasn't aware that such an important communication was going out to his customers, giving them false hope that their funds would be coming back to them. On the other hand, with his attention so focused on the disaster of the missing coins and how to resolve the issue, he may have signed dozens of things off without properly looking at them. We will never know, but Karpelès later defended his actions during this period by claiming that 'a lot of miscommunication' was taking place at the time, with both the internal and external customer service teams simply repeating the company line that had been doing the rounds ever since the transaction malleability bug had been discovered: they were working on a fix which should be implemented soon.

The statement ended with the promise of an update by the 19th, when bitcoin withdrawals, as far as customers were concerned, might resume. While some were hopeful of getting their funds back imminently, others were more circumspect:

> *Something is very strange with this exchange. If someone is holding your money and they tell you that they can only release a fraction of it at a time (or none at all, as is the case right now)... you should be very cautious. It would not surprise me one bit if they actually no longer had access to the assets that they claim they control. Good luck to everyone who still needs to get their bitcoins out of Mt. Gox.*

Some went further, calling out Karpelès and MtGox for their malpractice as well as hinting that all was not well:

> *This is all complete bullshit. When are they going to address the delays in withdrawing money via wire transfer? I've been waiting 4 fucking months*

now, with no real explanation for the delay. There's something fishy going on with Mt. Gox. They used to be adequate.

Coindesk noted that the 'small but determined protest' by Burges and his cohorts outside the MtGox office had continued over the weekend and into the following Monday, with some questioning its merits now that MtGox had promised that withdrawals were set to restart. Burges says that there was a very good reason why the protest continued:

> At this point, MtGox was really panicking about the protest and trying to stop it. To me, it's fairly obvious that the message was put there to attempt to diffuse the momentum around the protest. I remember an online comment saying, 'Why are you still protesting when the problem is fixed?' At that time MtGox was resorting to writing comments pretending to be MtGox users.

Indeed, allegations have been made that someone on the MtGox team posted fake comments on online forums talking up the exchange at this time and denying that the issues were as bad as the press and the Bitcoin world were making out. These comments made it as far as inclusion in lawsuits and were even referenced in bankruptcy reports, but conclusive proof has never been forthcoming.

Knowing he had a week's grace to plug the gargantuan hole in the company's accounts before the bankruptcy court pulled down the shutters, Mark Karpelès went to work. He assumed that other big players in the Bitcoin world, chiefly the operators of other major exchanges, would be willing to bail him out in order to protect their own businesses; while Bitcoin itself may not have been at fault for MtGox's issues, trust in Bitcoin exchanges would be shattered, potentially beyond repair, if MtGox collapsed with the loss of hundreds of thousands of coins. Bitcoin users around the world might denounce the ecosystem as inherently unsafe, an assertion that might stifle or even kill the sector before it was even out of short trousers. The not unfounded concern among the MtGox hierarchy was that the collapse of MtGox could precipitate an exodus that could set Bitcoin adoption back years, at best.

On a mission to save MtGox, Karpelès began approaching these major players to try and secure a bailout for the exchange. These calls and emails were soon supplemented by a prospectus called the Crisis Strategy Draft, which outlined the state of the exchange and what it planned to do to save itself:

> *For several weeks, MtGox customers have been affected by bitcoin withdrawal issues that compounded on themselves. Publicly, MtGox declared that 'transaction malleability' caused the system to be subject to theft, and that something needed to be done by the core devs to fix it. Gox's own workaround solution was criticised, and eventually a fix was provided by Blockchain.info. The truth, it turns out, is that the damage had already been done. At this point 744,408 bitcoins are missing due to malleability-related theft which went unnoticed for several years. The cold storage has been wiped out due to a leak in the hot wallet.*

This figure of 744,408 is, in fact, more than 67,500 bitcoins short of what had actually been lost to hacks by this point, but the September 2011 hack was likely not taken into account, seeing as it hadn't yet been discovered. Again, however, we see MtGox blaming the massive theft on the transaction malleability bug, although it also blamed a 'leak' in the hot wallet, an exploit it dropped in without further explanation. MtGox then produced a table listing its assets and liabilities. Needless to say, it made very uncomfortable reading:

Assets

Bitcoin: 2,000, in hot wallet.

Cash:22.43 million US dollars, plus 5 million US dollars held by Coinlab and 5.5 million US dollars held by the Department of Homeland Security.

Liabilities

Bitcoin: 624,408 (customers) and 120,000 (MtGox), minus 80, 208 from banned or suspicious account.

Cash: 55 million US dollars (but still unclear at this point).

The document admitted, 'The reality is that MtGox can go bankrupt at any moment, and certainly deserves to as a company', but warned that a collapse of MtGox could set Bitcoin back '5-10 years', adding, 'At the risk of appearing hyperbolic, this could be the end of Bitcoin, at least for most of the public.' The recipients of the draft were then treated to a plan for how to save MtGox without it having to go public about the loss. First, it would need an injection of bitcoins in order to shore up its reserves and clear the withdrawal backlog. Second, the company would close for a month while it rebranded, with Karpelès 'admitting his errors and expressing a desire to fix the situation by stepping back as a CEO [and] blaming the technology implementation, which was not sized and designed to deal with such [a] level of transactions or to deal with malleability'. Of course, this ignored the fact that Karpelès was the de facto head of MtGox's IT department, given that it was he who signed everything off and had agreed to have MtGox coded in a way that ignored the potential impact of transaction malleability. Third, the newly rebranded 'Gox' exchange would also seek to 'inspire confidence' by refreshing its social media and communications channels with its new image and message, and fourth, it would get a new development team to rewrite the codebase. This, the document predicted, could all be completed as soon as 1 April.

While potential suitors assessed MtGox's offer, MtGox customers awaited their promised update and their bitcoins. On the evening of 19 February, they got their update, but it wasn't what they expected:

> *In addition to the technical issue, this week we have experienced some security problems, and as a result we had to relocate MtGox to our previous office building in Shibuya. The move, combined with some other security and technical challenges, pushed back our progress.*

Many saw this relocation as more delaying tactics by Karpelès, who they said was using the peaceful MtGox protest by Burges and co. and anonymous online threats by frustrated customers as an excuse to kick the can down the road by moving offices right when the team should have been focused on resuming withdrawals; after all, sort the withdrawals and the protests would stop. Of course, Karpelès and his management team knew that this was now impossible; they just hadn't told anyone else yet. The update promised further information 'as soon as possible' and left it at that.

Ignoring the criticism, or perhaps fueled by it, Burges and his fellow protestors gathered once again at the MtGox office, where they were told that the staff had left the premises, although the parent company, Tibanne, was still present. Some protestors got so angry that they began shouting at the building, which was captured by the news cameras still following their endeavours. The swift escalation in the scale of the protest and the fact that some protestors were now upgrading it from a quiet protest to a more vocal one was the tipping point for the Japanese authorities, who were likely becoming embarrassed by the events playing out on television and computer screens all around the world. Within forty-eight hours of MtGox announcing that it was moving offices, police had closed the protest down. Kolin Burges flew home, knowing that while he may not have gotten what he came for, he had at least alerted the world to what was going on at MtGox.

While Burges was flying back to the UK, the Bitcoin world was begging Karpelès to open up about what was really going on with the world's best-known Bitcoin exchange. Chris Ellis, the creator of the cryptocurrency Feathercoin, added his voice to those who now believed the jig was up and that it was in Karpelès's best interests to lay his cards on the table:

I think the guy needs to come clean. He needs to just fess up. I wouldn't be surprised if he's lost all the coins, and it's some big fuck up, but whatever it is, he just needs to come clean because the real theft now is the theft of everybody's time and attention.

While others were calling for him to come clean, Karpelès was channelling former Lehman Brothers CEO Dick Fuld and trying frantically to rescue his company by any means necessary. However, as Bitcoin blogger Ryan Selkis would reveal after the crash, Karpelès's meetings with the Bitcoin exchange operators were a disaster:

A source who met with the Mt. Gox team the day after the 'Crisis Strategy Draft' was created, confirmed that Bennefla and another person joined Mark Karpeles for a meeting to discuss an emergency bailout of Mt. Gox. This meeting triggered a chain reaction of events in which the solicited investors rebuffed Karpeles and his colleagues, demanded they come clean to customers and stakeholders immediately, and then notified other industry executives, including those at the Bitcoin Foundation, of the catastrophic losses at Mt. Gox. This group of executives promptly reached out to regulatory authorities and began crafting a joint statement condemning Mt. Gox.

Like Lehman Brothers prior to its collapse in September 2008, MtGox was now considered toxic by the CEOs who didn't share Karpelès's belief that a collapse of MtGox would also sink Bitcoin. As a result, and in a clear indication of just how much MtGox's cachet had fallen in a matter of months, the individuals he approached all professed a preference to let MtGox go under rather than rescue it. These newer, better-run exchanges, such as Kraken, Coinbase and Bitstamp, had been taking the market share away from MtGox since 2013, and the fact that all their owners turned their noses up at MtGox's huge customer base showed the extent to which MtGox's star had waned.

It was about to be swallowed up by a black hole.

Chapter 10 – Collapse

With nobody willing to bail out MtGox, the Monday, 24 February deadline imposed by the bankruptcy court rapidly approaching and the executives of the other top exchanges preparing to spill the beans on what was going down, Mark Karpelès went into the weekend knowing that he needed a miracle to save the company and his skin. There was already talk of a class action lawsuit against him on Bitcoin forums, although he knew this would be the least of his worries if he couldn't replace his customers' deposits. Karpelès spent the weekend in dialogue with various individuals, including Charlie Shrem, who had been kicked off the Bitcoin Foundation board following his arrest on 26 January on money laundering charges related to Bitcoin. The pair tried to think up a way to extricate Karpelès and MtGox from the waves that threatened to engulf them. Every avenue failed, however, and late on Sunday, the first domino fell:

> *Effective immediately, Mt. Gox has submitted their resignation from the board of directors. We are grateful for their early and valuable contributions as a founding member in launching the Bitcoin Foundation. MtGox Co. Ltd. (Japan) held one of the three elected industry member seats. Further details, including election procedures, will be forthcoming.*

Shrem lauded the resignation, saying that following 'lengthy' conversations with Karpelès and the MtGox team, he predicted 'good news on the horizon for people who have funds stuck on MtGox', leading to speculation that a takeover was in the offing. When *Coindesk* reported the falling of the second and third dominoes late on Sunday night, however, the potential for good news took a massive hit:

Mt. Gox has removed all posts from its official Twitter feed. Readers started noticing the missing tweets just a short time after CEO Mark Karpeles resigned his seat on the Bitcoin Foundation's Board of Directors.

Indeed, Karpelès had followed MtGox off the Bitcoin Foundation board, and the exchange had wiped its entire Twitter feed with no warning or reason given, sending Bitcoin forums into meltdown. Multiple theories were given for the wiping, ranging from a potential rescue and rebrand to the latest sign that the exchange was on the verge of collapse. A BitcoinTalk poll found that the majority of voters, 43%, believed that MtGox was 'dead in the water', while 35% believed that it would survive. As Monday dawned, MtGox customers held their breath and waited.

At the same time as Karpelès and Shrem were trying Hail Mary phone calls to save MtGox, Ryan Selkis was walking his dog when his phone notified him of an incoming email from Bitcoin angel investor Ben Davenport. Davenport said he needed to talk to Selkis urgently about the MtGox situation. Selkis called him and was told something extraordinary: MtGox was short around 745,000 bitcoins. Selkis was initially dismissive, but Davenport said he had proof, which he emailed over. Once home, Selkis opened this email to find a document attached. It was the Crisis Strategy Draft. Selkis read through the document but found the stated losses so staggering that he initially considered it a fake. After all, everyone knew MtGox was incompetent, but surely it hadn't been *that* incompetent. However, after ringing around purported other recipients of the document and receiving vague non-answers as opposed to outright denials, Selkis realised that it was almost certainly true; MtGox had lost nearly half a billion dollars worth of bitcoins, but worse, it hadn't told anyone.

Selkis wasn't sure what to do with the information, wondering if he should post the document in its entirety or seek more thorough clarification of its authenticity first. Should he even post it at all, given that it would mark the exchange's death knell and crash the Bitcoin price? Whatever he was going to do, he realised, he would have to do it soon: MtGox was due to post a company update in a matter of hours, where it might try and once again reassure customers rather than telling them the truth. Alternatively, Mark Karpelès could do a runner with what was left in the kitty. Selkis sold his bitcoin holdings, uploaded the Crisis Strategy Draft and penned a hasty blog post under his pen name, Two-bit Idiot, reaffirming that the document was unverified but that he believed it to be true. Selkis signed off the post by saying:

> *This is catastrophic, and I am sorry to share this. I do believe that this is one of the existential threats to bitcoin that many have feared and have personally sold all of my bitcoin holdings through Coinbase. To do so, and not give you the same information, would be dishonest and immoral. I am a risk tolerant investor, but I believe this will be catastrophic for Bitcoin, both as a currency and as a fledgling industry. If this is a hoax, it is one that I am fully blindsided by. I fear, however, that it is not.*

The blog post and the Crisis Strategy Draft flew around the Bitcoin community, leading to fervent debate about its merits. Selkis was praised and pilloried in equal measure, with a few hopefuls praying that MtGox would deny that the document was genuine and that the exchange hadn't suffered anything like that level of loss. The numbers were breathtaking, too, so large that many simply couldn't comprehend them, while others were simply in denial, and for a very good reason: it wasn't just any old bitcoins that had gone missing – it was *their* bitcoins. The idea that their holdings might have been wiped out under the noses of the custodians was unthinkable for some, who clung to any slivers of hope they could rather than face that prospect.

Once again, MtGox left an informational vacuum at the worst possible time, keeping the communication shutters firmly pulled down in the wake of the leaking of the Crisis Strategy Draft and leaving the Bitcoin and non-Bitcoin worlds to debate its content and merits. Naturally, the rumour mill went into overdrive, with Karpelès's silence on Monday 24th attributed to him having gone to ground with hundreds of millions of dollars in customer funds. Those who had predicted MtGox's downfall waited for confirmation of the same, but the few that retained hope pointed to an interesting fact: the Crisis Strategy Draft featured a timeline which stated that should a buyer emerge, the exchange would be shut down for one month for rebranding from Tuesday, 25 February. Optimists argued that the Twitter clearout could be related to this rebrand, a belief that was reinforced when it emerged that Karpelès had snapped up the domain gox.com, the name for the rebranded entity, on the 24th. Everything was starting to point towards a buyout, at least for those who were determined to see it that way. This contingent even saw his stepping down from the Bitcoin

Foundation and lack of comment on events as a natural part of the succession process, which the document also said was to take place on the 25th. The fact of the matter was, however, that Karpelès's role with the Bitcoin Foundation had been rendered moot by this point, given that he was hardly ever in contact with the other members and had never gone to a Bitcoin Foundation conference outside Tokyo. His position had become almost ceremonial, and the ceremony was well and truly over.

Karpelès, too, still retained hope, at least publicly. In an online chat with New York-based Bitcoin consultant Jon Fisher late on the 24th, Karpelès opined that he had not given up on MtGox, saying, 'Giving up is not a part of how I usually do things.' He even posted a picture of his keyboard, with his beloved cat, Tibane, also in shot and seemingly assisting with the efforts. Karpelès said he could not disclose whether or not he had stepped down as CEO of MtGox, although at this point, the question seemed like a fait accompli. He added that the Crisis Strategy Draft posted by Selkis was 'more or less' legitimate, ending the argument that had sprung up since its publication that Selkis had been duped or had created it himself, and also confirmed the massive bitcoin loss. In an attempt to keep the flame burning as long as possible, Karpelès defined the customers' funds as 'temporarily unavailable' rather than lost, but the only person he was kidding was himself.

As 25 February dawned in Tokyo, the Bitcoin world waited for any sign that the exchange was either doomed or saved. They got it at around 11 a.m. (10 p.m. the night before in New York) when a statement was published by the CEOs of six major cryptocurrency exchanges, including Kraken's Jesse Powell, Bitstamp CEO Nejc Kodrič and Coinbase founders Fred Ehrsam and Brian Armstrong. The statement, titled 'Joint Statement Regarding MtGox', didn't say outright that MtGox was insolvent, but the authors distanced themselves from the exchange and its operations, cryptically referring to a 'tragic violation of trust'. The CEOs added, 'As with any new industry, there are certain bad actors that need to be weeded out, and that is what we are seeing today.' The statement had, in fact, initially been titled 'Joint Statement Regarding the Insolvency of MtGox', but seeing as the exchange hadn't publicly filed for bankruptcy yet, this was ruled premature. Nevertheless, this was merely a technicality; a spokesman for the group told CNBC that MtGox had confirmed its intention to file for bankruptcy that morning.

Having teetered on the edge of a cliff for so long, the speed with which MtGox finally plummeted caught many by surprise; within minutes of the statement being published, MtGox suspended trading on its site and then took it offline entirely, leaving visitors greeted by nothing but a blank page. Even those wearing the most rose-tinted of glasses realised that the end was now near. Sure enough, several hours later, MtGox confirmed the worst when it came back online with a simple, terse statement on its homepage:

> *In the event of recent news reports and the potential repercussions on MtGox's operations and the market, a decision was taken to close all transactions for the time being in order to protect the site and our users. We will be closely monitoring the situation and will react accordingly.*

For many, this confirmation came as something of a relief. After months of tension and guessing games, everybody finally knew the truth: MtGox was dead. Bitcoin advocate and future exchange owner Erik Voorhees warned of what was to come:

> *MtGox is gone. So let's prepare ourselves. On Tuesday, and for the rest of the week, all hell will break lose in the media. It will be blamed on MtGox, it will be blamed on Bitcoin, it will be blamed on the 'bug,' and it will, more than anything, be blamed on the 'lack of regulation.' Pundits and 'experts' of all types will weigh in on the calamity. It will be world news in a matter of hours. Get ready, because it will be an ugly week.*

He wasn't wrong. MtGox's collapse made headline news all around the world, marking the first time many had heard about Bitcoin at all. Such was its novelty that many news reporters had to explain what both MtGox and Bitcoin were before they could tackle the notion of just how the former could lose $475 million worth of the latter. Some experts tried to discuss the transaction malleability bug, but the lay audience was much more receptive to the idea of a hack by outsiders or a theft by Mark Karpelès. As Erik Voorhees predicted, the knives came out for Bitcoin; *The Guardian* complained that 'Bitcoin still has long-term issues regarding transaction speed, price volatility, and ease of use, as well as finding a killer app which isn't online drug sales', while Senator Joe Manchin claimed that Bitcoin was 'disruptive to our economy' and urged regulators to 'work together, act quickly, and prohibit this dangerous currency from harming hard-working Americans.'

Inside the Bitcoin bubble, Kolin Burges, who had almost become the face of the MtGox crisis, told reporters how he was resigned to the fact that his holdings were definitely gone, although he had known deep down that this had been the case for some time. Messageboards and social media platforms exploded with responses to the news that ranged in emotion from pure rage to reluctant acceptance, despite there being no official confirmation yet that the company had lost its customers' bitcoin holdings. By this point, however, nobody was in much doubt. Threats against the company and Karpelès himself were immediate and vicious, with most users in no doubt that Karpelès was to blame for the disaster, questioning how the exchange could have been talking up restarting withdrawals while knowing, or at least heavily suspecting, that it was bankrupt. Speaking to the World Crypto Network, Andreas Antonopolous suggested that 'legally imposed audits from the outside' would be mandated within forty-eight hours, following which 'we might see certain people go to jail over this'.

While some were venting their fury, others were questioning MtGox's version of events. Rick Falkvinge, who had been keeping tabs on the withdrawal situation since late January, summed up the thoughts of many as MtGox began to slip beneath the waves:

> *So the question is; how can you not notice one billion dollars gradually disappearing from your company over several years, as has been claimed to be the case? The answer is simple: you can't. It's practically against the laws of physics to not notice this. You can't close the ledgers on a fiscal year without every cent accounted for. There would be a faint theoretical possibility it could have taken place entirely within a fiscal year, but even that is improbable to the level of the moon being made of cheese.*

Charlie Shrem, the man who had spoken of his hope that MtGox was going to survive, now questioned Karpelès's story over the transaction malleability bug on an episode of the *Let's Talk Bitcoin* podcast with fellow Bitcoiners David Perry and Adam B. Levine, where the trio summarised their thoughts on the matter:

> *We find it hard to believe those coins are missing and the basic math alone should refute this. 740k btc since malleability became known in '11 is 20k+ btc per month, about 675 btc per day. Even at current prices that's*

over 300k USD per day, that's not the kind of money you just misplace and don't notice.

The piece concluded that it would have taken the equivalent of stealing $48,629.01 worth of bitcoin from MtGox every day for four years to arrive at the figure MtGox said it had lost, which was impossible given that this many bitcoins didn't even exist in 2011. Another theory put forward by a listener posited that Karpelès had lost the private keys to the cold wallets, hence his suggestion that the issue was a temporary technical one and not an irretrievable theft and that the Frenchman was playing for time, thinking he could get them back. Selkis, who some still inexplicably blamed for the downfall, added more fuel to the fire:

> Mt. Gox has allegedly never conducted a single audit of its customer deposits, and it is believed that Karpeles may have been the only one within the company to have knowledge of how to actually tap the exchange's cold storage. It remains unclear exactly how this type of storage leak could have happened over a multi-year period without any knowledge on the part of the executives at Mt. Gox.

Selkis had also heard a theory regarding Karpelès taking advantage of these lower prices:

> ...one source believes that Karpeles knew about the pervasive damage of the transaction malleability attacks for several weeks and was engaging in an arbitrage scheme that leveraged the depressed Mt. Gox price to reap gains on other exchanges. This was allegedly happening well before the exchange's breaking point this past weekend.

As the Bitcoin world struggled to grasp the scale of what had happened with MtGox and what it might mean for the wider ecosystem, talking heads weighed in with their suspicions over MtGox's conduct. Andreas Antonopolous noted that funds couldn't leak from cold storage if properly implemented, leading to only two possible scenarios as far as he was concerned: either there was no leak, or there was no cold storage. Roger Ver took the view that Bitcoin was stronger than MtGox and claimed to know where the issues lay at the exchange:

> I'm very sorry for the people around the world who have lost money because of this, but we need to understand the whole picture. This issue was caused by poor programming skills and a total lack of bookkeeping on the part of

MtGox. It was caused by a single mismanaged company, not by any problem with Bitcoin itself.

Jesse Powell, who, like Roger Ver, had seen firsthand just how ramshackle the operation had been back in 2011, opined that 'how the damage got to be so severe without anyone noticing is unfathomable'. Powell revealed that both Karpelès and Gay-Bouchery had been 'upbeat and excited about their Bitcoin Café' despite their banking woes when the trio had met for coffee just weeks before, as if they believed they were going to make half a billion dollars back in pastry sales. Powell also revealed that there were no indications that the pair were concerned for the exchange's future at their meeting:

We talked about how we were in it for Bitcoin, and the greater good, and how we should work together. They certainly gave no indication that they were worried about insolvency. Perhaps it was something they'd come to live with, or perhaps they really were oblivious.

Like many, Powell wasn't satisfied with the transaction malleability story and offered up his own theory, suggesting that MtGox was robbed of all its bitcoins in June 2011 and had been operating as a 'fractional reserve' ever since. He suggested that either MtGox knew of the loss and pulled out the transactional malleability line when it was finally exposed, or it didn't know the full extent of the loss because it never reconciled its books. He also posited that MtGox might have spent its fiat reserves to bolster its bitcoin balance, hoping to hold out until it was rescued.

The attitude of customers within MtGox's forums at this critical moment was telling; rather than anger, the common emotion in evidence was a sense of resignation, with the announcement coming as confirmation of what they had suspected for months rather than a terrible shock. Some were still trying to put the gloss of a potential buyout and rebrand on the bankruptcy filing, with one such optimist calling the 'leaks' from Fisher and Selkis 'part of a strong arm tactic' by the potential buyer, while the 'insolvency, if real, is not as bad as the [Crisis Strategy Draft] describes'. These levels of optimism represented the minority, however, with the overriding emotion being grim acceptance that MtGox had indeed lost all its customers' money.

One man who *was* angry was Roger Ver, who was on the receiving end of a fresh torrent of abuse over his 'hostage' video. In a BitcoinTalk post on 26

February, Ver said he was 'sorry he led people to trust Mtgox' but defended himself over the claims that he was lying about MtGox's financial position:

But I'm sick of people claiming I said Mtgox was solvent!

I NEVER SAID THAT, EVER!

Liquidity != Solvency

I chose my words very carefully.

That is why I read them from my own script.

I said Mtgox had lots of **LIQUIDITY** *7 months ago when I made that video.*

That was certainly true, but is completely different from saying that they were solvent.

On the same day, MtGox customer and New York-educated lawyer Daniel Kelman penned an open letter to Karpelès in which he proposed building a community-run exchange from the ashes of MtGox, saying that if Karpelès was willing to work with customers, they could 'save Mt. Gox and provide the Bitcoin Community with what it truly needs: an exchange that has everyone's trust'. The reaction to this was mixed, with some saying that they would no longer trust anything connected to MtGox, whoever was in charge, while others welcomed the opportunity to rebuild it, seeing it as their only chance of recouping at least some of their lost funds. Though initially well supported, this idea never made it further than a couple of online posts, although Kelman would have a big part to play in the bankruptcy process and beyond.

More disappointment for MtGox customers came through the actions, or inactions, of Japan's financial overseers, the Financial Services Authority (FSA). Mark Karpelès had stated on several occasions that MtGox was operating within Japanese law, and for many, this meant the company being registered with the FSA, which would have meant that their cash holdings at least were protected. They were to be sorely disappointed, however, when the FSA told *The Wall Street Journal* on the 24th that 'Bitcoin isn't a currency' and that 'The FSA is in charge of currency-based services. Therefore, bitcoin exchanges are not subject to our regulatory oversight.' The Bank of Japan, the Ministry of Finance and the Ministry of Internal Affairs and Communications also washed their hands of having any jurisdiction over MtGox because the exchange dealt with bitcoins, not fiat currencies. Except, of course, that it *did* deal with fiat currencies, and the evidence was there for anyone to see:

- MtGox had made headlines around the world for its fiat deposit and withdrawal issues in recent months
- MtGox had been working with the extremely well-known and regulated Mizuho bank since 2013
- MtGox had $5 million seized by American authorities because it was handling US dollars without a license
- MtGox had $22 million worth of cash deposits when it filed for bankruptcy
- Mark Karpelès had several meetings with the FSA to ensure that it was meeting regulations

Given this wealth of evidence, there is simply no way that three departments of the Japanese government, together responsible for financial oversight in the country, managed to miss the fact that MtGox was accepting, holding and transmitting fiat currencies.

If we are to believe Mark Karpelès, the authorities had actually given him the all-clear to operate, at least informally. As far back as April 2011, MtGox was boasting that it had 'worked our way through all the requirements needed to run our exchange legally' at the time, sentiments that Karpelès echoed even at the time of its collapse, telling *The Wall Street Journal* that he had 'discussed the company's business model with Japanese authorities to ensure the firm was operating within the law.' However, if MtGox *had* been operating within the law, then Karpelès would have been registered as a currency handler as part of the Payment Services Act. This means that Karpelès either lied to *The Wall Street Journal* about speaking to the FSA, told the FSA that MtGox didn't handle currencies and hoped they wouldn't notice, or the FSA didn't investigate properly and failed in its duty. Whichever way the truth lies, Karpelès was never pulled up before or after MtGox's collapse for illegally operating a money-handling business, despite it being an immensely simple crime to prove. The FSA simply tried to skate under the entire affair, with the suggestion being that it had no idea how to handle MtGox at the time and wanted to save face by not admitting complicity following its collapse.

In the days after MtGox went offline, Karpelès was, as would be expected, inundated with demands, complaints and interview requests as he and his top team tried to work out if there was any way to save the exchange. On 26 February, Karpelès tried to reassure customers that he was 'still in Japan, and working very hard with the support of different parties to find a solution to our recent issues.' However, he then took another leaf out of the PR for idiots guidebook when he asked customers to 'kindly…refrain from asking questions to our staff'. This was followed by a later request to customers that struck a very different tone:

> We're working very hard…to find a solution to our recent issues. Stop asking us questions.

Rick Falkvinge summed up the impact of this statement:

> In what must surely rewrite the handbooks for the entire field of Public Relations, MtGox's trailblazing handling of public concerns over the missing billion dollars at this point amounts to 'stop asking us questions'.

In the afternoon of the 25th, Karpelès had told Reuters that MtGox 'should have an official announcement ready soon-ish', adding, 'We are currently at a turning point for the business.' He could say that again. While Karpelès was working on this announcement, the first lawsuit arrived. On 27 February, Illinois citizen Gregory Greene filed a class action suit against Karpelès and MtGox in the United States District Court for the Northern District of Illinois, citing 'systematic misuse and misappropriation of its users' property' and seeking unspecified damages. Greene would add Mizuho Bank to the list of defendants a month later for its part in the collapse of the exchange, by which time a second class action lawsuit had also arrived, this one from Canada. This was in addition to the $75 million Coinlab lawsuit that was still trickling its way through the legal system.

In his live blog covering the events, Falkvinge expressed the thoughts of many around this time:

> You can feel the noose tighten around Karpeles' neck as the picture becomes clearer, both in a figurative and literal sense.

Indeed, attention was already shifting from the collapse of MtGox to the role of its CEO, a shift that was only gathering momentum.

Chapter 11 – Sorry

On Friday, 28 February 2014, MtGox took the first step towards dissolution:

MtGox Co., Ltd. made today an application for commencement of a procedure of civil rehabilitation (minji saisei) at the Tokyo District Court. This application was accepted on the same day.

The communication added that MtGox now had bankruptcy protection and listed liabilities twice that of its assets:

Total amount of assets – ¥3.84 billion ($37.7 million), including ¥2.8 billion ($27.5 million) in cash reserves

Total amount of current liabilities – ¥6.5 billion ($63.8 million)

The letter added that a future increase of liabilities 'may be linked to a loss of bitcoins and customer funds', a situation that was being 'investigated by an expert' and that 'all efforts are made to discover the truth'. It also laid the blame for the loss squarely on the transaction malleability bug:

Although the complete extent is not yet known, we found that approximately 750,000 bitcoins deposited by users and approximately 100,000 bitcoins belonging to us had disappeared. We believe that there is a high probability that these bitcoins were stolen as a result of an abuse of this bug and we have asked an expert to look at the possibility of a criminal complaint and undertake proper procedures.

These figures were, of course, vastly different from the figures quoted in the Crisis Strategy Draft, with 100,000 more customer bitcoins and 20,000 fewer company bitcoins lost. There was some confusion over the distinctions between 'outstanding debt' and 'total liabilities', but most were only interested in one thing:

> *I want to know where every single one of those missing 750k Bitcoin have gone to. MtGox should publish full details of all their compromised cold storage wallet addresses so we can see what happened. Right now for all I know Mark simply decided to keep all the coins for himself – he needs to prove he didn't do this.*

Conspiracy theories increased in scope, some of which involved the long arm of the US government, while others proposed theories that would end up being mightily close to the truth:

> *I think you are very deluded and it's probable that most of the theft happened at a time when the bitcoins were much lower in value and Gox never came out about it.*

The formal acknowledgement of the loss brought forth more volleys of criticism, scepticism and disbelief from the Bitcoin community. Bitcoin blogger and future General Partner at crypto investment firm Andreessen Horowitz, Arianna Simpson, called the fact that MtGox hadn't realised it had lost hundreds of millions of dollars worth of bitcoins 'mind-boggling' and offered an alternative:

> *In their crisis strategy document, they state that the theft went unnoticed for years. It is challenging to imagine ineptitude at such a grandiose scale, so the logical alternative is that they had been aware of the issue for a long time and voluntarily chose to hide this information from their investors and the public at large.*

Simpson added concisely, 'If you're doing it right, the cold storage should not be accessible via the hot wallet, leak or no leak. That's the whole point of separating the two.' Computer scientist Emin Gün Sirer was of a similar mindset, stating that 'a hacker, no matter how good, cannot jump over an air gap and gain access to coins in cold storage'. He put forward a theory that he felt explained the massive loss in a much more feasible way, following the discovery of the transactions that were created by the malleability bug:

> *...Mt.Gox went through their keys and deleted the private keys corresponding to addresses for transactions that they thought never took place. This is a disaster scenario, as the money then suddenly and irretrievably disappears.*

Karpelès's claims over transaction malleability were further harmed when researchers at the Swiss Federal Institute of Technology concluded that the first such attack on MtGox didn't take place until 9 February 2014 and that as few as 386 of the 850,000 missing bitcoins were lost this way, with the report claiming that 'while the [transaction malleability] problem is real, there was no widespread use of malleability attacks before the closure of MtGox'. This immediately eviscerated Karpelès's claims that the attacks had been going on for years and were the reason for the massive loss. One of the institute's researchers, Christian Decker, later gave his opinion of the real reason for the bitcoin black hole, bringing up a theory that was already starting to do the rounds as a viable alternative:

> *The alleged theft is due likely to insecure handling of funds by MtGox in their internal systems. This would have been the case even if their allegations that transaction malleability was to blame, since they were using faulty network nodes internally.*

These assertions would be backed up once again by Gün Sirer, who observed that it was 'quite difficult to drain 850,000 BTC' through malleability as 'the double-spend requires massive social engineering'. If anyone still had any vestiges of hope that transaction malleability was to blame for the loss, it had now been erased. Of course, the stated liabilities didn't include the lost bitcoins, which carried a valuation of $475 million on the day MtGox filed for civil rehabilitation. Shortly after the letter announcing its losses was published by MtGox, Mark Karpelès was told that he would need to give a press conference at the Tokyo District Court to explain what had happened. If Karpelès was under any illusions about the impact of the collapse of MtGox on Bitcoiners and non-Bitcoiners alike, the press conference brought this home.

The press conference took place in a small room at the Tokyo District Court, with a table and five chairs laid out in a row overlooking the open floor. Reporters and photographers crammed into the space, with the table soon festooned with microphones and dictaphones. At 12.30 p.m., Mark Karpelès entered with his legal representatives, looking distinctly uncomfortable in a grey suit, lilac shirt and blue tie. This was only the third time he had ever worn a suit in his life, and it showed. He sat, gazing around at the assembled mass in a dazed, almost robotic manner, no doubt avoiding everyone's eye as usual before the conference began. A short introduction from Karpelès's chief counsel, spoken in Japanese, was followed by a quick nod of understanding between the pair. Karpelès stood, took a deep breath, and offered a low bow in a traditional Japanese show of apology, the move lit up by a barrage of flashbulbs. He then tried to offer some words to go with the gesture, but it didn't quite work out as planned, as he explained in 2019:

> *The press conference was very stressful. I mean, I did try to go and say that I'm sorry, in Japanese at the same time and completely messed my words. Basically, it was my first time doing a press conference...on MtGox civil rehabilitation and I'm saying that I think that Bitcoin was stolen. So that was not a very much a good experience.*

Karpelès's verbal apology, spoken in muted Japanese and, indeed, terribly garbled, was drowned out by the phalanx of camera shutters that continued throughout. His apology over, Karpelès returned to his seat and began answering questions, blaming 'a weakness in our systems' for the loss of the bitcoins and still claiming that the transaction malleability bug was the cause, even though this had been almost completely discounted. News of the bankruptcy and the huge loss had spread like wildfire, with Karpelès rocketing to the top of the news agenda, his face and his apologetic bow seen all over the world. At the same time, Bitcoin's reputation was also dragged through the mud, as many had feared it would be.

Unsurprisingly, Karpelès's apology cut no ice with victims, with a Reddit thread entitled 'Real life stories of people screwed at Gox' soon sprouting up, compiling the personal stories of many who had lost money on the exchange. There was talk of life savings, retirement money, and student loan repayments all going down the drain. One labelled their loss a 'complete disaster' while another said that they could not 'reasonably afford to lose' the funds they had on MtGox. Talk of MtGox-related suicides wasn't long in coming, either. Autumn Radtke, the CEO of another Bitcoin exchange, First Meta, was found dead in Singapore on the same day as the MtGox announcement after falling from her apartment. This was ruled a suicide six months later, and many linked the collapse of MtGox to her death, although this was never proved. In 2015, a MtGox customer would reveal that he 'almost jumped off an overpass in my city' the day that MtGox went under, while another lengthy Reddit post on the impact of the collapse was taken by many readers to be the author's suicide note, especially considering this was, and remains, the last post ever made on the site by the account. More explicit posts would be published in the weeks following the bankruptcy; one poster admitted that they were 'Checking into a motel to end it all tonight' having lost 150 bitcoins on MtGox, money they said had been intended to 'put my kid through school'. Fortunately, this individual was talked out of such horrific action. Clearly, the event of having small fortunes and big plans suddenly ripped away was proving too much for some, although in 2018, Karpelès said that he had 'investigated all such claims [of suicides linked to MtGox] and so far haven't came across anything'.

Amid the stories of loss and despair, there appeared on Reddit a summary of a conversation that one user claimed to have had with Mark Karpelès two weeks prior. Bruce Fenton, a former Vice President at Morgan Stanley and future Executive Director at the Bitcoin Foundation, had tried to urge Karpelès and Gonzague Gay-Bouchery to strip back MtGox and start again from scratch, getting rid of Karpelès as CEO and rebuilding its reputation, starting with honesty over the status of user accounts. Karpelès and Gay-Bouchery didn't think such a move was necessary, with Fenton's experience of the pair echoing Jesse Powell's from around the same time:

> ...the entire time it did not seem at all that Gox had lost the coins. Why would they have bothered even talking to me? Surely they didn't think an investor would cover the coin losses...Part of me is still optimistically hoping that Mark is just being profoundly bad with PR and trying to under-promise and over-deliver and has at least a good chunk of coins and will try to 'fix' things. His behavior and manner and communications were not at all like that of someone who either 1) lost 800,000 coins or 2) was pulling a major con.

In the immediate aftermath of the bankruptcy filing, Karpelès continued to go to work to try to find a way to rescue the company. The intention behind civil rehabilitation was to allow him to try and save the business, with the Frenchman still planning to follow the process laid out in the Crisis Strategy Draft and resuscitate MtGox. The atmosphere in the office was, obviously, vastly different to that before the collapse, with most of the staff no longer required and only a skeleton crew installed to handle key operations. This included manning a newly installed support line, which, as callers soon found out, offered them nothing more than was publicly available.

Protesters soon gathered around the MtGox office again, joined by reporters who also tried to catch Karpelès entering and exiting his apartment block, fighting to get some insight from the man who had crashed the Bitcoin Titanic. Karpelès, however, refused to talk, instead spending more and more time at home, working virtually and living on takeouts, quiche (of course) and food bought by his few friends. There was a good reason for his regression into a hermit-like status: death threats were appearing on online forums, and people clearly knew where he lived.

According to Karpelès, on 7 March, after a day spent discussing various issues with his lawyers, he was about to enjoy an evening of blissful solitude when he noticed something on the computer on which he was still running the cold wallet scans. Rather than the typical '0', one wallet balance was instead showing a rather staggering number: 200,000. He checked the wallet and verified that it indeed contained 200,000 bitcoins that it had somehow not found before. Karpelès immediately told his lawyers of the discovery, with the court informed the following morning. Karpelès was advised that until the coins could be safely transferred into their custody and all the legal issues sorted out, the discovery could not be made public. Given that the Tokyo District Court had never handled bitcoins before, this would not be a quick process. Finally, however, Mark Karpelès would be able to give his beleaguered customers some good news. Or so he thought.

The day after the bankruptcy court was told about the 200,000-bitcoin find, things took a potentially devastating turn. Late on Sunday, 9 March, the Reddit account and personal blog belonging to Mark Karpelès proclaimed:

> *That fat fuck has been lying! It's time that MTGOX got the bitcoin communities wrath instead of Bitcoin Community getting Goxed.*

The posts, which contained a link to a 750MB zip file, added, 'This release would have been sooner, but in [the] spirit of responsible disclosure and making sure all of [the] ducks were in a row, it took a few days longer than [we] would have liked to verify the data.' Clearly, Karpelès's accounts had been hacked, with the hackers claiming to have stolen MtGox's entire transactional history. This, they said, had been analysed before being posted for the public to see, with the results of their investigations proving that Karpelès had been lying about the number of bitcoins the company held upon its collapse. Their evidence for this was a transactional line that suggested a balance of plus 951,000 bitcoins rather than minus almost this number. While it would transpire that the zip file was, in fact, malware designed to steal bitcoins from anyone who ran it, the data itself was legitimate and would come to play a very important part in the story in just a few weeks' time. The same day this was revealed, Japanese newspaper *Yomiuri Shimbun* cited MtGox lawyers as claiming that, in the days leading up to its collapse, the exchange was fending off an astonishing 150,000 attacks per second from hackers. Assuming this is accurate, credit has to be given to Karpelès and his team for at least keeping this tsunami at bay.

On 10 March, MtGox took the next step in its attempts to protect itself. As its newly found 200,000 bitcoins were in the process of being transferred to the custody of the Tokyo District Court, it filed for bankruptcy through its US outfit in Delaware. This move, which protected it from creditors for around five weeks, outraged some customers, with many believing it was simply a way to halt the lawsuits building up against it. Gregory Greene, the lead plaintiff in the Illinois class action suit against MtGox and Karpelès, had been scheduled to ask a federal judge to freeze MtGox's US-based servers and other computer equipment and to set up a trust over its assets. The bankruptcy filing made this impossible, however, with Greene's lawyer making his feelings very clear to the judge on the astuteness of such a move:

> [MtGox] *claim incredibly that they will preserve assets and protect assets by entrusting the servers and other property to Mr. Karpelès. Respectfully, your honor, that is the definition of the fox guarding the henhouse.*

Karpelès was also scheduled to be deposed later that month in the $75 million Coinlab lawsuit, but the introduction of bankruptcy protection halted that one, too. Even the darkest of clouds, it seemed, had silver linings for Mark Karpelès.

On 20 March, nearly two weeks after its discovery, MtGox was finally allowed to go public about the 200,000 discovered bitcoins. In the announcement, Karpelès revealed that he had found the haul in one of the 'old format wallets which were used in the past and which, MtGox thought, no longer held any bitcoins'. These wallets, stored in the cloud, had been untouched and their contents seemingly forgotten about since their creation in 2011. News of the find had the opposite effect that Karpelès was hoping for, with various theories emerging as to where they had actually come from. Kolin Burges, for one, wasn't buying it:

> It barely needs to be mentioned that the idea of MtGox suddenly finding 200,000 missing bitcoins is ludicrous. I have strong faith in the incompetence of Mark Karpeles but I don't believe for a second that he was unaware of these coins. There are few people in the history of the world who could claim to have lost all their assets yet completely forgotten about $150 million they had lying around.

Emin Gün Sirer didn't mince his words, or his accusations, in his summary of the event following the 'discovery' either:

> But the simplest explanation of all, the one that serves as my default in the absence of a clear technical explanation from the Mt. Gox techies, is that Mt. Gox's collapse involved simple fraud and/or theft, with insider assistance. The latest discovery of 200K BTC could be a simple case of cooling the mark out.

This idea of 'cooling the mark out' is when scammers give their target a little something after they have been conned in order to appease them. A Reddit user suggested that it was, in fact, someone else who had found the money on the blockchain and forced Karpelès to declare it:

> Other people, not at MtGox, discovered them in your back pocket, by looking at transactions, and then you go 'Oh, I didn't know those were still there'. Right, we should trust that you would have 'found' them yourself. What we know for certain is that you claimed all the bitcoins had gone, until other people discovered you still had 200,000 BTC left.

BitcoinTalk users were also revelling in the unlikelihood of the discovery:

> This is like seeing you're about to get pinched for shoplifting by the security guards at the exit of the mall and you 'suddenly remember' you have merchandise in your pocket that you didn't pay for.

> One does not simply LOSE what at one time was over $200 Million+ dollars of Bitcoin and 'suddenly' discover it later when the heat is on...

It was clear that almost no one believed that Mark Karpelès had simply stumbled upon the 200,000 bitcoins, but the media reporting the story failed to ask any questions and simply moved the conversation along to what was going to happen to the discovered coins. As for Karpelès himself, despite the final stash reducing customer losses to some 647,000 bitcoins, it would end up being the rope in the nine-year tug-of-war that was to follow, and, as Karpelès himself would later say, he frequently wished he'd never found it.

Chapter 12 – Willy

If the collapse of MtGox was the Bitcoin equivalent to the sinking of the Titanic, the weeks following its shuttering were a little like the aftermath of the ship's submergence into the icy Atlantic. After the clamour of its death throes, the ship had finally gone down, and an eerie calm settled over the Bitcoin sea. Following legal advice, Mark Karpelès was now saying nothing, and the only moves he made publicly in the weeks afterwards were to ignore that demand to appear before the US Bankruptcy Court in Delaware and a subpoena from FinCEN, with which MtGox was still registered as a money service business. Karpelès maintained a hope that someone would come and rescue MtGox, but his phone was hardly ringing off the hook with offers.

There was one potential rescue boat on the horizon, however, in the unlikely shape of Brock Pierce. Pierce had already tried to acquire MtGox from Karpelès twice, once in 2012 and again in 2013, with the intention of bringing it to China, where he had met with great success by helping to launch Alipay. When MtGox collapsed, Pierce saw an opportunity and teamed up with venture capitalist William Quigley to form Sunlot Holdings, which began private discussions with Karpelès about buying what was left of MtGox soon after it filed for civil rehabilitation. Karpelès was amenable to a deal, obviously, and keen to get an advantage over the competition, Pierce sent Karpelès a Letter of Intent on 11 March 2014, which Karpelès signed. Karpelès says that he drew up a contract to sign MtGox over to Sunlot and sent it to the company for signature, but he never got a signed copy back. In the event, the Tokyo District Court rejected the sale, leading to Karpelès sending a second letter to Pierce scrapping the deal. Pierce, however, never signed the second letter, which would be important years down the line.

On 16 April, with the Sunlot deal dead, along with his plans to rejuvenate the company, Karpelès went back to the Tokyo District Court and filed to have

MtGox moved from civil rehabilitation into bankruptcy, pursuant to liquidating it. His application was accepted, with the case handed to Tokyo-based restructuring and insolvency group Nagashima Ohno & Tsunematsu, who appointed Nobuaki Kobayashi, a partner in the firm, as the administrator of the MtGox bankruptcy process.

Karpelès, having lost the battle to keep MtGox afloat, handed everything over to Kobayashi and vacated the MtGox office forever. He still had MtGox's parent company, Tibanne, to run, and, grateful to have something to keep him busy, he turned his attention to its operation. This wasn't easy, however, given that he was continually bombarded on social media with insults over his leadership of MtGox and accusations that it was he who had stolen the company's bitcoins, accusations that, for legal reasons, he rarely replied to. In typical Mark Karpelès fashion, however, he didn't help himself by actively discussing other more whimsical matters online and even posted a video on YouTube showing how to make his celebrated tarte aux pommes, the kind he had hoped, not so long ago, to serve in his Bitcoin Café. These posts only angered the MtGox customer base, leading to the abuse ramping up to the next level. Once again, Mark Karpelès had spectacularly misread the situation.

On 25 May 2014, three months after MtGox's implosion, a report was posted online which threw a million-watt spotlight on the actions of Mark Karpelès. The Willy Report focused on the presence of two bots, or automated trading algorithms, present on MtGox, which, between them, had heavily manipulated the price of Bitcoin on the exchange and, therefore, the entire Bitcoin market in 2013. The first of these bots, dubbed 'Willy', appeared to have been implemented in April 2011 but saw its main deployment in late 2013. During this time, and possibly beyond (buying records didn't stretch past January 2014), Willy went on a rampage, buying up bitcoins like there was no tomorrow. However, it was the pattern of the buying that intrigued the report's author. Using leaked trading logs from the March hack on Mark Karpelès's Reddit and blog accounts, the report found that a random number of between 10 and 20 bitcoins were purchased every 5-10 minutes, non-stop, throughout November and December 2013 and into January 2014. In total, the report said, Willy spent $112 million on 270,000 bitcoins, mostly bought in November 2013, typically in $2.5 million allotments, although almost 30% of this total was bought in a concentrated spurt in December 2013 and January 2014 alone. Until this report surfaced, there had been several theories as to why Bitcoin's price rose so spectacularly in 2013: some suggested a wave of Chinese buying was behind it, while others believed that people were simply riding the wave of speculation. The answer, argued the report, was much simpler and more insidious: market manipulation.

Not only was Willy at least partially responsible for the late 2013 run-up in the Bitcoin price, it may also have been to blame for exacerbating the collapse in early 2014 as well; the report found that, from 3 February that year, Willy had begun to 'run in reverse', selling around 100 bitcoins every two hours until the exchange collapsed later that month. This led the author to note, 'More than likely, the entire dump down to double digits was the handy work of this dumping bot.'

Willy hadn't been the only bot in town, either. A second, which the report's author dubbed 'Markus', appeared to have been active since at least April 2013, controlling multiple accounts that were buying up coins at completely random prices. Markus's activity ramped up in late 2013 along with that of Willy, with Markus also buying hundreds of thousands of bitcoins, but there was something about Markus that disturbed the Willy Report's author more than the actions of its counterpart: Markus was acquiring the bitcoins 'without spending a dime'. This suggested that either a hacker had managed to compromise the servers and was awarding themselves free coins, or someone on the inside was faking purchases. To make things worse, Markus, too, was in the business of selling, accepting cold hard cash for bitcoins it was getting for nothing. As far back as June 2013, Markus had sold 31,000 bitcoins for $4 million and bought back 15,000 bitcoins for absolutely nothing, all in the space of one and a half hours. This was more than just market manipulation – it looked like outright fraud.

The Willy Report noted that there was a customer name associated with Markus' MtGox account number, a name that was hard to ignore: MagicalTux. The researchers also noted that there had been efforts by someone with access to the database to change the details of this account:

Everything points to these values having been manually edited, presumably to erase traces of suspicious activity...all other logs have been altered to a different ID not traceable to MagicalTux to cover up fraud in a very lazy way (by setting all Money spent to whatever was the last trade), and someone forgot there was still a zip file lying around with the unaltered data.

The Willy Report calculated that Markus bought a cumulative 335,203 bitcoins and sold 37,575 bitcoins, which took the total bought by the two bots to around 570,000, although the author suspected that there were further secrets out there:

> *Although there are no trading logs after November, Willy was observed by multiple traders to be active for the most part of December until the end of January as well. Although this was at a slower, more consistent pace (around 2000 BTC per day), it should roughly add up to another 80,000 BTC or so bought. So that's a total that's suspiciously close to the supposedly lost ~650,000 BTC.*

The report reached a theory as to the fate of the missing bitcoins:

> *...the straightforward conclusion would be that this is how the coins were stolen: a hacker gained access to the system or database, was able to assign himself accounts with any amount of USD at will, and just started buying and withdrawing away.*

However, the author noted one important thing:

> *There are a lot of things that don't add up with this theory; in fact there is a ton of evidence to suggest that all of these accounts were controlled by MtGox themselves.*

The report concluded:

> *It needs to be recognized that, whether intentional or not (though plausible ignorance only goes so far), MtGox has effectively been abusing Bitcoin to operate a Ponzi scheme for at least a year. The November 'bubble' well into the $1000's – and possibly April's as well – was driven by hundreds of millions of dollars of fake liquidity pumped into the market out of thin air (note that this is equivalent to 'with depositors' money').*

Despite the Willy Report's author stressing that their findings were 'not intended to make accusations', the finger was pointed instantly, and with some vigour, at one man: Mark Karpelès. The MagicalTux connection was the smoking gun as far as many were concerned, and given Karpelès's all-controlling power at MtGox (the 'Wizard of Oz' as many termed him), it was surely impossible that he would have missed this level of account activity taking place on the exchange, especially as it used his moniker. The theory that Karpelès was behind the bots also fitted with the perception many already had of him as the guilty party when it came to the theft, and this was just a stepping stone on the path to that inevitable conclusion.

An alternative theory emerged that the trades were real and were conducted by a so-called 'dark pool', institutional traders operating in the shadows in order to hide their purchases, but this option had been removed on MtGox back in 2011. The one man who could answer the question definitively was, at that time, hidden behind a wall of lawyer-instructed silence. While the discovery of Willy and Markus indicated that a fraud may have been perpetrated on MtGox, the report didn't answer the all-important question of how the coins left the exchange. If the withdrawal logs could be obtained and matched to accounts, then the MtGox investigators might have their man.

With three months having now passed since MtGox's collapse, questions were being asked as to why Mark Karpelès wasn't being spoken to by police. The scale of the loss, combined with Karpelès's level of control, left many feeling that it was obvious he should have been brought in for questioning immediately. Every day that he wasn't detained was another day he could flee Japan and hide out somewhere that didn't have an extradition treaty, a feat that someone with access to almost half a billion dollars would find very easy indeed. While everyone wanted answers as to the extent of Karpelès's role in the collapse of MtGox and his association with Willy and Markus, hardly anyone outside of law enforcement was qualified to (or even able to) obtain them. With the FSA and other government agencies unwilling to get their hands dirty over the MtGox affair, it would be left to the Japanese police to investigate the loss, and there were immediate concerns that they wouldn't know how to untangle the complex world of Bitcoin and the blockchain in the attempt. This wasn't surprising, given that blockchain technology was an unknown quantity to authorities in 2014 and nothing like this had ever needed investigating before. Such was its lack of knowledge that the Tokyo Metropolitan Police Department had to create a whole new blockchain division in order to learn how the technology worked before it could investigate MtGox. While it was doing this, the thief could be liquidating the assets they would soon be tasked with recovering.

The MtGox case had already attracted amateur blockchain sleuths from all over the world who were trying their hand at decoding the available information to try and prove once and for all where the missing bitcoins had gone. One man who had the desire and the investigative talents was thirty-two-year-old Swedish MtGox customer and software engineer Kim Nilsson. A Tokyoite like Karpelès, Nilsson, known in his field for being able to solve the most complex programming problems, was keen to get to the bottom of the MtGox affair, not just for his own peace of mind but because of the challenge it presented. He was also one of those acutely aware that Japanese authorities had zero experience in this new world and so doubted whether they would be up to the task of finding his, and everyone else's, money. There was one problem, however, which was that Nilsson had never analysed blockchain data before either. He was sure, though, that he could bring his investigative skills to bear in this most testing of environments, especially given his geographic proximity to it in the form of the MtGox office. But he wouldn't be able to do it alone.

Chapter 13 – Private Investigations

In March 2014, while the Bitcoin world was still trying to come to terms with the astronomical losses at MtGox, three men sat around a table at Teddy's Bigger Burger restaurant in Tokyo and discussed how they could find out what everyone concerned wanted to know: who stole the MtGox bitcoins? Kim Nilsson was there, as was security researcher and fellow Bitcoin enthusiast Jason Maurice, known as 'Wiz', and Daniel Kelman, he of the short-lived MtGox community takeover attempt. Kelman and Maurice had met at a Bitcoin meetup shortly after the MtGox collapse, where Kelman had mentioned that he was keen to hunt down the MtGox millions. This was understandable, given that Kelman held $400,000 worth of bitcoins on MtGox at the time of its collapse.

Maurice had mentioned that Nilsson might be a useful ally in the attempt to track down the bitcoins, and, following preliminary discussions, the trio were now sitting at a table in the burger bar, mapping out their campaign. What had started as a plan to crack the MtGox case in isolation had quickly expanded as the three men came up with an entire business model based around the concept of tracing cryptocurrency thefts on behalf of exchanges and law enforcement agencies. With other cryptocurrencies emerging and the space seemingly on the verge of a growth explosion, there could soon be a huge demand for such blockchain forensics. The three decided on the name Wiz Security (WizSec), and the self-styled Bitcoin security specialists got to work.

Nilsson realised that while the amount of MtGox data made available through leaks and other sources following its collapse was voluminous, it was also fragmented (a 'ticker tape of Mt Gox trades' as Maurice would later call it), with only bits and pieces of the puzzle available online. The group decided that their first port of call should be to Mark Karpelès to try and get a complete dataset. As Nilsson explained during a presentation at the 2017 Breaking Bitcoin meetup in Paris, the trio put on their 'best smiles' and went to see Karpelès to ask if they could have a copy of the full MtGox database for their analysis. Unsurprisingly, Karpelès declined their request, leaving the three investigators with only what they could find for themselves. This also put the group at a disadvantage compared to the Japanese investigators who had naturally been afforded access to the full database from the outset, although the WizSec gang did have something going for them, something that Nilsson explained in a 2015 presentation of his MtGox findings to The Foreign Correspondents' Club of Japan:

> *The MtGox case is huge, there's a huge amount of data. There are millions of addresses, millions of transactions, and this is simply not possible to analyse and investigate manually. You need to have some sort of specialist tools, and…since Bitcoin is so new, these tools basically don't exist yet, so you need to create them yourself.*

While these requirements set law enforcement on the back foot from the outset, the WizSec trio had no such issues, given that its team members possessed the expertise to develop the tools necessary to find the patterns they knew would be there. They did just that and began looking into the data surrounding Willy and Markus's activities to find answers to the missing bitcoins. The group based their analysis on the data from the Willy Report and looked not only for patterns in the activities of the bot itself but also the person running it, concluding that it was more than likely 'an automatic bot which was at times controlled by its operator' who would occasionally tweak the parameters. The team speculated that the presumed working pattern of the operator meant that they worked Asian hours, although they slept 'somewhat irregularly', unless there was more than one user and they were working in shifts. They also noted that nearly all the activity took place on weekdays, which led them to suspect that those weekdays on which the bots were not very active may have been days when the owner or owners were otherwise occupied or at times of national holiday. Willy and Markus's operators were also able to control the bots from their work environment as well as from home, meaning they needed a certain element of privacy at work in order to do so, although the trio realised that there was a possibility that the owners didn't have a job. However, the weekday pattern indicated a regular work schedule.

Nilsson and his team concluded their research with a list of pertinent questions that needed answering to allow for further investigation, but fell short of being able to pinpoint an actual individual behind Willy and Markus. They handed their findings to Karpelès, who thanked them for their efforts but declined to take WizSec on board to carry out any further work despite the fact it might exonerate him. Nilsson wasn't entirely surprised by this; throughout the data analysis and his conversations with Karpelès, Nilsson's suspicions that it was indeed Karpelès who was behind Willy and Markus had only grown, and so his reticence to allow WizSec to investigate further with the full dataset might have resulted in what Nilsson called the Frenchman's 'dirty laundry' being aired. There was, however, no smoking gun to confirm his suspicions. WizSec also provided a copy of its report to the Cybercrime Division of the Tokyo Metropolitan Police Department, where it was received as if it were a freshly detonated glitter bomb rather than a detailed forensic report into MtGox.

The twin knockbacks from Karpelès and the police were a blow to the WizSec trio, who were starting to realise that the hurdles which now needed clearing might be too high. The group's headquarters was Nilsson's 650-square-foot Tokyo apartment, and with only a semi-powerful gaming computer to work on, Nilsson simply didn't have the processing power required to scan the blockchain in the manner needed for an efficient investigation. The group made their work public through a *Coindesk* piece shortly after the rebuff from the police, where they unveiled their progress on the bot investigation and made it clear that with the full database, they could do so much more to help MtGox customers.

By this time, however, there was another investigative team in town. MtGox trustee Nobuaki Kobayashi had initially appointed Deloitte Touche Tohmatsu and ReEx Accounting to help hunt for the missing bitcoins (an appointment that, as we'll see, was not well received by creditors), but in a tacit admission that this appointment hadn't panned out, Jesse Powell's Kraken was hired to assist the two firms as well as assisting with the customer claims which had started to come in. Kraken had gained a solid footing in the Bitcoin world since its launch in 2011 and, in a blog post announcing the appointment, said that it 'possesses the skill and expertise required to properly carry out an investigation of the lost bitcoin and the distribution of assets to creditors.' Powell said he was 'very humbled' to have been asked to help the Bitcoin community following the shock of MtGox's collapse and handed the daunting task to Chief Operating Officer Michael Gronager. Gronager contacted Oxford University postgraduate economist and friend Jonathan Levin, who had written several papers on cryptocurrencies, and the pair set about planning just how they would tackle the mammoth task. While some may have considered the scale and novelty of the project overwhelming, Gronager and Levin were, in fact, overjoyed to have been handed the job; they had been knocking around the idea of creating blockchain tracing software that they could license to law enforcement agencies for a little while, and they had just been handed the ultimate environment in which to build and test their theories. The pair came up with a name for the fledgling offshoot, Chainalysis, and they soon had their hands inside the MtGox database... except when they did, things weren't quite as they seemed:

Many records of trades were missing the "counterparty"—the buyer or seller on the other side of the deal—and many more entries seem[ed] to have been deleted altogether.

Gronager challenged Karpelès over the missing data, with Karpelès telling a story that had never been made public: in early 2014, someone had physically broken into the MtGox servers, where they most likely deleted the missing data. An incredulous Gronager asked about a backup system, but Karpelès insisted this had failed, too. Gronager didn't believe Karpelès, but he had no authority to formally challenge him, and so the issue was dropped (tellingly, Karpelès has still never publicly aired this theory).

In contrast to the freedoms afforded to Chainalysis, the WizSec team was made to sign an NDA by the Japanese police that would ensure their report stayed under wraps until February 2015, with the explanation being that the authorities didn't want it to interfere with their investigation. From what they had seen, however, Nilsson and Maurice thought the term 'investigation' was a gross exaggeration.

Chapter 14 – Fallout

While WizSec, Chainalysis and the Japanese authorities were conducting the mind-breaking work of blockchain analysis for the first time, the MtGox bankruptcy proceedings were taking shape. Suggestions were being made about how to share out the 200,000 bitcoins, which represented all that was left of the previously dominant empire, with several schools of thought on the best way forward. Given the huge divergence between the number of lost bitcoins and those recovered, it was clear that nobody was going to get all their coins back. It wasn't even possible to pro-rata the recovered bitcoins out to customers in the form of the bitcoins themselves, partly because Japanese bankruptcy law didn't allow for such remedial action and partly because it wasn't just customers who were owed money; MtGox had outstanding bills to pay, too. Then there were those lawsuits waiting in the wings, most pressingly the $75 million claim from Coinlab.

With questions swirling around the bankruptcy process and what it meant for creditors, a meeting was arranged for 23 July, which would see aggrieved MtGox customers able to air their grievances in front of those who mattered and ask the most burning questions. Nobuaki Kobayashi would be present to advise on how the bankruptcy was likely to proceed and how the recovery of the lost funds was going, while Mark Karpelès would also appear, most likely dreading the experience even more than his February press conference. All proceedings were to be held in Japanese, with non-Japanese attendees told to provide their own interpreters.

The meeting, attended by hundreds of creditors from all over the world, was an emotionally charged affair, and it didn't get off to a great start; Mark Karpelès offered a short apology to the sea of angry creditors, which cut very little ice and only increased the palpable frustration in the room. Kobayashi took over and spent twenty-five minutes running through the details of the case as it stood, revealing little of any actual substance, although he was able to confirm that he had taken possession of 202,105 bitcoins and ¥698 million ($6.83 million) on behalf of MtGox, which left MtGox with assets worth a total of ¥779 million ($7.68 million) and liabilities of ¥8.73 billion ($86.1 million). It was during this meeting that Kobayashi announced that Deloitte Touche Tohmatsu and ReEx Accounting had been hired to investigate the disappearance of the bitcoins, which at that moment could not technically be classified as 'missing'.

Once Kobayashi had finished, he opened up the floor for questions, at which point the floodgates opened. The creditors seemed of one mind, all inherently dissatisfied with the lack of solid information provided by the trustee, which left them barely any further along than they had been despite five months' worth of supposed investigation. What leads did Kobayashi have on where the stolen coins were? What was the status of the police investigation? When would the remaining holdings be distributed? Time after time, Kobayashi answered, 'That's still under investigation' or, 'That's confidential', increasing the frustration levels in the room as creditors were left feeling no further forward in their quest to understand what was being done to help them. Some questioned the merits of the two firms hired to search for the missing coins, asking why Kobayashi wasn't deploying the kind of computer security resources available to the FBI or Interpol. Again, Kobayashi simply stated that the matter was under investigation. Among the few positives from Kobayashi was his pledge to do all he could to arrange bitcoin repayments rather than have the remaining holdings liquidated into cash. This would be no mean feat, he added, given that bankruptcy law dictated that the assets had to be liquidated rather than being returned in their original form. He also announced that he hoped to create a 'reasonable and smooth method' through which MtGox customers could file their claims, which he hoped to have in place by November with a view to starting appraisals in February 2015.

From Karpelès, creditors wanted to know one simple thing: What the hell had happened? The Frenchman, however, could offer little to appease them or help explain the situation, given his legally mandated silence. One of the few things he could do was agree with the suggestion that any future profits from MtGox's parent company, Tibanne, should go towards making creditors whole. This was a noble gesture but ultimately a futile one, seeing as Tibanne would go out of business ten months later.

Among the attendees, many of whom had flown in from overseas for the occasion, were Kim Nilsson and Kolin Burges, the man whose snowy protest had caught the attention of the world's media and turned the MtGox affair into a global story. Burges was unhappy with how the meeting had gone, saying that those on the panel 'didn't give out the answers they should have done', which reflected the sour mood in the room. Nilsson said after the meeting that the bankruptcy team was 'very careful about giving out any information at this stage', adding that as a customer, he had been 'hoping for more'. Also present at this first meeting was Daniel Kelman, who informed Kobayashi of his plans to form a creditor group which could, under Japanese law, involve itself in the bankruptcy proceedings so long as it satisfied certain conditions and was recognised by the court as representing the interests of creditors en masse. His group, he said, would work towards an alternative settlement that better reflected creditors' wishes. Kelman had good reason to help settle the creditors' claims apart from getting his own holdings back: prior to the meeting, he had informed Kobayashi that he was planning to buy MtGox and relaunch it in partnership with Chinese ATM producer BitOcean and New York-based exchange technology provider Atlas ATS. This new Bitcoin exchange, which would also be based in Tokyo, would be called BitOcean Japan and would, under his proposal, distribute the 200,000 found bitcoins on a pro-rata basis to creditors in addition to a 49% equity stake in the new exchange. Kelman claimed at the meeting that he was 'very close' to the 50% creditor support threshold needed for representation.

However, Kelman's wasn't the only bid in town. Also still vying for the remains of MtGox was Brock Pierce and his Sunlot group, which had reignited its 2014 bid. Three months before the first creditor meeting, Pierce had managed to convince the individuals behind the American and Canadian class action lawsuits against Karpelès and MtGox to provisionally settle their cases on the understanding that Sunlot would immediately distribute all victims' holdings proportionally. Pierce's plan had received a boost on 9 May when a Chicago judge gave his preliminary approval to the settlement plan, only for Coinlab to formally object, claiming that Sunlot had 'crafted a procedural manoeuvre that attempts to cram down the proposal upon creditors while avoiding competitive bidding or other meaningful creditor safeguards'. After the July creditor meeting, Sunlot's CEO John Betts told the *Financial Times* that he was still talking to Kobayashi about the deal, saying the company had 'stayed the course as the longest standing serious offer'. As we know, of course, Kobayashi eventually rejected this bid.

The meeting broke up with more questions than answers, but with the promise that, under Japanese bankruptcy law, there would be meetings every few months to give updates on progress, with the next one scheduled for November. Many drew up plans to attend, hoping for more answers five months down the line. They needn't have bothered. On his website, mtgoxprotest.com, Burges revealed a complete lack of progress at the November meeting, describing how 'the whole [bankruptcy] process looks like it's just stumbled drunkenly over the starting line'. He later summarised the meeting:

The meetings are supposed to be about giving out information but the feeling is they're about conforming to the requirement for a meeting but with the aim being to give away as little as possible.

Indeed, there was little for creditors to cheer in the second meeting, apart from Kobayashi announcing that a few more bitcoins had been recovered, taking the total to 202,149, and ¥671 million ($5.7 million) had been retrieved from third parties. When it came to tracing the missing bitcoins, Kobayashi was only able to report that Deloitte Touche Tohmatsu and ReEx were encountering 'obstacles' in their reading of the database, which didn't fill those present with any optimism, while there were more groans when he announced that the opening of the claims portal had been pushed back to April 2015.

The meeting also threw up some concerns that Kobayashi addressed a month later in a filing to the court. Among these were payments that MtGox was making to Tibanne, payments that were coming out of the creditor kitty. The payments themselves weren't itemised on Kobayashi's expenses, but they had nevertheless been picked up by creditors who wanted to know what the defunct MtGox was doing to earn its customers' money. Kobayashi revealed that he still needed to rent the office space, servers, Internet connection and services of Tibanne employees in order to carry out the bankruptcy duties, claiming that the amount being paid to MtGox was 'appropriate'. For many creditors, however, this was simply rubbing salt into the wounds.

The creditors present for this second meeting left with their spirits raised not one inch, with many bemoaning the lack of information coming their way nine months after MtGox's collapse. What creditors didn't know, however, was that they were about to get more information on the lost MtGox millions in a single blog post than they would get in a hundred creditor meetings.

Chapter 15 – Answers

On Valentine's Day 2015, WizSec was allowed to release its initial findings on the MtGox trading bots. The report, now somewhat out of date given the months of research that the team had conducted since the embargo was placed upon it, was noncommittal on the suggestion that Karpelès was the operator of Willy and Markus but still noted the links between the former CEO and at least one of the bot accounts:

> The [Willy] report dubbed this user 'Markus,' and later concluded that it was using the MtGox trading account of CEO Mark Karpelès, though the log data was inconsistent and may have been intentionally manipulated specifically to conceal or obfuscate this account activity. Ultimately the relationship between Markus and Willy remains unclear.

Kim Nilsson also stated to the media that it was 'more plausible that [the bot operator] was an insider rather than an external hacker'. This was catnip to those who already suspected Karpelès; given that nothing went on at MtGox without him first signing it off, there was, the argument went, no way that anyone else could have cleaned out those wallets without him spotting it.

The team also addressed the question of exactly how Willy and Markus could have been responsible for the 647,000-bitcoin loss, assuming that they were. Nilsson had spotted signs that the loss was down to more than just algorithmic trading or a transaction malleability bug, having found unrecorded withdrawals from the hot wallet that followed a recognisable pattern, all flowing to the same destinations and for which no trading bot activity or transaction malleability attacks would have been responsible. As far as Nilsson was concerned, a compromised hot wallet was ground zero for his research. Nilsson had set his overworked and underpowered computer to the task of scanning the Bitcoin blockchain using his bespoke software, which quickly searched each transaction's input, output and addresses and compared the data to the transactions and wallets used by MtGox customers. He was even able to match them with the thousands of Reddit and BitcoinTalk posts complaining about unprocessed withdrawals, all of which allowed him to reconstruct the more than two million Bitcoin addresses associated with MtGox. Unfortunately, he had no idea who owned these addresses or what each one was used for, but it was a start.

Karpelès himself was largely quiet on the WizSec report, although he spoke to the *Financial Times* to echo WizSec's belief that the time zone patterns could 'show the way to new theories', such as multiple bot operators or a team working in shifts. Nilsson noted at the end of the report that 'Since putting together this report, we have continued to dig deeper into both Willy and other aspects of the case, though, as mentioned earlier, we have to be careful with what we reveal.'

As Nilsson conducted more blockchain investigations, Daniel Kelman went the direct route and tackled Mark Karpelès face to face, accusing him of embezzling the money, more out of frustration than with the aim of actually achieving anything. However, Kelman's argument seemed to hit home with Karpelès, and desirous of clearing his name, he agreed to meet Kelman and Nilsson at another Tokyo burger bar. There, he agreed to help match up Nilsson's addresses with individuals from the MtGox database, allowing Nilsson to create a comprehensive list of MtGox users and their activities. Despite this apparent new willingness to help, Karpelès's contributions were frustratingly limited, given that he wasn't technically supposed to be sharing anything, and he still didn't fully trust WizSec's motives. Much of the work was carried out at Karpelès's apartment, where Nilsson would often encounter the Frenchman making more tarte aux pommes or coding a new application rather than preparing to help him analyse the MtGox database. Plus ça change.

Karpelès's sporadic input and the various data leaks that continued to find their way to journalists and onto the Internet allowed Nilsson and Maurice to spot the first hints that a malicious act might have taken place on MtGox. As they dug further, they became more and more alarmed; like most other people, the pair had expected the bulk of the bitcoins to have gone missing in late 2013 or early 2014 (although they didn't buy the transaction malleability line), but as they analysed the data they found that the disparity between expected bitcoins and actual bitcoins in the MtGox wallets predated this anticipated timeframe by quite some margin. It didn't take long for them to realise that neither the transaction malleability bug nor the concept of a single, destructive hack could have been responsible for the loss of all those bitcoins. However it had been done, the theft, for that was almost certainly what it was, had started much earlier than anyone had realised.

To get a clearer idea of how the wallet balances had changed over the years, Nilsson formatted the exchange's Bitcoin holdings into a chart that showed at one glance how the total balance of bitcoins on MtGox had changed since the start of his dataset in June 2011:

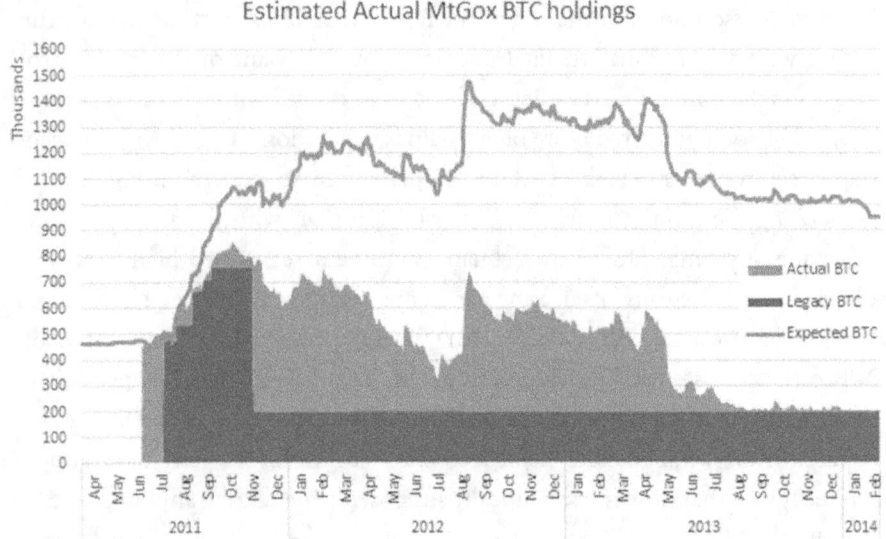

Credit: WizSec

When the last field had been populated, Nilsson refreshed the chart and sat back in astonishment, feeling like an archaeologist who had just discovered a human femur bone among the remains of a fossilised T-Rex. The outflows between mid-2013 and February 2014 were nothing like most pre-existing theories suggested they should have been, and for one very simple reason: by this time, there were hardly any bitcoins left to be stolen.

Nilsson was shocked to learn that MtGox had been haemorrhaging bitcoins since late 2011, two years earlier than first thought, with its October 2011 holdings of 850,000 coins reduced by 61% over the following nine months, leaving MtGox with just 300,000 bitcoins when it should have had over one million. But it was worse than this; that figure included the 200,000 bitcoins found in 2014 that, Mark Karpelès claimed, had been stuck in a legacy wallet since November 2011. This meant that MtGox, in fact, had only 100,000 readily accessible bitcoins to its name in June 2012, rather than the million-plus it should have had. This led Nilsson to comment in the resultant report that 'Barring any major hidden fiat or bitcoins reserves, the all but inescapable conclusion is that knowingly or not, MtGox was technically insolvent since at least 2012.' Crucially, Nilsson's data also revealed that the exchange's reserves had been picked clean by August 2013, which was when the bitcoin withdrawal issues started, meaning that MtGox had indeed been operating as a Ponzi scheme for the last seven months of its life. This being the case, Nilsson realised that Willy and Markus could not have been involved in the theft of the 650,000 bitcoins because the coins were already virtually gone by the time the bots hit their stride. He didn't know, of course, that the 'Gox Bot' had, in fact, been in use since early 2011 to cover the 1Feex loss.

Nilsson compiled the data into a report and published it in April 2015, finally shedding some light on the questions that had plagued anyone with an interest in MtGox for over a year. By this time, WizSec was almost solely Nilsson's baby, with co-founders Maurice and Kelman having since stepped away from the operation. The report began by noting that while the reception from readers over its February report had been 'very encouraging', interest from officials had been 'pretty low'. This was a veiled way of saying that Japanese police hadn't shown any interest in Nilsson's findings despite not being able to achieve them by themselves. Now, however, they would have no choice but to sit up and take notice.

Nilsson summarised the scale of the loss and confirmed the final figures, which came out higher than initially calculated by MtGox:

> *For reference, the expected bitcoin holdings when MtGox collapsed were roughly 950,000 BTC. Out of those, 200,000 BTC were later found in an old wallet, and possibly up to 100,000 BTC belonged to MtGox itself (and would presumably be excluded during bankruptcy proceedings), leaving some 650,000 BTC ultimately missing.*

Nilsson elected to focus on the mammoth 2011-2014 hack and chose not to reference the 77,500-bitcoin theft of September 2011, telling me that there was 'not much to say' about it because very few clues were left about where the coins went or who stole them. The loss was reflected in the chart, however, marked by a sharp deviation in the number of assumed and actual bitcoin reserves at that time.

Nilsson was also able to make another important conclusion: all the bitcoins going into MtGox were real customer deposits, meaning that there could be no accusations of someone inside the company cooking the books. Instead, the discrepancy was likely caused by bitcoins leaving MtGox without going through a valid withdrawal process. The most likely reason for this was theft, which was the inescapable conclusion that Nilsson's data led to. Nilsson was also able, through painstaking work, to identify where the stolen coins were typically sent: crypto exchanges Bitcoinica and BTC-e, MtGox itself and other unidentified wallets.

Nilsson then turned to the question of how the coins had been taken. Clearly, no one had raided Mark Karpelès's security boxes for the wallets and then siphoned off the bitcoins, so how had it been done? While Nilsson was missing a couple of the key pieces needed to complete the picture, the one thing he knew for sure was that the source of all MtGox's problems was its hot wallet, the wallet into which all deposits arrived and from which all withdrawals went out. This wallet, Nilsson said, had been seriously compromised in some way very early on, and somehow, all the cold wallets had been ransacked as a result. This would have been particularly concerning for Karpelès, seeing as he had implemented wallet encryption in September 2011, after which he believed that no other hacks had taken place.

Nilsson offered his thoughts on the idea of how the bitcoins were stored at MtGox, but stressed that 'we don't know enough details about the handling and historical use of MtGox's cold storage' and that he was therefore 'forced to speculate'. Nilsson proposed the theory that electronically held private keys were compromised by hackers but seemed to favour a different setup which involved both manual and automatic operations:

> *Our understanding is that MtGox did not have continuous monitoring of its cold storage, which consisted of paper wallets generated ahead of time and stored away. These locked-up paper wallets would then gradually and automatically be filled one by one by the system, by depositing surplus bitcoins out from the hot wallet. Vice versa, whenever the hot wallet ran*

low, staff would manually scan a paper wallet, refilling the hot wallet with stored bitcoins.

One possibility is that without any monitoring of the storage or comparing incoming and outgoing amounts, MtGox staff may have blindly kept pouring their cold storage into their leaking hot wallet, assuming that they were just dealing with frequent swings in deposits/withdrawals and that on average the cold storage was being refilled at roughly the same rate they were draining it.

This theory is a version of what had already been dismissed by many informed observers, with Nilsson suggesting that either MtGox staff were going back and forth to the security boxes to collect the paper wallets or they had copies in the office ready to use at a moment's notice but weren't bothering to (or were instructed not to) check the amounts in the wallets before they used them. As far as Nilsson was concerned, this lack of monitoring would have given Karpelès an out when it came to his level of complicity:

As crazy as it may sound, I don't think it's at all impossible that [Karpelès] really didn't know the full extent of the problems until the very end.

When it came to identifying who was behind the attack, Nilsson was, unsurprisingly, unable to point the finger:

The truth is that as independent investigators, something like narrowing down actual suspects is close to impossible without proper access to all available data. There will be follow-ups and refinements to this report, but as it stands, if anyone is to continue where we leave off and anyone is to eventually get caught, then it's up to officials and law enforcement at this point (as well it should be).

One reader of Nilsson's report was far from shocked at the data, although he was surprised and impressed at how Nilsson had reached it with his comparatively meagre resources. Just a month earlier, Chainalysis' Michael Gronager had had the idea of trying to fill the plentiful holes in Karpelès's data with blockchain records, hoping that, when combined, they would form a comprehensive picture of the inflows and outflows at MtGox. Gronager used the data to produce two charts – one showing the balance of bitcoins on MtGox and one showing the movements of coins on the blockchain – which, when overlaid, produced an identical chart to Kim Nilsson's. Gronager emailed Karpelès, but the Frenchman could offer nothing to explain such a huge and consistent outflow. Clearly, this had been a theft of gargantuan proportions carried out over an extraordinary length of time.

With Nilsson publishing his identical findings in April 2015, Gronager gauged the reaction. The response from the Bitcoin community to the WiZsec report was surprisingly muted, mainly because Nilsson had only managed to answer a selection of the most burning questions. One respondent on BitcoinTalk opined that it 'doesn't really tell us much' before propounding a theory that, bit by bit, was becoming common thought:

> *At least [we] know we are starting to get the full picture: a mix of lack of security, fear, and not really knowing what to do with so many Bitcoins on one's control.*

This comment reflected a slight shift in sentiment towards Karpelès that took hold in the wake of the report; while many were still convinced the Frenchman was involved in the mass theft somehow, more and more people were coming around to the idea that this involvement extended to incompetence and bad stewardship rather than malice. Karpelès, as he had attested on the few occasions he had spoken about it since MtGox's collapse, had said that he was responsible for a failure of duty to his customers rather than for the bitcoins actually going missing, a theory that Nilsson's report helped to bolster. This theory was far from all-pervading, however, with many still convinced that his supposed connection to Willy and Marcus pointed to deeper involvement and that the police were finalising their case against him.

They didn't have to wait long to be proved right.

Chapter 16 – Arrest

2015 had begun for Mark Karpelès in a manner that was, even for him, unusual. During the trial of Ross Ulbricht, the mastermind behind Silk Road, that January, Karpelès's name was once again brought up as an alternative candidate for the moniker Dread Pirate Roberts, the site's pseudonymous creator. During the trial, lead Silk Road investigator Jared Der-Yeghiayan repeated his belief that Karpelès could well have been Silk Road's creator and operator, a theory that Ulbricht's counsel was using as a form of defence. Following Der-Yeghiayan's claims, which he made under oath during the trial, Karpelès had quashed such rumours in an email to *Motherboard* where he said, 'This is probably going to be disappointing for you, but I am not Dread Pirate Roberts', suggesting, rightly, that Ulbricht's attorney was 'trying everything he can to point the attention away from his client'. Indeed, the idea that Karpelès was the Silk Road mastermind disappeared when the judge in the Ulbricht case ruled that key portions of Der-Yeghiayan's testimony would be retroactively declared inadmissible because they were based on his beliefs rather than 'competent evidence' and thus should be considered hearsay or unsubstantiated rumour and should be struck from the record. This, needless to say, included the notion that Mark Karpelès was Dread Pirate Roberts.

Karpelès could have done without the attention, given that he had bigger fish to fry at this time. While Der-Yeghiayan was on the witness stand suggesting that Karpelès had created Silk Road, the *Yomiuri Shimbun* newspaper was reporting that Tokyo's Metropolitan Police Department believed that no more than 7,000 bitcoins from the missing MtGox haul could be attributed to the transaction malleability issue, blaming the rest on 'internal system manipulation' rather than an external attack. The article didn't name Karpelès directly, but the inference was clear, building on the mounting accusations that the CEO had indeed carried out the manipulation on MtGox following the release of the Willy

Report of the prior year that first tied him to the trading bots. This was despite Kim Nilsson's report showing that the bots were not responsible for the loss of the coins.

In between the first and second WizSec reports, the spectre of Silk Road had reared its head once again and in the most sensational fashion. In March 2015, after Ross Ulbricht had been sentenced to double life imprisonment plus forty years, it was revealed that two federal agents tasked with bringing down the marketplace had, in fact, stolen and solicited large numbers of bitcoins from the site. But that wasn't all. The first, Secret Service agent Shaun Bridges, was accused of stealing around $820,000 in bitcoins from Silk Road, which he sold on MtGox, emptying his account in March 2013, right before he himself signed the seizure warrant for MtGox's Dwolla and Wells Fargo accounts. If this wasn't shocking enough, the name of the second man involved gave Karpelès a seismic jolt: DEA agent Carl Force. Force had, of course, tried to ingratiate himself with Karpelès and petitioned for a role as the US front for MtGox, only to taunt Karpelès with the 'Told you should have partnered with me!' email following the seizure signed off by Bridges. Further revelations in the Force indictment made sense of these activities: Force had been selling information about the Silk Road investigation to Ulbricht in return for bitcoins, which he too sold on MtGox, and even claimed to Ulbricht that Karpelès had given investigators Ulbricht's name as the Silk Road kingpin. Ulbricht had been desperate to contact Karpelès in September 2013 as a result of the investigation that he knew was closing in on him to find out what Karpelès had said to the police, but Karpelès, either wisely or through sheer luck, never responded to Ulbricht's entreaties and has forever maintained that he had no contact with Ross Ulbricht either personally or as Dread Pirate Roberts.

The actions of Bridges and Force, meanwhile, and their supposed connection to Karpelès and MtGox, led to growing suspicions that the pair were also involved in the theft of the MtGox bitcoins. Understandably, the underhanded activities of Force and Bridges stung Mark Karpelès, so much so that in July 2015, he penned a blog post which outlined his theory about the pair's intentions behind their actions, most notably the $5 million DHS seizure in 2013. Karpelès argued that there were two main possibilities: either Bridges was trying to destroy MtGox to erase any record of his Bitcoin activities on the site, or someone paid Bridges/Force to 'harm' MtGox for their own means. Neither theory has been conclusively proven, and, in the words of Ashley Barr when discussing the theory, 'If you know Mark, you'd understand it's easy for him to be lost in his own mind, and it's hard to bring him out of wherever it is he is.'

As the sideshow of the Ross Ulbricht trial died away, Karpelès returned to the issue of trying to run Tibanne and, where possible, help the police with their investigation into MtGox's missing bitcoins. 'The Mounties always get their man' is a famous saying about the Royal Canadian Mounted Police, and according to Jake Adelstein, an American journalist, crime writer and friend of Mark Karpelès who investigated and covered the MtGox case in depth at the time, the same could be said of the Japanese police in the MtGox case, but for a very different reason. Adelstein says that the National Police Agency's Second Investigative Division, which took over the MtGox case from the Cyber Crimes Unit in late 2014, was fighting an uphill battle from the outset. Prime Minister Shinzo Abe had very public ambitions to make Tokyo a cryptocurrency hub at the time of the MtGox collapse, and, as the FSA was finding out, the affair threatened to become a national embarrassment. The police were, therefore, under pressure to get their man – or, more to the point, *a* man. What made things worse was that the unit was, as Kim Nilsson had correctly identified, ill-equipped to deal with the technicalities of blockchain investigation. This meant that vital evidence was at risk of getting misinterpreted, bypassed, or, worse, ignored altogether if it didn't fit the theory that investigators had already decided to work towards: Mark Karpelès was the thief. According to Adelstein, the highest echelons of the Japanese police force decided early on that Karpelès was the prime suspect for the MtGox hack and that, as a result, Japanese investigators didn't bother to chase down any other leads in case they threw up contrary evidence.

The Japanese police were also still smarting from an extraordinary case involving IT worker Yusuke Katayama, who had been charged with making multiple death threats against various Japanese institutions and companies. Tech wizard Katayama used timed text messages from an unregistered mobile phone to his phone, which he claimed were from the real perpetrator, texts which his counsel said exonerated him. The judge agreed, and Katayama was released. When it was discovered that Katayama was the sender of the texts, having been caught retrieving the unregistered phone from where he had buried it, he was re-arrested and tried, where he changed his plea to guilty. He was eventually imprisoned, but the episode was acutely embarrassing for all echelons of the Japanese legal system. Fearing a repeat of this episode, the police wanted to bag a quick, reputation-enhancing win, especially given Karpelès's standing as a tech-savvy operator.

Rumours about the possible arrest of Mark Karpelès began circulating in Japanese media in June 2015. Reporters, hopeful of catching the act live, had begun once again to occupy the narrow street below Karpelès's apartment, which represented the only entrance and exit, but they were to be disappointed. An uneventful month for Karpelès ended with a phone call from his lawyer following a tip-off from a reporter at the *Nikkei* newspaper that the arrest was imminent. Again, nothing happened. A few reporters remained in situ regardless, hovering like a pack of lions waiting for their prey to step out into the open. One of the reasons speculation was gathering was because police were now finalising witness testimonies. Ashley Barr, who had already given two statements to the Tokyo Metro Police the prior April, was contacted by the Second Investigative Division and asked to go over some of the details in his statements. The first statement had focused on Barr's refusal to accept the CEO position after he wasn't allowed to see all the financial records and his firing weeks afterwards, but it was the second that the police were most interested in; this one related to the exchange's financial operations. Barr had highlighted the multiple instances of suspected negligence from Karpelès and the veil of secrecy he kept over key elements of MtGox's operations, in particular surrounding its financial standing, and officers wanted to know more.

In the interview, Barr revealed how he had received a phone call in April 2013 from one of his hires at MtGox telling him of a troubling discovery he had just made. The employee said that a customer deposit had gone into the wrong account and that when they approached Mark Karpelès about it, the CEO refused to send it to the correct account. Upon further investigation, the employee noted that the account into which had been deposited was buying up bitcoins at something above the market rate and doing so in a consistent, timed manner. The amount, Barr told the police, had been something in the region of 2,000 bitcoins each time. When the Willy Report was released in 2014, Barr knew at once that this was what his former colleague had seen. When he informed the lead investigator how the discovery by his former colleague linked to the actions of Willy and Markus, he was stunned to learn that the official had no idea what he was talking about; the Japanese police had no knowledge of the Willy Report or the existence of the trading bots. Barr provided them with a link to the report, and the investigators went off to read up on something that everyone else with a passing knowledge of MtGox had known about for almost a year.

The arrest whispers increased throughout July to the point where, on the 31st, Karpelès had had enough; he phoned investigators to ask whether or not he was about to be taken into custody, saying that if so, he would rather come down to the station and hand himself in to avoid a scene. He was reassured that no one was going to arrest him and that, if anything changed, he would be informed beforehand. Karpelès hung up, placated. After all, these rumours had been doing the rounds for months, and nothing had come of them. Plus, he'd had plenty of meetings with Japanese authorities recently, and they had all been perfectly cordial, with the idea of him being involved in the hack itself never brought up.

Karpelès went to bed around midnight, relieved that he wasn't about to have his face plastered over every newspaper and TV network in Japan, and possibly the world, as the chief suspect in the MtGox hack. He was in for a shock. At 5.30 the following morning, he was woken by a phone call from the police telling him that they were on their way to arrest him. *That* was his advanced warning. Karpelès said he needed time to shower, which he also used to try and get ahead of the story, telling the *Wall St Journal* that the allegations of grand theft were 'false' and that he would 'of course deny' them. The police arrived half an hour later, by which time a media scrum had convened at the entrance to Karpelès's apartment block. The police erected a cordon and allowed the arresting team through. Once they were in his flat, Karpelès was shown the arrest warrant, his rooms and possessions were photographed, and his electronic devices were seized, tagged and bagged. He was taken down the stairs and out through the entrance right in front of the phalanx of journalists, a white cap pulled down over his eyes, and his dark hair pulled back into a small ponytail. Reporters and cameramen jostled to get pictures and video footage, with more stationed at the end of the alleyway where the police car was waiting. They shouted questions at Karpelès in Japanese and English as cameras flashed away, but wisely, or perhaps out of pure shock, Karpelès remained tight-lipped as he was escorted to a waiting police car. While the cameras may have added ten pounds, it was clear that the

Frenchman had nonetheless been enjoying the culinary delights of being a wealthy man, amply filling the 'Effort Less French' t-shirt he had thrown on.

Given the weeks of rumours regarding his potential arrest and the conclusions many had already drawn about him, the detention of Mark Karpelès was far from unexpected. Jake Adelstein had seen it coming since day one and had warned Karpelès just days before the arrest of what to expect if he were detained, offering some advice into the bargain:

> *Do not confess to anything. Do not sign anything...They will bully you, threaten you, promise you a lighter sentence if you confess, block you from talking to your lawyer, lie to you about testimony they don't have and evidence they don't have and will do everything to break your spirit...Don't confess.*

While the arrest itself may not have been a surprise, the reason behind it was: it was soon revealed that Karpelès had been arrested not for the theft of any bitcoins from the exchange but instead for abusing his position to illicitly add one million dollars to an account under his control with which he had allegedly bought up the hundreds of thousands of bitcoins through Willy and Markus. The response from those affected by the MtGox collapse was, understandably, a mixture of confusion and disappointment. One Reddit user said that the arrest represented 'a tiny amount of justice served' while others baulked at the lightness of the five-year prison sentence Karpelès could get if found guilty. One portentous comment said that 'The only thing that will be good for mk is that he will weight 30kg less when he leaves his Japanese prison' and pointed to a YouTube video showing the military-style way in which Japanese prisons operate. Ashley Barr, believing that he was now safe to break his NDA ('Mark has other things to worry about'), also took to Reddit, this time to conduct an Ask Me Anything (AMA) over his time at MtGox where he made no bones about his feelings towards Karpelès and what he expected to happen:

> *We plan to eat pizza in front of Mark while he is in prison. We always assumed that was where he'd end up.*

Incredibly, Karpelès's arrest was the moment when his mother first found out that he was running MtGox, the job he had held for over four years. Reporters trying to interview Anne Karpelès about her suddenly famous son needed first to explain to her what MtGox and Bitcoin were before they could quiz her about him.

Karpelès was taken to Shibuya police station, where he was told that he was alleged to have manipulated MtGox's books to run Willy and Markus, but this was just a cover; what they really wanted was a confession that Karpelès had stolen the 650,000 bitcoins taken between October 2011 and January 2014 to which Willy and Markus were connected. Karpelès was put before a public prosecutor, where his lawyer, Noboyusu Ogata, asked for bail, citing Karpelès's cooperation with authorities as an example of the kind of person he was. In contrast, prosecutors painted Karpelès as a kind of evil genius who, if freed, had the potential to remotely destroy evidence or perhaps even flee the country, even though Karpelès had had over a year to do both. The judge, as is typical in Japan, sided with the prosecution and issued a warrant of detention. This gave investigators up to twenty-three days to question Karpelès, after which he would be freed if he wasn't charged. This is the time when, according to critics of the Japanese judicial system (of which there are many), prisoner abuse is most likely to take place; detainees are cut off from contact with the outside world, including with their legal representatives, and authorities are known to use the lack of detainee protection to try and elicit a quick confession through whatever means available to them. Karpelès, however, didn't envisage it this way:

> *It wasn't what I expected. I expected a three-week visit to see how a police station worked, then I could go home.*

Indeed, Karpelès took to his initial interrogation with a detached mentality that many former colleagues and employees would have recognised; he began observing everything and everyone around him with a tourist-like interest, even making sketches of what he saw and experienced, including schematics of his cell and its furniture. He took the experience, as he would later say, as a chance to see a side of Japan he hadn't yet witnessed.

Karpelès was interrogated on each of the twenty-three days about the injection of money into MtGox to fund Willy and Markus, with the police claiming that the Frenchman had used the bots to buy and steal the 650,000 coins. Karpelès, as Adelstein had recommended, denied everything, resisting the immense pressure to confess that was exerted on him day after day. With little progress being made, at least to him, Karpelès expected to be freed on day twenty-three, where he could get on with rebuilding his life. On the 23rd day, 21 August, he was indeed released, only to be rearrested in the hallway on new charges. This, he had been warned by both his lawyer and Jake Adelstein, was a tactic that Japanese police liked to employ because it gave them another twenty-three days to question a suspect, again without charge, allowing them to carry on where they had left off. Only now did Karpelès start to realise that this was no holiday.

When news of his rearrest broke, many MtGox customers assumed that it was based on information gleaned from the first interrogation and would result in charges related to the theft or other misdemeanours regarding the stolen bitcoins. But the new charges didn't relate to the missing bitcoins, instead focusing on a transfer of ¥321 million ($3.14 million) from MtGox to Karpelès's personal bank accounts, which police alleged constituted embezzlement of company funds. The money, they said, was mainly spent on buying licenses for 3D-rendering software and also Karpelès's $40,000 custom-made bed. Karpelès's interrogation over these new charges commenced immediately, but the focus was still on soliciting a confession over the missing bitcoins, with prosecutors even asking at points if he was Satoshi Nakamoto, the creator of Bitcoin. Karpelès's initial faith in his release evaporated as he was relentlessly interrogated, with police demanding again and again that he confess to the theft. At points, Karpelès felt like giving in so that the 'nightmare' could be over, as he told CNN in 2019:

> *It's very tempting when you are not free and facing a system that every morning tells you just cooperate and everything will be simple, to just go with the flow and say: okay, okay.*

It is beyond the scope of this book to cover the inadequacies or otherwise of the Japanese legal system, but the subject bears at least a passing mention because of the impact on Karpelès and his case. The concept of 'hostage justice' in Japan has been well documented, and there have been many in the past who have observed that the system exercises a 'guilty until proven innocent' approach, stretching the law to its limit to obtain confessions and punishing those who choose to defend themselves. In a 2018 documentary, Jake Adelstein gave an insight into how this affected Mark Karpelès:

> *Japanese prosecutors are not interested in a fair trial. They're not interested in justice. So Karpelès's mistake may have been that he believed*

the system is about justice. No, it's about finding someone to take the blame and getting them convicted.

This approach goes some way to explaining Japan's 99.9% conviction rate for those indicted, a club that the majority felt Karpelès was destined to join. The mood among the cryptocurrency fraternity was mixed, with some, like the Japanese police and media, pronouncing Karpelès guilty already, while others said that his 'crimes' were nothing but trumped-up charges designed for law enforcement to claim an easy win and, in the best case scenario, force a confession over the missing bitcoins. Many of those who know or have worked with Karpelès have since publicly criticised the way he was treated by the Japanese justice system, viewing his treatment at this stage as incommensurate with the crimes with which he was actually charged. With the world watching on, however, Japan was desperate to obtain a quick confession.

On 11 September 2015, another case of embezzlement was added to the charge sheet, allowing police to detain Karpelès for a further three weeks, which they could once again extend if required. Karpelès denied the new charges to local media, saying that he had intended to pay back the money he was supposed to have embezzled, while his legal team offered its take to *The Daily Beast*:

> *The money that our client used for investments came from his company's income, $28 million in total, not from his clients'. Mr. Karpeles therefore did not commit embezzlement by law.*

His team also used the FSA's shortcomings to bolster their argument, saying, 'If a bitcoin exchange in Japan, under Japanese laws, is not considered operating as a bank, then it's even more far-fetched to say he committed embezzlement.' Kim Nilsson, who was possibly better placed than anyone to offer an opinion on the level of Mark Karpelès's culpability, offered his opinion to Agence France-Presse:

> *[I am] happy the police have made breakthroughs on investigating the missing fiat money, but it would be unsatisfying if after all this time all we get is a conviction for manipulated records and embezzlement only amounting to a fraction of all the money people lost...It may be better than nothing for the people who want to see someone held responsible, but I think we should be expecting more.*

Three days after this development, Nilsson and a group of other 'white hat' hackers spoke at the Foreign Correspondents' Club of Japan over the MtGox hack and Karpelès's potential role, with Nilsson saying that 'the theft itself would certainly have been possible to do by one person', but the laundering of the proceeds 'would at least hint at possibly a more organised effort'. Nilsson noted, 'There could have been multiple hackers in multiple countries' who carried out the manipulation of which Karpelès had been accused, but added that 'there is a lot of evidence pointing to inside Japan'.

Following Karpelès's new charges, Duncan Riley of the tech website Silicon Angle offered this dark take on the Frenchman's fate:

> *Japan is said to have a high rate of court convictions, meaning Karpeles is likely going to end up living in a deep, dark, metal cage, forgotten about, much to the joy of many of those who lost millions when the exchange failed.*

Karpelès endured more than six weeks of further interrogations before, in December 2015, he was finally shipped off to Kosuge prison, otherwise known as the Tokyo Detention House, a pre-trial detention centre where he would wait out his bail application. Karpelès was singled out because of his celebrity status and was placed in solitary confinement on the eleventh floor, away from the general population, sharing the floor with around fifteen individuals on death row and another fifteen waiting to be tried or sentenced for such crimes. He was refused contact from the outside world and was only allowed limited conversations with his legal team. Detainees were, as the informed Reddit user had said, made to march in a military fashion when being taken from place to place, and there were also only two ways of sitting permitted: 'Japanese' style (kneeling) or sitting cross-legged on the floor. Detainees in solitary confinement, like Karpelès, had to follow other strict rules, such as no contact or communication of any sort with other detainees, even eye; no making of any noise in cells, such as whistling or singing; no slouching; and no sleeping outside of proscribed times. On one occasion, Karpelès 'freaked out' and 'punched a door', which led to harsher measures:

> *About fifteen guards arrived as reinforcements. I was tied up and taken to the cells...they have special cells for this.*

These 'special cells' were the padded 'punishment rooms' where Karpelès's hands were tied behind his back, and he was kept sitting on the floor for four hours. On completion of this, Karpelès was returned to his regular cell where all privileges, including books and writing materials, were withdrawn for four days, leading to him sitting for up to ten hours a day with nothing but the occasional guard check and mealtimes to break the monotony.

Outside of this punishment, Karpelès passed the time in the detention centre by writing his diary and reading (helped by the fact that the light in his cell was never turned out). He even allegedly somehow managed to teach English to other detainees. He dreamed, were he to be released on bail, of making the most of his freedom by buying a bus and turning it into a 'giant camper van'. Prison food was, to a Frenchman used to the finer side of the culinary world, worse than unsatisfactory: cereal and packet milk for breakfast; a lunch consisting of two slices of bread and jam; and dinner of soup, fish and rice or barley. Karpelès's spell in Kosuge prison was conducted, as the quirks of the Japanese law dictated, in ten-day spells; every ten days, on the tenth day, Karpelès would be handed another detention order for the same period of time. This process can go on indefinitely in Japan, with Karpelès explaining in a 2022 interview that one of his fellow detainees had been kept in the detention centre in this manner for over a year. The only maximum term that applies is that a charged individual's trial must start within two years of their charges being filed, but until that day arrives, the perpetual ten-day process is adhered to, a psychological trick intended to demoralise detainees and, ideally, persuade them to plead guilty. However, such was the lack of information that Karpelès was allowed to receive from the outside world, he had little idea of any of these finer points of Japanese law beforehand. To him, life was just an endless procession of ten-day cycles.

Just six weeks into his stay, Karpelès was hit with another charge of embezzlement, this time of ¥20 million ($170,000), some of which was allegedly spent on prostitutes. Karpelès's lawyers denied this charge, too, saying that the money had come from Karpelès's salary, meaning he could do whatever he liked with it. Needless to say, they also denied that company money had been spent on such activities.

In early 2016, *The Daily Beast* received what writer Jake Adelstein would later describe as a 'giant envelope full of papers' which appeared to have been sent from near the Tokyo police headquarters. These papers, which he believed were sent from either the police or the prosecution team, related to the buyout of MtGox in 2011 and the surrounding era. They included the email exchange between Karpelès and Jed McCaleb from April 2011 discussing the 79,957 bitcoins lost in the 1Feex hack and the use of the Gox Bot to buy them back. *The Daily Beast* published the email, representing the first time that the 1Feex hack had been made public, with customers realising that Mark Karpelès intentionally hid the theft from them, even after the exchange had collapsed. Worse was the fact that both the Willy Report and Kim Nilsson's research had dated Willy and Markus' inception to no earlier than 2013, exonerating Karpelès from the accusation that he used the bots to buy up and then withdraw the coins. The knowledge that Willy had actually been in use all the way back to March 2011 was a shocking twist that revived the theory that Karpelès could have been the one who ransacked the exchange after all.

Fortunately for Mark Karpelès, Jed McCaleb drew most of the ire for having handed his successor a live hand grenade, although Karpelès's naivety over the takeover didn't go ignored. Nor did the way he set about trying to repair the damage, as one online commenter noted:

> *This is a tiny amount. I mean really, that is what amazes me...It should take next to no time to raise that kind of capital...Karpeles thought that if the most popular exchange at the time was $62k in the hole, the fucking market would implode.*

Many readers opined that Karpelès's attempts to fill the hole through the Gox Bot had massively manipulated the Bitcoin price to the detriment of his customers, as the *Financial Times* explained:

> *In some cases, a self-fulfilling feedback loop might even occur in which no matter how much bitcoin you pre-buy to sell to your customers at a premium, the underlying capital needed to acquire the bitcoin becomes proportionally ever larger in ratio terms. So you end up short-squeezing yourself to ruin.*

While there was no denying that the email looked bad for Karpelès in terms of his use of the trading bots, here, at least, was evidence that they had been created with one initial purpose: to fill the hole left by the 1Feex hack. Whatever they might have been used for afterwards was going to be down to prosecutors to prove (potentially), but it was clear that the motive behind their origin was the betterment of the company. There was also the fact that there was still no evidence of the 650,000 coins leaving MtGox and ending up with Mark Karpelès. Ogata, it seemed, planned to use the email to back up his claim that Karpelès did nothing wrong and that he was only trying to get the company back on an even footing to rescue it and protect investors' funds, a defence that might protect him from the harshest of the state's accusations.

The man at the centre of the article, however, was almost certainly unaware of its publication, meaning he had no idea that the world now had confirmation from his own lips that he had operated Willy and Markus. Unbeknownst to Karpelès, he had an advantage: prosecutors had almost no idea how to read the MtGox database and, therefore, they were hard put to back up their accusations of embezzlement and data manipulation, especially where the transactions related to bitcoins rather than fiat. The only person investigators knew who could translate everything and offer anecdotal insight was Mark Karpelès, the very man they were trying to bring down with the information. They had, of course, asked MtGox staff and associates for inside information on Karpelès and his dealings, but, ironically, the Frenchman's 'walled garden' approach ensured that they knew next to nothing and could offer very little insight whatsoever.

What Karpelès really needed in order to work on his defence was a copy of the MtGox database. This would allow him to see exactly how the police had come to their assertions over embezzlement and the injection of cash and try to work out, as his lawyers were attempting to do at that very moment, how he could counter them. The police had an eight-week head start, but Karpelès's legal team was eventually allowed to provide him with the MtGox database, albeit on paper. Some 20,000 pages of transactions, deposits, withdrawals and more from three years of activity on MtGox were printed, packed up and shipped to Kosuge prison, where Karpelès took receipt of them and then realised he was missing something very important: a calculator. Prison rules stated that detainees could buy an abacus if they needed to make calculations, but Karpelès discovered that a calculator was available in cases that involved accounting or finance. Accordingly, he spent ¥15,000 ($120) on the best calculator the prison shop sold, and, armed with his new acquisition as well as his existing treasure trove of pencils and a notepad, took the first box from the stack that occupied almost a third of his cell and set about trying to prove his innocence.

Chapter 17 – The Russian

While Mark Karpelès was using the MtGox database to work out what prosecutors had against him, Kim Nilsson was using it to work out who had committed the theft. Nilsson had already identified three exchanges that had received stolen MtGox funds – MtGox itself, Bitcoinica and BTC-e – and had since been able to pin down some of the addresses that had previously proved elusive, discovering that they belonged to TradeHill, a San Francisco-based exchange that launched in 2011. There were no signs that MtGox had laundered the bitcoins returned to it, and both TradeHill and Bitcoinica had shut down in early 2012, the latter after a hack. This left BTC-e.

Through his research, Nilsson found that many of the stolen MtGox coins had been transferred to addresses controlled by one individual on BTC-e, with some of the stolen funds being deposited back into MtGox accounts used between 2011 and 2014. Allied to this were seventeen instances where stolen MtGox funds and funds from other hacked exchanges, such as Bitcoinica, were sent to Trade Hill and then back to another MtGox account. This account had a note attached to a lone cash deposit made to it, a note made up of three letters: WME. The owner of the WME account instantly became Nilsson's prime suspect. Using the MtGox database and some good old-fashioned Internet trawling, Nilsson came across a BitcoinTalk user by the name of WME who regularly discussed Bitcoin activities and, crucially, the exchanging of bitcoins into various fiat currencies. In one post from October 2011, WME wrote [translated]:

Hello.

I have been engaged in exchanges for more than ten years, now I have started working with bitcoins.

> *I can trade them for anything. I give preference to cash in Moscow, but without any problems I will exchange it for vmz, vmr, epese, paxum, ecoin, paypal, ruble bank transfer from an individual (alfa, telebank, etc., etc.), dollar bank transfer from an offshore company and other options.*

Nilsson did some more digging and found that the person he was seeking was a Russian currency exchange facilitator who had been on the scene for around a decade, likely putting him in his 30s or 40s. He continued searching WME's posts for more clues, watching him rant about one exchange, CryptoXChange, after his account had been 'suspended due to suspicious circumstances'. This gave Nilsson further confidence he was on the right track. He scrolled through the lengthy post from WME criticising CryptoXchange, which included screenshots of WME's account... and suddenly, clear as day, Nilsson was staring at the name of the man who just might have hacked MtGox.

At the same time, a task force made up of Japanese federal investigators and the Criminal Investigation branch of the US Internal Revenue Service (IRS-CI) was itself looking at suspects for the MtGox theft. This task force included the man known in IRS-CI circles as the 'Blockchain Wizard', Tigran Gambaryan, who also helped to take down Silk Road in 2013 and who would prove influential in outing the activities of Carl Force and Shaun Bridges two years later. Shortly after publishing the second WizSec report in April 2015, Nilsson had been contacted by Gary Alford, a special agent in the IRS-CI who was famous for being the first member of law enforcement to finger Ross Ulbricht as a possible Dread Pirate Roberts candidate. Alford had done what Japanese authorities hadn't and had taken notice of Nilsson and his findings, asking the Swede if he would assist in their fledgling investigation into the MtGox affair. Nilsson was wary about getting into bed with the IRS, given that they might use the data against Bitcoin traders on MtGox, but he realised that the agency could be the muscle he so badly needed to finish the job and nail someone for the hack or series of hacks. However, despite giving them 'everything', all that Alford and the IRS would offer Nilsson in return was encouragement that he was 'on the right track'. So much was already obvious, and Nilsson received none of the assistance he had hoped for. At the time of the first communications between the pair, however, Alford's involvement had given Nilsson fresh impetus to continue his laborious task of tracing the flow of funds out of MtGox.

After confirming his findings through several other posts, having initially been sceptical that his target would have published their real name, Nilsson informed Gary Alford of his find. Nilsson's tip came just at the right time; the IRS-CI investigation into the MtGox hacks was gathering pace, with the Washington D.C.-based team having at that time just joined forces with Japanese authorities, and names were beginning to pop up. Like Nilsson, they, too, had zeroed in on BTC-e and WME, but they didn't yet have a real-world name to go with it. Through their own blockchain analysis, honed following its debut during the Silk Road investigation, and using the long arm of the US legal system to subpoena bank records, the team determined that a BTC-e account owned by a Russian national was involved in cash transfers to banks in Cyprus and Latvia, known waypoints to major banks in Europe and further afield, between 2013 and 2015. They, like Nilsson, knew that WME was controlling MtGox accounts that had received and sent stolen MtGox bitcoins, so they were sure this was their man. All they needed now was a name.

In an attempt to match WME to a real person on MtGox, the US team had asked its Japanese counterparts for a full copy of the MtGox database and were stunned when the request was refused. An anecdote from Jake Adelstein, retold in his book *Pay the Devil in Bitcoin*, explains how he personally had to break it to one of the members of the US investigation team that the reason for this denial was because US authorities would 'make idiots' of Japanese investigators if they uncovered evidence of someone else other than their man, Mark Karpelès, being behind the MtGox theft. When the agent asked why Japanese investigators would prejudice the case in this way, Adelstein explained, 'Japanese prosecutors put saving face above justice'. This put an end to any cooperation between the two nations, but the IRS-CI team found a back door to get what they wanted: a Secret Service agent who had been part of a former Tigran Gambaryan-run operation recalled that a suspect with the pseudonym WME had been associated with stealing and selling credit card information. One look at the Secret Service's database confirmed what Kim Nilsson's forum scrolling had also revealed: WME was Alexander Vinnik.

Alexander Vinnik was born in the provincial town of Kurgan in western Russia in 1978. Choosing not to follow in his father's carpentry footsteps, Vinnik grew up instead assembling radios and learning to program computers on a rented ZX Spectrum, ironically not unlike Mark Karpelès. The budding tech entrepreneur moved to Moscow with his mother in the early 2000s, where he pursued various Internet ventures before pivoting to a more lucrative business model: online payments. Vinnik established Wm-Exchanger.com in 2004, a website that allowed people to convert rubles and E-Gold (an early electronic currency) into WebMoney, another digital currency that was popular in Russia. Wm-Exchanger grew, and Vinnik marketed his skills as an electronic payments aficionado in online forums before taking on extra work for WMExpress, a company that helped clients exchange digital and physical currencies, in 2006. The services of Wm-Exchanger became increasingly sought-after, with part of the appeal down to Vinnik himself, who was one of just five or six online currency brokers in Russia that had offshore bank accounts at that time, making him a very popular option for all types of customer. Foreign exchange traders and Internet professionals were the first to use digital currency exchange services, but it wasn't long before they were joined by cybercriminals and credit card scammers. Vinnik learnt about Bitcoin in 2009, not long after it launched, and recognised the huge opportunity it presented to payments professionals like him, especially those who worked with the darker elements of the cyber world.

In August 2011, Vinnik and Aleksey Bilyuchenko, a then thirty-seven-year-old former IT manager for a furniture shop chain, launched BTC-e in Crimea. This was four months before Vinnik's first appearance on BitcoinTalk and just three months after Mark Karpelès had taken over MtGox. BTC-e got off to a slow start, securing only 20,000 customers by the end of 2012, while MtGox had around ten times that. However, BTC-e's share was lower because it attracted a very specific kind of clientele: criminals. BTC-e actively obscured user accounts and activity, anonymised transactions and the source of funds and lacked any anti-money laundering controls. In short, it was designed for the perpetrators of financial crimes to cash out their ill-gotten gains almost totally anonymously, not unlike Liberty Reserve. BTC-e proved to be a very popular service, with hackers, ransomware scammers, identity thieves, corrupt public officials and narcotics distribution rings all making use of its money laundering facilities to the tune of billions of dollars. As MtGox stuttered and then collapsed in 2014, BTC-e was there to pick up the pieces; by October 2014, it had grown to almost 570,000 users, with many praising its slick performance compared to MtGox's crumbling infrastructure in its final weeks.

By the autumn of 2016, BTC-e was the third biggest Bitcoin exchange in the world by daily volume, and it looked like Vinnik and Bilyuchenko's operation was going to be challenging for the top spot before long. The fact that BTC-e had launched right around the time of the first major MtGox hacks and had received much of the stolen haul had not escaped investigators', or Kim Nilsson's, notice. Neither had the fact that it had also scooped up much of the MtGox customer base following its collapse, something that Chainalysis had noted, too, with Michael Gronager spotting that a great deal of the criminal activity took place in Russian timezones. With Vinnik and BTC-e now identified as being hugely complicit in the MtGox thefts, the task force's next job was to find out how deep Vinnik's involvement in BTC-e went; was he just a cog in the machine, or was he controlling the entire operation?

The sprawling nature of the investigation into BTC-e and the breadth and scale of Vinnik's apparent criminal activities had necessitated the involvement of more and more departments of the US government as it had progressed. This led to the Justice Department's Criminal Division, the Immigration and Customs Enforcement's Homeland Security Investigations division, the Federal Bureau of Investigation, the United States Secret Service, the Federal Deposit Insurance Corporation, the Office of the Inspector General and FinCEN all going after one man. The expanded task force utilised data from Texan travel data giant Sabre, which had been gathering global travel information since the 1950s to carry out what Forbes would later call 'an unprecedented use of a U.S. surveillance power' as it tracked the movements of Vinnik and his suspected accomplices.

The need for so many agencies and such unprecedented surveillance was evidenced by the fact that the more the task force looked into BTC-e, the wider they realised the net spread; individuals from all over the world were using it for all sorts of illegal reasons. It was also up to its virtual neck in the affairs of Russian cybercriminals, affairs which would become global news just weeks later when Russian hacking group Fancy Bear got hold of Hilary Clinton's emails as part of their attempts to meddle in the 2016 US election, with funding for the operation coming in the form of bitcoins received into BTC-e.

Armed with all the evidence gathered so far, a grand jury was convened in early 2016 to assess whether there was enough to charge Vinnik, his associates and BTC-e with various crimes centring around money laundering. Prosecutors laid out the laundering pattern that had taken place in the wake of the hacks on

MtGox: 530,000 of 647,000 bitcoins stolen from MtGox between September 2011 and February 2014 had been sent to accounts held by Vinnik at TradeHill, BTC-e and MtGox itself, with BTC-e receiving the majority (300,000). Vinnik, an administrator of BTC-e, was also identified as the co-owner of Canton Business Corporation, the Seychelles-based company that owned BTC-e and which, through a network of shell companies under its umbrella, was the recipient of much of the laundered money. Three other individuals were named as Canton co-owners and fellow BTC-e operators: Andrey Nikonoriv, Alexander Buyanov and Stanislav Golovanov. Together, the foursome was allegedly responsible for the laundering of billions of dollars in bitcoins through BTC-e and other avenues from all varieties of online criminal activity.

The grand jury sat through the first quarter of 2016 and returned its verdict in May: there was enough evidence to indict the four individuals and Canton on three charges, namely operation of an unlicensed money service business, conspiracy to commit money laundering and criminal forfeiture. Arrest and seizure warrants were drawn up, but things quickly reached a sticking point: being Russian citizens, arresting and extraditing the four was out of the question. US authorities, therefore, requested that the indictments and arrest warrants be sealed, knowing that the gang could go to ground if they were charged before authorities could move on them. This request was granted on 31 May, leaving the task force to try and find an opening.

As the task force sought ways to apprehend Vinnik and his cohorts during the second half of 2016, a raft of new evidence threw a very different light on what they thought they knew. As they dug into bank statements, traced money flows and analysed corporate documents, the task force realised that, far from this being a four-man effort, it was all down to Alexander Vinnik. Almost everything, from the setting up of fake companies in London to the shifting of money through the Seychelles, had been down to Vinnik, who had used the identities of Buyanov, Nikonoriv and Golovanov without their knowledge to try and minimise his involvement. This wasn't to say that the three were squeaky clean, but the evidence that had been used to indict them was undetermined by new evidence that showed Vinnik's hand behind the curtain. The sealing of the indictment in May had prevented Buyanov, Nikonoriv and Golovanov from having their names splashed across the newspapers, but Russian BBC journalist Andrey Zakharov had done some investigating of his own and had discovered that Buyanov was listed as the most recent person with significant control of Always Efficient LLP, one of Canton's shell companies registered in Britain. When Zakharov tracked Buyanov down to the Moscow nightclub where he worked as a DJ and confronted him about his role in laundering the MtGox money, Buyanov said he had no idea what Zakharov was talking about. Similarly, when *Coindesk* spoke to Andrey Nikonoriv, he claimed to have been just a BTC-e customer and that Vinnik must have used his identification documents to conduct bank transfers in his name.

Just five months after the first set of charges were sealed, a new grand jury was convened, this time looking at the activities of Vinnik and BTC-e in isolation. The swathe of new evidence that exonerated Buyanov, Nikonoriv and Golovanov made things a whole lot worse for Vinnik: the grand jury believed there was sufficient evidence to charge him and BTC-e with twenty-one counts relating to multiple financial crimes, including money laundering, conspiracy to commit money laundering, unlawful money transactions and criminal forfeiture. Once again, the indictment referred to the laundering of 530,000 of the 647,000 MtGox bitcoins, but this time, Vinnik was named as the sole actor, with US authorities alleging that he had used other people's identities across multiple cryptocurrency exchange accounts and company bank accounts to funnel the cash out to Canton's shell companies. As well as facing more than fifty years in prison, Vinnik was looking at a $12 million fine while BTC-e was in line for a separate $88.6 million penalty. Buyanov, Nikonoriv and Golovanov were all absent in the superseding indictment, with 'individuals known and unknown' listed in their place, showing that Vinnik hadn't worked alone but that there wasn't enough evidence to add anyone else to the charge sheet. An arrest warrant was sealed on 17 January 2017, with US authorities still scratching their heads over how to actually get their hands on Vinnik, although one was at least easier than four.

It didn't take too long for an opportunity to fall into their lap; six months after the indictment had been sealed, Vinnik and BTC-e co-founder Aleksey Bilyuchenko both booked summer holidays to the Mediterranean. The pair stayed apart to avoid suspicion, with Vinnik and his family staying on the Greek peninsula of Halkidiki while Bilyuchenko ended up hundreds of miles away on the island of Crete. With Greece and the US having an extradition agreement dating back to 1937, this was going to be the best chance that the investigative team would possibly ever get to grab Vinnik. Agents from the US task force informed their Greek counterparts, the Cyber Crime Unit of the Hellenic Police, of Vinnik's holiday plans, and between them, they forged a plot to arrest him and shut down BTC-e.

On 24 July 2017, Vinnik, along with his wife, Alexandra Shevchenko, and their two boys – a three-year-old and a newborn – checked into a luxurious beachside hotel in Ouranoupoli, a tranquil area located in the easternmost of the three prongs comprising the Thessaloniki peninsula, unaware that they had been watched by Greek police ever since they had arrived in the country. The following day, Alexandra was swimming in the sea while the couple's children played on the sand. Vinnik was relaxing on a sun lounger, shielding himself from the scorching thirty-five-degree heat. A wiry man with short, light brown hair, Vinnik's pale skin showed that natural sunlight, especially that offered by the relentless Greek sun, wasn't something he was accustomed to. As Alexandra swam, the idyll was shattered by a battery of urgent shouts from the beach. She turned quickly to see several surfers and beachgoers converging on her husband, yelling at him to lie down and put his hands behind his back. Panicked, she waded ashore as quickly as she could and made her way towards the group, gathering up her terrified children as she did. She approached the gaggle of men, imploring them to leave her husband alone, but she could do nothing but watch helplessly as Vinnik was handcuffed. She demanded they release him, but there was no room for negotiation. Vinnik was permitted to dress – a pair of light grey trousers and a black t-shirt emblazoned with a boxing gloves motif – before being ushered into the back of an unmarked car and driven away.

While Vinnik was taken to the Thessaloniki Administrative Courts, the couple's hotel room was searched, with police seizing two laptops, two tablet computers, five mobile phones and, rather surprisingly for a holiday, an Internet router. At the court, the US charges were read to Vinnik, who denied any involvement in money laundering or any association with BTC-e and even professed surprise at his arrest. He phoned his mother, who herself then made a phone call to Bilyuchenko, warning him of what had just happened. Panicking that he might be next, Bilyuchenko took his laptop to the coast near his hotel, smashed it to pieces against the rocks, threw it into the sea and caught the first flight back to Moscow.

News of Vinnik's capture made international headlines, with the grand jury findings affording the world an astounding glimpse into this shadowy world of which most knew very little. Vinnik was accused of laundering some $4 billion in illicitly obtained funds, including 65% of all the coins stolen from MtGox across its various hacks. The Japanese press, which had all but convicted Mark Karpelès by this point, had to perform a careful balancing act when reporting the news, lest anyone even remotely suspect that the police might not have the right man. They were aided in their efforts by the briefing published by the US Department of Justice, which went only as far as suggesting that Vinnik 'operated' BTC-e and that he 'obtained funds from the hack of MtGox', with no suggestion that he was complicit in the hack itself.

Vinnik's arrest also spelt trouble for BTC-e, which learned pretty quickly that it hadn't been thorough enough with its efforts to hide itself. The web hosting company that supported the exchange's operation rented server space from an American company called Equinix, and it didn't take the FBI long to find out where Equinix's data centre was; an agent located in its Newark field office would only need to look out of any high east-facing window with a pair of binoculars to see a squat, dark blue building perched in the middle of an industrial area five miles away over the Hackensack River. Four days before Vinnik's arrest, the agents had obtained a search and seizure warrant from a New Jersey District Court for this building, a warrant that was executed following confirmation of Vinnik's capture on 25 July. Having driven the nine miles to the data centre, the FBI carried out its raid, taking the servers away and forcing BTC-e offline. Despite this action, BTC-e was still able to withdraw 66,000 bitcoins, at the time worth some $169 million, from its cold storage wallets to multiple addresses hours before the FBI could seize them. Only once the coins had been safely moved out did BTC-e tell its users that it was undergoing 'unplanned maintenance'; within three days, the FBI had taken over the BTC-e domain and posted a takedown and seizure notice on its website. In a statement reproduced on BitcoinTalk, BTC-e tried to distance itself from Vinnik and his activities, declaring that 'Alexander Vinnik never was the Head or Employee of the BTC-e service', but no one who knew anything about the inner workings of BTC-e was fooled.

With Vinnik arrested, the world finally had a name to definitively link to the massive loss of the MtGox bitcoins. This helped take the spotlight off Mark

Karpelès and finally solidified in the minds of those not prejudiced against the Frenchman that the MtGox haul had undoubtedly been stolen by outside forces. The question now was: how had Vinnik and his associates done it? One man who knew more than most about Vinnik's involvement with MtGox, of course, was Kim Nilsson, who was now able to publicly name the man he had helped authorities identify more than a year prior. In a report dropped in the wake of Vinnik's arrest and which covered more than two years' worth of further analysis of the MtGox hack, Nilsson revealed how he had been supplying authorities with the results of his work since 2015 (and getting nothing back in return) and named Vinnik as 'our chief suspect for involvement in the MtGox theft (or the laundering of the proceeds thereof)'. This, again, fell short of directly pinpointing Vinnik as the hacker, with Nilsson saying in 2018 that his data told him everything about the hacks except 'who shot JFK'.

One thing Nilsson *was* able to do was to offer up a theory as to how the massive hack on MtGox between 2011 and 2014 had taken place. The hot wallet was confirmed as the conduit by which the hackers had managed to rob the exchange of all its bitcoins, but unlike with the 1Feex attack, where the hackers had gotten away with just the contents of the hot wallet, on this occasion, they had also swiped the keys to 100,000 deposit addresses tied to it. This meant that when anyone had deposited funds to any of those 100,000 addresses, the hackers had been able to siphon them off the second they arrived. As a result, all customer deposits into those addresses had gone directly into the hackers' pockets, with the same fate meted out to the coins sent to those addresses from MtGox's cold storage.

As for how no one at MtGox had been able to spot this, there was a little mitigation for Mark Karpelès in the fact that the limitations of the Bitcoin blockchain didn't (and today still wouldn't) allow MtGox to monitor the bitcoins it supposedly owned to see if they were being moved elsewhere. As far as MtGox was concerned, those coins were real, and they were being handled as expected: the cold wallet balances were assumed to be growing and were used to top up the hot wallet when withdrawal levels demanded it. This was the pouring of cold wallet funds into a leaky hot wallet, as Kim Nilsson had suspected, although the report did not speculate whether this was done manually or automatically. The theft of the coins in the hot wallet and the compromising of the 100,000 addresses allowed the hackers to syphon off the 647,000 bitcoins

Vinnik had allegedly laundered between October 2011 and January 2014, taking the total number of bitcoins lost to hackers to almost 810,000. The scale of the theft was brought home by the fact that this hack alone, never mind the others that went on before it, was worth a staggering $1.43 billion on the day Nilsson released his report in July 2017.

Nilsson's investigations also reinforced his theory that, for whatever reason, when Karpelès created a new Bitcoin wallet, he kept the private key but discarded the public key, necessitating the long-winded way of recovering the public key when it was needed. This, he had told the Foreign Correspondents' Club of Japan in 2015, was a basic mistake:

> ...[the process] is definitely not how cold storage and private keys are supposed to be used. There would have been very safe ways of dealing with that.

What had also previously troubled Nilsson was that the bitcoins didn't start leaving the hot wallet until October 2011, *after* the wallet encryption had been activated by Mark Karpelès, which should have been impossible. By tracing the dates of the fraudulent withdrawals, however, Nilsson was able to pinpoint the date and even the time that the hot wallet had been compromised: 9.30 p.m. GMT on 11 September 2011, *before* Karpelès had implemented the wallet encryption. By sheer good fortune for the hackers, they had escaped with both the money in the vault and a copy of the keys right before it was locked down.

Nilsson's research also revealed that a separate issue with MtGox had compounded an already bad situation. The existence of two separate yet identical wallets working in tandem, one owned by MtGox and one by the hackers, had confused the MtGox system. The upshot of this was that when the hackers removed bitcoins from the hot wallet, MtGox would sometimes treat these withdrawals as additional deposits. Not only was MtGox losing bitcoins through repeated thefts, therefore, but it simultaneously credited some of those same stolen bitcoins to other users. This helped mask any issues with the hot wallet balance and resulted in forty-eight MtGox users receiving a total of 44,300 bitcoins from the exchange's cold storage, many of which were simply withdrawn straight away. Some of these bitcoins were recovered, but about 30,000 were quietly removed by the lucky recipients and merely added to the losses.

With so much more now known about the hack on MtGox, including how its own systems had compounded the issue, and with Alexander Vinnik under arrest for laundering the spoils, it remained to be seen whether Japanese authorities would recognise Vinnik's involvement and Nilsson's research. These questions, and more, would only be answered at the trial of Mark Karpelès, which was rapidly approaching.

Chapter 18 – On Trial

A year earlier, as Mark Karpelès had been methodically working through the boxes and boxes of documents containing his paper copy of the MtGox database, he began to see how the police had arrived at a charge of embezzlement. At first glance, it seemed that MtGox's profits weren't enough to cover its spending and its losses, but through further investigation, he concluded that the authorities had missed, either through incompetence or intent, a whole heap of booked profits. This amounted, by Karpelès's calculations, to some ¥650 million ($5.5 million) worth of revenue that wasn't accounted for, although he realised that this was only part of the final tally and that far larger discrepancies lay between prosecutors' numbers and his.

Karpelès tried to communicate his findings to his legal team, but the rules of his detention prohibited this. Realising that these rules were actively hampering his case gave his legal team an idea, and they used it to play their last remaining card to get him out on bail. Japanese law states that a defendant must be given a proper chance to defend themselves to make any conviction valid, and Karpelès's legal team, armed with this new insight over the financial discrepancies from their client, renewed the push to release him on bail to allow them to work with him on his findings. They petitioned the court, claiming that wading through thousands of transactions by hand in a detention cell with a single calculator was not an effective form of defence. To form a proper defence, they argued, Karpelès needed better equipment, such as a computer, and the assistance of his legal team. Despite protestations from prosecutors, the court agreed, and on 14 July 2016, Mark Karpelès was freed on bail to work on his defence, on the condition that he didn't leave the country.

At the bail hearing, the judge took the unusual step of criticising the prosecutors for the delays in bringing Karpelès to trial and the time it had taken to prepare their brief. This would have come as no surprise to the state's team;

they had already been criticised by the Cybercrime Division for ignoring large amounts of data around the case (as Karpelès had just discovered) and for having an incomplete, and possibly completely misguided, case. When pressing the judge to deny bail, prosecutors were forced to admit that they were not ready for trial, which worked in Karpelès's favour and showed that he might have the upper hand, at least for now. Karpelès left Kosuge prison with a bone in his hand still broken from his altercation with the door. He also left some 35kg slimmer than when he went in, prompting one wag on Reddit to retort, 'He can get a job promoting a Japanese diet for weight-loss. He has a good track-record for making stuff disappear....'

While freedom was, naturally, better than being locked in a detention centre, Karpelès found it harder to adapt to life outside than he had thought. As an accused criminal, finding an apartment and a job was a struggle. Given that he was still getting death threats and that he was a recognisable figure even on the busy streets of Tokyo, Karpelès spent his time as a semi-nomad, moving apartments every few months in case an aggrieved customer spotted him or uncovered his address and decided to exact retribution. He was desperate to see his ailing mother, whom he hadn't seen since leaving France for Tokyo in 2009, but of course, he couldn't. Japan's two-year arrest-to-trial protocol meant that his trial would start no later than July 2017, so he was likely to be confined to Japan for another year at least and potentially many more if things didn't work out in his favour.

Karpelès and his team spent the following twelve months working on his defence from his various temporary homes before, on 11 July 2017, he and his entourage arrived at the Tokyo District Court for the first day of his trial. This was a court that Karpelès knew well, having visited it many times in 2014 throughout the MtGox bankruptcy proceedings. The plentiful Western press and observers, eager to report on the case, had been advised not to expect the same kind of courtroom drama that they were used to back home. Japanese trials are typically carried out in stages, with each stage often being just days in length but months apart; stage one constitutes opening proceedings, stage two sees evidence examined and hears witness testimony and stage three sees closing arguments presented to the court. Verdict and sentencing then take place weeks or months later, usually together. The whole thing, the journalists were told, was more of a presentation of arguments and evidence rather than a battle between wily attorneys, with much going on behind the scenes.

As expected, the press was out in numbers to capture Karpelès's arrival, with many photographing the Frenchman in the back seat of a black saloon car as it made its way through the gates to the courtroom car park. The trial was technically open to the public, but the disparity between the size of the courtroom and the demand for seats meant a lottery system was put in place to see who could attend the first day. Of the twenty-four audience seats in the tiny court, six were taken up by police working on the case, leaving journalists, creditors, and everyone else wanting to see the action first-hand fighting over the remaining eighteen. To outside observers, the use of such a small courtroom for such a huge trial was illogical, but, as one Japanese journalist pointed out to Kolin Burges (who was only able to get a seat after a cryptocurrency exchange gave him one of their winning tickets), the Japanese government may have intentionally chosen a small court in an attempt to minimize the number of media outlets who could attend and report on it. Like many, Burges was hopeful that the trial would provide answers to the questions that Karpelès had been rebuffing for over three years, so he was thrilled to have obtained a front-row seat.

Alongside Kolin Burges in the courtroom was Kim Nilsson, who was there to observe the man whose actions had consumed his life for the best part of three years and in whose house he had helped consume innumerable tarte aux pommes while poring over the MtGox database together. Nilsson, of course, was one of the few in the world who knew that Karpelès almost certainly had nothing to do with the theft, having recently helped authorities identify Alexander Vinnik, the man who, as Karpelès stepped into the courtroom, was still two weeks away from having his holiday so drastically cut short by the police.

Once the formalities had been observed and Karpelès had been read his rights, the charges against him were laid out. Karpelès faced three charges: two of embezzlement of funds, representing the use of company money for private purposes, and one of manipulating the balance of his account on MtGox for the purposes of buying bitcoins (the use of Willy and Markus). The prosecution was pushing for embezzlement of customer funds rather than company funds, which carried a heavier penalty, although the latter would be its fallback if that venture failed. What was more important, of course, was what Karpelès was *not* being charged with: being personally responsible for any of the missing 647,000 bitcoins stolen between October 2011 and January 2014. Despite Alexander Vinnik's name not being on anyone's lips at that point, the passage of time and the publication of Nilsson's research since the collapse of MtGox had all but proved that the coins had been stolen through a series of hacks between 2011 and 2014 and not by exploitation of the transaction malleability bug. Karpelès was still in the frame as the thief as far as some were concerned, but sentiment on this front was continuing to shift away from this idea as it had become clearer that he was simply terrible at his job rather than having his hands perpetually in the till.

What also helped this shift in perception was the fact that Japanese prosecutors, unable to force a confession from Karpelès, seemed to be steering clear of accusing him of having anything to do with the hacks despite having publicly linked the operation of the bots and the theft right back to their first suspicions in 2014. This theory, however, ignored the research of Kim Nilsson, Chainalysis and US investigators, which showed that the furious buying and selling of coins in late 2013 had nothing to do with the loss, as it had already been going on for one and a half years by that point. Vinnik's arrest would help set the seal on this perception shift for all but a few holdouts, although it couldn't disguise the fact that Karpelès had kept the series of thefts, losses and missteps to himself for three years and almost certainly knew about the exchange's perilous position before it was revealed following MtGox's demise.

After the charges had been laid out, Karpelès was asked to enter his plea and was given a chance to make an opening statement, which he took:

I am innocent of all charges. I absolutely did not manipulate any data for personal gain, or fraudulently use any customer funds. What is being called 'fraudulent creation of private electronic records' was in reality a business function called 'obligation exchange', by which MtGox's bitcoins and USD liabilities towards its customers could be exchanged at market value for the purposes of keeping MtGox's debt portfolio reasonably balanced.

This 'obligation exchange', Karpelès went on, was his way of rebalancing the books to try and get the company solvent at the outset of his tenure, not to enrich himself. He then went on to throw Jed McCaleb under the bus:

Regarding these problems, Jed McCaleb directed me to implement this 'obligation exchange', and as a result, part of operating MtGox came to include dutifully running the 'obligation exchange' to protect customers. Any investigation will readily show that it was not for my or MtGox's own benefit.

Karpelès also denied the charges of embezzlement, saying that any money used in this way was money already transferred to him and had been correctly registered in the company accounts, stating explicitly, 'These were not customer funds', before lamenting the fact that the trial wouldn't be dealing with the actual collapse:

> *It is regrettable that this trial is concerning matters entirely unrelated to the cause of the MtGox collapse. The entire world is observing, and this trial is not about revealing the cause of the bankruptcy. At the same time, through the efforts of a handful of talented experts around the world, the principal cause for MtGox's collapse is already being made clear as a bitcoin theft by outside hackers...As for me, in this trial which has no relation to the MtGox collapse, I want to prove my innocence.*

Karpelès ended his statement by saying that, although he wasn't responsible for the theft, he was responsible for allowing it to happen:

> *I am deeply aware of my unavoidable responsibility for the collapse, and for the sake of all the harmed customers, I am determined to continue to work together with various law enforcement agencies and investigation groups to further the investigation into clarifying the cause of the collapse and attempting to recover any bitcoins.*

Nilsson, too, noted in his summary of the day's action that it was unbelievable that the loss of the 647,000 bitcoins didn't feature:

> *...if you're thinking it's a farce for the trial over MtGox, a case three years in the making, to focus exclusively on Karpelès and not provide any satisfactory explanation for the collapse that ended up with half a billion dollars missing, you're not alone.*

Karpelès's admission that he had been running Willy and Markus made headlines all over again, confirming what the world had known for a year thanks to the 2011 email between himself and Jed McCaleb that had been printed in *The Daily Beast*. As for the intentions behind Willy and Markus, Karpelès would finally get around to a detailed explanation in a 2022 interview; the grand plan had simply been to turn the 80,000 bitcoins lost in the March 2011 hack into a dollar debt, which Karpelès said was more 'stable' and could have been repaid by buying bitcoins to sell at a higher price later on. The necessity of keeping this activity secret was, according to Karpelès, imposed on him by Jed McCaleb as a condition of the takeover. Karpelès had used Willy and Markus to try and cover the 80,000 bitcoins stolen in the 1Feex hack, plus the other debts that had accrued over time, with McCaleb urging Karpelès to 'slowly buy more bitcoins' and fill the hole 'before the price got out of hand'. Karpelès had followed this process but forgot the 'slowly' part, and as the price rapidly increased, he was forced to use Willy and Markus to buy back the bitcoins at higher and higher prices, defeating Willy and Markus's purpose and leaving MtGox massively out of pocket as a result. By this point, however, Karpelès had already filled the gap left by the 1Feex hack many times over, leaving us with only suppositions as to why he didn't shut the bots off. One theory is that he knew that 647,000 bitcoins had been lost in the catastrophic 2011-2014 hack and was trying to fill this gap, too, but this doesn't explain the mass selling in 2014. Another is that he fully expected a 'run' on the exchange if it ever opened up bitcoin withdrawals again, which would almost certainly have happened, and so he was trying to buy up enough bitcoins to have a buffer and ensure that the exchange didn't collapse that way. A third theory is that he simply got greedy and wanted to hoover up as many bitcoins as possible, perhaps believing Bitcoin was set for more gains, and was forced to sell when the market turned.

Whatever the reason behind Willy and Markus's continued operations past their initial parameters, Kim Nilsson revealed in his 2017 report that, rather than making 80,000 bitcoins as planned, plus whatever other debts Karpelès may have tried to cover, Willy and Markus, in fact, *lost* MtGox a whopping 22,800 bitcoins and $51.6 million in cash, largely because of Markus dumping hundreds of thousands of the bought bitcoins in early 2014 as the market crashed. This was yet another epic disaster to add to the catalogue of catastrophes, but conversely, it was also more proof that Willy and Markus were not used to siphon bitcoins off the exchange. At the time of Karpelès's courtroom admission, this information wasn't known, however, and MtGox creditors were left with the uncomfortable realisation that if Karpelès was able to rationalise the use of the bots against his own customers, what else might he have allowed himself to do?

To this end, Nilsson noticed on the first day of the trial that the court was only interested in the use of Willy and Markus up to November 2013, the time when the bulk of the bots' 650,000 bitcoins were picked up, and not when the mass selling started. It was clear that MtGox customers were not going to come away from this trial any more informed about the fate of their bitcoins than they had going in.

The first stage of Karpelès's trial lasted two days, with the prosecution setting out its stall on day one using facts that were already known or assumed, much of which related to Karpelès's alleged embezzlement, which was of no real interest to the Bitcoin community, and nothing whatsoever about the hacks and the monstrous losses. By the second day, Burges and Nilsson had learnt their lesson concerning the lottery system and bought a team with them to increase their chances of getting a seat. It worked, and both got in again, but they were to be disappointed; the second day lasted just five minutes, with Karpelès's defence team handing its evidence over to the judges, explaining their reasons for Karpelès operating Willy and Markus and insisting that the money he spent was fully justified and in line with corporate law. A date of 12 October was set for continuation, and that was that. After three years of waiting, no one was any closer to solving the puzzle of who stole 810,000 bitcoins from MtGox, and it didn't look like the trial of the only man who had control over them was going to bring any closure on that matter.

Three months later, the court reconvened, with Burges once again expecting to battle for space in the courtroom. However, the attention paid to the trial this time round was negligible, requiring no lottery system and with few journalists reporting on events. Across 12 and 17 October, both sides were given the chance to present and cross-examine witnesses, with Karpelès not expected to take the stand. Karpelès's side didn't produce any witnesses, while three were slated to appear on behalf of the state, including Ashley Barr, who, if anything, was sure to provide some colour to what threatened to be otherwise quite stale proceedings. In the event, these two days proved to be largely uneventful; procedural discussions, a handover of more documentary evidence and a blow-by-blow account from one of the investigators as to how MtGox and Mark Karpelès were investigated were of little value to anyone but the judges, with Barr not called to the witness stand after all. It was becoming clear to Western onlookers that public court proceedings were just the tip of the iceberg in Japan and little more than an opportunity to formalise discussions that were evidently going on behind closed doors. The court was adjourned until December 2018, when further examination of the evidence would take place, and closing arguments would be made before the judges retired to consider their verdict.

Despite the arrest of Alexander Vinnik in July 2017 having brought the MtGox story back to the headlines again, coverage of this second part of the Karpelès trial was almost non-existent, especially from Western media outlets. All the hype from the opening day had firmly died away, with little of any substance reported after Karpelès's dramatic opening statement. The Bitcoin world had moved on, which was little solace to MtGox victims who were no closer to understanding what had happened to their holdings. There was plenty to keep them occupied while they waited, however... like trying to get their money back.

Chapter 19 – The Tokyo Whale

A mile north of where Mark Karpelès was standing trial, Nobuaki Kobayashi was going through a trial of his own. Ensconced in his office at the law firm Nagashima Ohno & Tsunematsu, located on the first floor underneath the KITTE Marunouchi shopping centre, the MtGox bankruptcy administrator had spent more than a year trying to get his head around the tens of thousands of claims that were coming through from MtGox customers. The numbers involved were simply staggering, and it didn't take him long to work out that a not-insubstantial number of people were simply trying their luck.

Kobayashi and his team had belatedly begun investigating customer claims in February 2016, comparing them with the records they had to hand, and came to a final figure three months later: MtGox creditors were claiming a staggering total loss of $2.4 trillion. This was a particularly impressive amount considering that all the bitcoins in the world at the time were only worth $7 billion. Of this gargantuan figure, Kobayashi revealed that only $414 million worth had been approved, representing less than 0.02% of the total value claimed, with 24,750 claimants approved. With only $91 million in assets recovered from the exchange, it was obvious that customers would be lucky to get as much as a quarter of their funds back.

The creditors themselves, meanwhile, were becoming deeply frustrated by the slow nature of the bankruptcy process and the monthly costs which were eating away at the company's remaining assets, as well as the lack of progress in the actual investigation into the collapse of MtGox. The number of bitcoins held by the estate had stagnated at 202,185 while the cash assets, despite having increased by 28% since the first creditor meeting in July 2014, were being steadily drained to no tangible benefit, with over $1 million leaving the kitty between creditor meetings in 2016. Kolin Burges, still a vocal critic of the way things were being conducted, reiterated that he was 'disturbed by the amount of money which the bankruptcy process has burned through', adding that creditors had seen 'very poor results from the investigations, and the details have been constantly shrouded from the creditors.'

As 2016 progressed, there was even less to cheer about. A creditor-led lawsuit filed the year before in Japan, which had attempted to get the coins classed as property and therefore have them distributed in their original form, had been thrown out on the grounds that bitcoins could not be considered property in a legal sense. This meant that the 202,185 bitcoins remained in the hands of Kobayashi, who, under bankruptcy law, would soon have to start selling them, given that he was making no headway with a bitcoin-based rehabilitation solution. There was also little progress, publicly at least, from the investigations being carried out by Deloitte, ReEx and Chainalysis, with the companies producing nothing that pointed towards any person or group of persons who could be held legally responsible. In fact, Chainalysis had matched and, on occasion, exceeded the work of WizSec, but the company had been gagged by US authorities. It was a source of continued frustration for creditors that the efforts of the official investigators appeared on the surface to be outshone by the efforts of Kim Nilsson and WizSec, yet it was they who were further draining the funds from the creditor pot.

2017 didn't start much better with Coinlab CEO Peter Vessenes, the man whose lawsuit was already threatening to hold up any potential creditor-approved deal, warning claimants that they shouldn't get their hopes up over payouts that year. This was met with an angry reception from MtGox creditors, including a couple of death threats, and Vessenes deleted the post. He was to be proved right, however: a March creditor meeting offered no advances on the timescale for payouts or even if bitcoin payouts were on the horizon, a situation that hadn't changed by the September meeting either. By the time of this meeting, however, another crisis was threatening to derail the MtGox bankruptcy train.

The collapse of MtGox in 2014 had helped precipitate a lengthy bear market in the cryptocurrency space, but by 2016, the scars were fading, and new players were coming to the crypto casino who hadn't been impacted by it. As a result, the price of Bitcoin began to steadily recover in 2016 and continued its upward trend as it headed into 2017. This increase in Bitcoin's price had huge ramifications for MtGox and Mark Karpelès. Article 124 of Japan's bankruptcy codes says that liabilities must be registered at current market value when bankruptcy proceedings are opened, which, for MtGox, meant that the value of the remaining bitcoins was pegged to ¥50,058.12 ($484) each. This put the total value of the company's assets (primarily the 202,185 bitcoins) at just shy of $97 million at the time the bankruptcy was filed in 2014. By June 2017, however, the value of the recovered bitcoins had rocketed to around $500 million, thanks to Bitcoin's price reaching $2,500. This meant, amazingly, that MtGox was technically no longer insolvent; the assets in its possession now exceeded the dollar amount it owed creditors. This presented Kobayashi with a conundrum: he had already promised to repay creditors in bitcoins if he could, but he had suddenly been presented with an opportunity to make creditors whole in terms of cash value, which, after all, was his job.

There was a side issue to the increasing value of the holdings, however, and one that Karpelès and the creditors were keen to avoid. If the price of Bitcoin continued to climb, fewer and fewer coins would eventually need to be sold to make creditors whole. This would leave a surplus of coins, which, by law, would go back to MtGox's parent company, Tibanne. This left creditors with the highly unpalatable prospect of Tibanne's two owners, Mark Karpelès (88%) and Jed McCaleb (12%), receiving a bumper Bitcoin payout and leaving them nursing a massive shortfall. Karpelès was vocal in his arguments against this outcome, given the negative attention and lawsuits that would inevitably follow, telling an interviewer that 'Getting one billion dollars and having 100,000 people hating me sounds like a bad deal. I'd rather not get any money.' When McCaleb was questioned on how he would spend his $75 million windfall from the MtGox bankruptcy, he tweeted that he had sold his holding for just $1 in 2014 'to some people that were trying to save mtgox from bankruptcy when it came out that Mark had lost all the btc'. The buyer, according to press reports, was none other than Brock Pierce, who told *Coindesk* in 2019 that he had picked up McCaleb's interest for one bitcoin rather than one dollar.

Karpelès explored the possibility of digging MtGox up from the grave and using it to distribute the bitcoins to the 24,750 claimants, but this idea was vetoed by the bankruptcy court. It was left to Karpelès to explain the situation as often as he could and to try to shoot down any claims that he was looking to profit from the collapse of MtGox, accusations that were causing the pendulum of sympathy to swing away from him again. The situation came to a head at a

September 2017 creditor meeting, by which time the value of Bitcoin had increased to over $4,000, getting on for ten times what MtGox creditors would be in line for. This meant that the pot was now worth $808 million, potentially giving Tibanne a $333 million payday once the bitcoins were sold. At the hearing, Kobayashi reinforced the message that those market gains belonged primarily to MtGox as a company and not its customers, who had legally signed over ownership of their coins the moment they were entrusted to the exchange. As creditors were digesting this news, Kobayashi further antagonised them by revealing that he was no closer to securing permission to refund customers in coins rather than cash anyway, something that was becoming a particularly prevalent concern. The situation was complex and unsatisfactory for everyone, but a recent unexpected twist had thrown another wrench into the already stuttering works. In July 2017, the Bitcoin blockchain was 'forked', and a new coin, Bitcoin Cash (BCH or BCC), was created. The upshot of this was that every bitcoin held in every wallet around the world had received an equal amount of BCH tokens automatically, including the wallets in which the MtGox bitcoins were being held. Suddenly, there were even more coins to deal with, with MtGox's Bitcoin Cash holdings coming in at an initial dollar value of $153.4 million at the time of its launch.

The situation boiled over at the meeting, where the news that Mark Karpelès could profit handsomely from the collapse he helped precipitate brought forth levels of abuse that surpassed anything he had yet suffered. The creditors' fury was understandable, but Karpelès decided that he had had enough; he deleted his Reddit post history, leaving just one solitary post up to explain his actions:

This last creditors meeting ended exactly as I've been warning here for some time, trying to explain how laws work in Japan and what I heard from lawyers and trustees. Yet all I get is s***, and if that was only that I could do with it. Now people are threatening me because things aren't going as they had fantasized it'd go.

Karpelès signed off by saying that he would 'not be responding to questions on reddit anymore, and not providing information I gather directly or indirectly either. Same applies for private messages, emails, twitter, etc.' While this abrupt exit generally led, predictably, to more negativity, Kim Nilsson stood up for Karpelès, saying that, whatever the Frenchman did, 'a significant amount of people will just indiscriminately throw hate his way regardless of what he does at this point'. Nilsson added that he had been on the receiving end of death threats, too, from antagonised creditors:

> *Basically I seem to "know too much" and I keep bringing up facts and pointing out also the things that clear Mark instead of just confirming certain people's conspiracy theories, so they just expand the conspiracy theory to include me, I'm "Mark's friend" or I was "probably involved with the theft" and am now involved in a cover-up. For some people that's all the justification they need to send me messages telling me how they're going to hunt me down and torture me to get the "real truth".*

Emotions were clearly running high while morale was at an all-time low, and in the weeks after the September 2017 meeting, creditors began to arrange themselves into factions, with their interests represented by different law firms. The most popular of these were Mtgox Creditors, spearheaded by then management consultant Richard Folsom and represented by law firm Nishimura & Asahi, and MtGoxLegal, which was fronted by journalist and MtGox claimant Andy Pag and was represented by MHM Japan. The purpose of these groups was to give the creditors more power when it came to the process; as a group of disparate claimants, their voices carried little weight, but as recognised groups, they could call for more transparency from the trustee and challenge decisions, although they would not carry the power of veto. Both camps sought contributions from members to cover legal bills, with MtGoxLegal achieving its target of $30,000 in less than a week, but Mtgox Creditors was the first to formally request a switch back to civil rehabilitation, which presented certain benefits to creditors over bankruptcy and would avoid the looming spectre of Karpelès and McCaleb walking off with a huge payout:

> *...there is a possibility that any residual assets that arise through the Bankruptcy Proceedings will be distributed to Karpelès and others. However, it would be extremely unfair and unjustifiable for Karpelès and others to benefit from the increase in the price of Bitcoin and to receive a distribution of a large amount of residual assets at the expense of the bankruptcy creditors.*

This was particularly apposite given that the value of the surplus on the day Mtgox Creditors filed its request was a staggering $1.6 billion, more than three times the value of the payouts creditors could expect. Switching to civil rehabilitation would mean that the creditors would get much more of a say on the denomination of their payouts instead of being bound by bankruptcy laws, which dictated a cash-only payout at the April 2014 valuation. In a note to creditors acknowledging the Mtgox Creditors filing and the appointment of an examiner to look at it, Kobayashi warned that he was legally bound to carry on regardless, which could mean liquidating the BTC and BCH held by the estate:

> *Unless the court makes a new decision...the bankruptcy proceedings will proceed as before and, as the bankruptcy trustee of MTGOX, I will continue to have the right to administer and dispose of the bankruptcy estate as before.*

While the court was considering this request, Kobayashi discreetly approached the estate's exchange partner, Kraken, to seek advice on how to sell large amounts of the coins in its possession should it need to. Kraken told Kobayashi not to sell the coins given that the civil rehabilitation order was under consideration by the court, but that if he was forced to do so, he should sell them via an auction or 'over-the-counter' (a private sale at an agreed valuation that doesn't affect the market price). The one thing Kobayashi must not do, Kraken warned, was simply dump a whole lot of coins on the open market. This would crash the price and would ensure that less dollar value per BTC and BCH would be obtained.

Four months later, at the March 2018 creditor meeting, Kobayashi surprised everyone by revealing that earlier in the year, he had sold $400 million worth of BTC (35,841) and around $48 million worth of BCH (34,008), which would secure the value of all the claims made against MtGox and would mitigate against any further drops in cryptocurrency prices. This action resulted in mixed opinions, with some understanding the sense behind the move and others angry that their coins were being sold. Kobayashi, correctly predicting the potential backlash, explained his reasoning:

> *I considered it necessary and reasonable to sell a certain amount of bitcoins and BCC at this point and secure a certain amount of money for distribution resources, and thus, I sold the amount of bitcoins and BCC above. I made efforts to sell bitcoins and BCC at as high a price as possible in light of the market price of bitcoins and BCC at the timing of sale.*

Kraken CEO Jesse Powell took to Reddit to say that he and his team had had no forewarning of the sales but explained that Kobayashi may have ignored the advice they gave him:

> *We were explicit about not dumping a large amount of coins on the market. Unfortunately, it looks like the trustee made their own decision or was taking advice from elsewhere -- maybe whatever exchange they dumped those coins on.*

Bitcoin holders outside the MtGox environment weren't happy with Kobayashi's actions either, blaming him for the sharp price drops that Bitcoin experienced during the first weeks of 2018. Some creditors demanded that Kobayashi publish a report that outlined who he consulted as to the most appropriate sale method and how he sold the coins, to which he agreed, saying that it would be produced in the days after the meeting. There was some good news to come from this March 2018 meeting, however: a Tokyo District Court examiner had reviewed the application to move to civil rehabilitation and had found no reason for it not to proceed to a full review. The first barrier had been cleared, and, at last, there was a glimmer of hope that the MtGox creditors would be getting at least some of their coins back.

Ten days after this creditor meeting, Kobayashi released his report, revealing that he sold the BTC and BCH in batches from December 2017 to February 2018 and explained how he had sold them:

> *I sold bitcoins and BCC from December 2017 to February 2018 with the cooperation of a cryptocurrency exchange in light of the market price at the time of the sale. Following consultation with cryptocurrency experts, I sold bitcoins and BCC, not by an ordinary sale through the bitcoins/BCC exchange, but in a manner that would avoid affecting the market price, while ensuring the security of the transaction to the extent possible. The method of sale of bitcoins and BCC was approved by the court as well.*

Kobayashi added that he wanted to 'refrain from explaining the details of the method of sale, otherwise the future sale of bitcoins and BCC could be hindered' and urged people to 'restrain from analysing the correlation between the sale of bitcoins and BCC by us and the market prices of bitcoins and BCC based on the assumption that the sale was made at the time the bitcoins and BCC were transferred from bitcoins/BCC addresses that I manage, as such assumption is incorrect'. Perhaps unsurprisingly, Kobayashi's entreaties were totally ignored, with a group of creditors under the collective name GoxDox publishing a report which supposedly proved that Kobayashi had done exactly what he said he hadn't done and dumped the coins on the open market, crashing the value each time he did. GoxDox identified Japanese exchange Bitpoint as the platform on which Kobayashi had sold the coins, mainly because the company deposited billions of Japanese yen into the trustee's bank account in chunks from late February to at least early June, when records ended. GoxDox compared the withdrawals with the Bitcoin price and noticed a correlation: each time the Bitcoin price dumped during early to mid-2018, a handsome withdrawal from Bitpoint to the trustee's bank account followed. This led them to surmise that either Kobayashi had ignored Kraken's advice or Bitpoint had ignored Kobayashi's request. Of course, without a trading record, there was no knowing how late these sales had been conducted, but GoxDox gave its rationale for the staggered payments:

> *It seems fair to conclude that the reason for sending frequent wires was to prevent counterparty risk. A hack at Bitpoint could expose the MtGox Estate to a loss and the trustee didn't want to get Goxxed. It follows that the trustee would have instructed Bitpoint to wire JPY (Japanese yen) over as soon as he had it. This way, MtGox Estate assets wouldn't be exposed to any hacking incident at Bitpoint.*

If it were accurate, this would prove to be a wise move: in July 2019, Bitpoint was hacked, and $32 million in various cryptocurrencies was stolen.

With the cash value of the payouts now reached, creditors were hopeful that the Tokyo Whale was done selling, but they knew that nothing was certain. All they could do was pray for a ruling from the court over the move back to civil rehabilitation, knowing that this was the only thing that could legally stop Kobayashi from further depleting their dwindling pool.

Chapter 20 – A Greek Drama

As Mark Karpelès was preparing for his second hearing at the Tokyo District Court in December 2018, almost six thousand miles away in the maximum security Korydallos Prison on the outskirts of Athens, things were happening to Alexander Vinnik. Lots of things. His arrest in Greece on a US warrant the year before had been followed by strong denials from his lawyers that he was ever an employee or executive at BTC-e, but these denials fell on deaf ears. US authorities pursued extradition, which Vinnik fought, and on 6 September 2017, in his first interview following his arrest, he explained his reasons for doing so:

> *I believe that I have not done anything illegal…I don't understand what the United States has to do with me and what right they have to judge a Russian citizen.*

There may have been another reason why Vinnik was trying to delay a flight to the US: Mother Russia was coming for him. Not wanting to be seen allowing its avowed enemy to snatch Russian nationals away at will, Moscow was preparing its own extradition request, with Russian Deputy Foreign Minister Sergei Ryabkov making the country's position very clear on 12 September:

> *We simply cannot remain indifferent to the de facto abductions of Russian citizens, to their constant ongoing arrests in third countries on American warrants.*

The following day, Vinnik was told that his fate would be decided on 29 September when the Council of Judges in Thessaloniki would rule on whether he could be extradited to the US. Nine days before this ruling, however, Russian authorities filed their extradition request, with Russian prosecutors adopting a stance of 'voluntary extradition for the administration of justice' regarding an alleged theft valued at just $11,000, which was totally unrelated to anything involving BTC-e. Unsurprisingly, Vinnik agreed to this voluntary extradition the very same day, and a week later, on 27 September, he was charged in absentia by the Ostankino Court of Moscow for the crime. This would, naturally, have led to the lightest of punishments for Vinnik compared to the fifty-five years he could get if found guilty in America.

Russia's efforts failed, however, when, on 4 October, the Council of Judges approved Vinnik's extradition to the US. Vinnik's lawyer said he would appeal to the Supreme Court of Athens and duly did, but this seemed irrelevant when, on 11 October, the Council of Judges changed its mind and agreed that Vinnik's voluntary extradition to Russia took precedence. This time, it was the US that got the Supreme Court involved, with both sides recruiting witnesses to aid their case. One of those called to give evidence on Vinnik's behalf was Sergey Mayzus, the director of Mayzus Financial Services, the very company whose MoneyPolo platform MtGox had begun using in December 2013 to ease its cash deposit and withdrawal issues. Ironically, the reason Mayzus was there to give evidence was because of his alleged longstanding connection with Vinnik and BTC-e, a connection that is worthy of a book in itself, but we will have to make do with a summary.

BTC-e began working with Mayzus Financial Services in mid-2013, using its MoneyPolo service to launder some $100 million through a network of offshore companies using dummy invoices to justify the movement of funds, some of which were almost certainly the proceeds of bitcoins stolen from MtGox and sold on BTC-e. This means that when Karpelès hired Mayzus Financial Services in late 2013, he was hiring the company that had unwittingly laundered the proceeds of bitcoins stolen from his own company and sold by a fellow Mayzus client. The irony doesn't end there, either: right at the time when MtGox was hiring Mayzus Financial Services to resolve its fiat congestion issues, BTC-e was suffering its own fiat deposit issues, for which it blamed the company that had been hired to resolve them: Mayzus Financial Services. Clearly, Karpelès wasn't one for due diligence.

Sergey Mayzus denied that he had ever met Vinnik or that he was even aware of BTC-e before Vinnik's arrest, despite BTC-e already being a client with whom he was seemingly deeply connected. Mayzus and his company had actually been caught up in Vinnik's 2016 indictment, with authorities claiming that Mayzus Financial Services actively laundered money on Vinnik's behalf, but they were dropped in the superseding indictment. Mayzus eventually sued Vinnik and sixteen associated shell companies to which he sent the money for $200 million, claiming that Mayzus Financial Services had suffered reputationally due to the now public association with Vinnik and BTC-e. In response, Vinnik's lawyer claimed that Mayzus himself owned and ran those shell companies, not Vinnik. This completed a quite incredible loop for Mayzus: one client, BTC-e, had laundered bitcoins stolen from another client, MtGox, the proceeds of which Mayzus himself had helped funnel into bank accounts belonging to BTC-e, funds that would be used to pay him off in the event that he won. Indeed, in 2019, Mayzus was awarded summary judgment against the shell companies (he had dropped the case against Vinnik) and was awarded $38 million by the Cypriot court hearing the case.

We will never know whether the judge believed Mayzus' claims to have never met Vinnik, but on 13 December 2017, he ruled that the original verdict should stand and that Vinnik should be extradited to America. Getting desperate, Russian authorities stepped things up a gear. In May 2018, Vinnik 'confessed' to stronger charges that Russian prosecutors had magicked up, constituting $12.4 million worth of computer fraud. The charges were handed to the Council of Judges, which would, again, rule on them. Also around this time, startling rumours of a failed assassination plot against Vinnik began to do the rounds. The source was Sputnik News, a Russian state-owned news agency and radio broadcast service, which claimed via a 'source' that Greek law enforcement had received intelligence of plans to assassinate Vinnik by 'some unknown person from Russia' linked to the criminal underworld. Vinnik was allegedly informed of this by the head of the prison in which he was being held and the prosecutor of the city of Thessaloniki. As a result, his security was increased; any gifts that came from outside the prison would be prohibited, and Vinnik wasn't to be allowed any food or drink not prepared inside the prison. There were immediate doubts over the accuracy of these claims, however, and the whiff of propaganda got even stronger when Vinnik's lawyer said that the assassination attempt was evidence that the criminal fraternity was trying to silence his client, who was just trying to do his bit as an honest citizen and report the crimes he had witnessed.

If Russia thought that the US was going to secede from its efforts to snatch Vinnik, a development in June 2018 made it think again. Seemingly out of nowhere, France entered the frame as a third suitor, with authorities there accusing Vinnik of defrauding French citizens through his money laundering activities and of continuing to operate BTC-e even after he was detained by Greek authorities. The US would, of course, have known that extradition orders between EU members took priority over those involving non-members and required less red tape to be finalised. As a result, Russia accused the US of leaning on France in order to do a deal that would ensure Vinnik stayed out of their grasp. The Council of Judges was brought in to decide on this newest request, and on 13 July, Vinnik was indeed told he was going to France. He appealed, with the Supreme Court once again set to be the ultimate arbiters. Before this appeal could be heard, however, the Council of Judges came to its decision regarding Russia's newer and more serious charges against Vinnik: it ruled that the charges were serious enough for Vinnik to be sent there first. The chances of this happening were increased when, on 4 September 2018, the Supreme Court threw its weight behind the Russian extradition claim. Finally, both courts were in agreement; Vinnik was off to Russia.

Or was he?

On 19 December, the Supreme Court overruled its previous decision on Vinnik's extradition to Russia when it upheld the Council of Judges' verdict in favour of Vinnik's extradition to France, with the ultimate responsibility of Vinnik's fate left to the Greek Justice Minister Stavros Kontonis. In the intervening months, Vinnik had made a desperate effort to secure extradition to Russia by vowing to go on a hunger strike until a move to his motherland was rubber-stamped. Vinnik managed eighty days without food, which led, according to Russian human rights ombudswoman Tatiana Moskalkova, to him losing 30% of his body weight. A petition from Moskalkova to Kontonis requesting Vinnik's extradition to Russia claimed that Vinnik was 'on the verge of death' as a result of his hunger strike. Moskalkova spent the bulk of 2019 appealing to numerous bodies to seek Vinnik's extradition back to Russia, with the man himself turning up to one hearing in an ambulance, such was the apparently parlous state of his health. Moskalkova's efforts included an appeal to the new Justice Minister, Konstantinos Tsiaras, who replaced Kontonis in July 2019. All her efforts fell on deaf ears, though, and Vinnik remained in prison while the legal mess was sorted out. In the meantime, the US upped the stakes by announcing a $100 million civil complaint against Vinnik and BTC-e to add to the criminal charges he already faced.

The three-way battle for Vinnik finally entered the home straight in December 2019 when Tsiaras ruled that Vinnik should be extradited first to France, then to the US and, finally, to Russia. Vinnik launched another hunger strike in protest, but this did no good, and Tsiaras' decision was upheld by the Council of State in early January 2020, marking the official end of the saga. On Thursday, 23 January 2020, Alexander Vinnik and several agents of the Direction Centrale de la Police Judiciaire boarded a French government-chartered plane and departed Thessaloniki International Airport for Paris Charles de Gaulle, where Vinnik prepared to face money laundering charges that could see him spend up to five years behind bars. Undeterred, Russian officials still felt confident they could bring him home, persisting in their claims that the US was pulling the strings behind the scenes.

Having been disappointed by the absence of any mention of their missing bitcoins during the first part of Mark Karpelès's trial, MtGox creditors had high hopes for the trial of Alexander Vinnik, given that he was known to have handled the stolen funds and might be aware of who perpetrated the crime. As was seeming to be their lot, however, they were once again let down; the French case only dealt with a $159 million ransomware fraud targeting French organisations between 2016 and 2018. MtGox was never discussed, either from a money laundering or a hacking point of view. Vinnik was tried in Paris on money laundering charges in October 2020 and was found guilty two months later. He was given the maximum sentence of five years as a result, which he appealed but lost the following year. In a sign that Russia may have had a point after all, Vinnik served just one of those five years before being released in July 2022, whereupon he was shipped back to Greece so that authorities could execute the US extradition warrant. This was done in the blink of an eye, and Vinnik was flown to the US on 5 August and transferred to California's Santa Rita prison without Russia ever getting a look in.

Mission accomplished.

Chapter 21 – Gox Rising

In April 2018, while Russia, France and the US were fighting over Alexander Vinnik, Mark Karpelès was opening up on Reddit. He had decided to do an AMA to try to offer closure for customers, a move that garnered over 1,500 questions and responses. For several hours, Karpelès fielded accusations, complaints and queries on a range of MtGox-related topics, save the ones that he couldn't discuss because they were part of various court cases. Some interesting points were thrown up during the AMA, such as when Karpelès denied that he had ever blamed the transaction malleability bug on the loss of all the bitcoins, something that was easy to disprove. Karpelès also apologised for his distance following the collapse, saying that he had 'requirements to be tweeting' but that he wasn't allowed to discuss the collapse on legal advice. He added that he was 'Sorry if it appeared as if I didn't care' and reviewed his stay in prison thus:

Poor service, bad food. Would not recommend.

Karpelès partially addressed the plentiful allegations that he knew about the parlous status of the company's finances long before they were publicly announced, responding to a claim that he either lied to Roger Ver or paid him to make the 'hostage' video by saying that at the time it 'was not obvious' that the company was broke. The questioner complained, 'You avoided answering the question, obviously you cannot incriminate yourself', and then summed up the thoughts of many:

**It wasn't obvious you had 650,000 bitcoins stolen? ** Somebody could take almost 3/4 of your money and you merely didn't notice when supplying evidence to people that you are in fact liquid? I'm not sure what kind of bookkeeping you were doing, but he claimed he saw the proof you were liquid, so either you supplied false proof, or he lied on your behalf.

Indeed, the general tone was one of frustration at Karpelès's spectacular mismanagement of MtGox, with many still amazed (or not accepting) that he didn't know what had been going on at the company, especially concerning the fact that the exchange had been broke since mid-2012. Karpelès apologised repeatedly, proclaiming a wish to go back in time and do things differently. The exercise may have been cathartic for customers, but it provided little closure.

Eight months later, on 12 December 2018, Karpelès headed back to the Tokyo District Court for the resumption of his trial for data manipulation and embezzlement, where he got a bit of a shock: prosecutors were now arguing that he 'diverted company funds to such uses as investing in a software development business for personal interest' which 'played a great role in totally destroying the confidence of Bitcoin users', crimes that, they said, warranted a ten-year prison sentence rather than the five years they had been pushing for ever since he was first indicted. This, Karpelès felt, was totally unwarranted and was an attempt to jail him for the theft of the 647,000 bitcoins without doing so in name.

If there was a star of the show during this phase of the trial, it was the MtGox dataset, which both sides used to illustrate their points: the prosecution used trading data from Willy and Markus to illustrate that it could only have been Karpelès who controlled the accounts which used them, while Karpelès's team used the same data to try and prove that there had been no embezzlement of company funds. Ogata and his team augmented this data with the McCaleb email and other evidence to back up Karpelès's claim that he used the trading bots as the 'obligation exchange' to try and make the company solvent rather than abuse his customers for profit. These arguments were reiterated during Karpelès's closing arguments [translated]:

> *The remittance act accused of embezzlement was carried out as part of the company's business. The company went bankrupt. We have never been unable to respond to customer requests for refunds due to the loss of bitcoins due to hacking, and we have not caused any damage to customers or the company.*

When Karpelès addressed the court on 27 December, he once again reinforced his not-guilty plea, saying, 'I'm sorry I couldn't prevent hacking', but denied that he did anything malicious to hurt customers. With that, the court broke up, and the judges retired to consider their verdict, which was due in just over six weeks.

Karpelès may have hoped for a quiet time while he waited for the verdict, but he had no such luck. Right when he was telling the court and the world that he was innocent of all charges for the second time, Brock Pierce was preparing a media blitz over Gox Rising, the exchange that he wanted to build out of the ashes of MtGox, the ashes that he still maintained were his due to the Letter of Intent signed by Karpelès in March 2014 and his buyout of Jed McCaleb's Tibanne shares. Having been patient throughout the creditor process, Pierce was now pushing firmly ahead with his plans, which included:

- Valuing all claims at 100% of their contemporaneous worth
- Exploring avenues to recover more of the missing bitcoins
- Fighting the Coinlab lawsuit
- Distributing any existing funds to creditors
- Relaunching the exchange, with creditors receiving a 16.5% equity stake for free, enabling additional recovery via profits
- Having the entire thing settled within a year

Pierce was planning to file a competing civil rehabilitation plan, which was something anyone could do and which presented a very real problem: Japanese law dictated that for a civil rehabilitation plan to pass, it needed to be accepted by votes which represented over 50% of all determined claim value. In the MtGox case, this claim value was not in dollars or yen but was instead in what Kim Nilsson called 'goxyen', an 'arbitrary unit of measurement of the relative sizes of claims'. If multiple plans were submitted to the court, then there was more chance of the votes being diluted, potentially resulting in there being no clear winner. If this were the case, MtGox would fall back into the bankruptcy that creditors were fighting so hard to exit, which would leave everybody financially worse off. Pierce's advisors sought out the counsel of Mt.Gox Legal's Andy Pag, where they informed him, out of the blue, that they wanted to conduct an Initial Coin Offering (ICO) with MtGox, which would tokenise the claims. Pag was stunned and pointed out the manifold legal issues connected to such a plan, a plan that suggested that Pierce and his team either had no idea what they were doing or had intentions that didn't align with those of the creditors.

Pierce went on a PR binge, including conducting an interview in mid-February 2019 with Bitcoin podcaster Peter McCormack, where he was combative and evasive in the face of questions about what Gox Rising hoped to achieve. He also denied that his advisors had put plans for an ICO to Andy Pag, saying that 'there's probably a 0% chance that I would ever run an ICO'. McCormack would later say that he found it 'really hard to get to what [Pierce's] incentives are' regarding MtGox and that he found the Minneapolitan 'patronising'. Pierce's mood might be explained by the fact that at the time of the interview, he was involved in a Twitter spat with Mark Karpelès over Gox Rising and the 2014 Letter of Intent. When Pierce posted his MtGox plan on Twitter along with the headline 'Brock Pierce to revive Mt. Gox', Karpelès refuted the suggestion that he had sold MtGox to Pierce:

> *No. No purchase agreement was ever even drafted, and the court didn't approve the LOI. I didn't hear of the price until recently either, and Tibanne has no record of any payment for the shares. MtGox official shareholders list doesn't list Brock Pierce anywhere.*

Karpelès poured more cold water on Pierce's plans by saying that they were overly complex and would likely just create more division, while Daniel Kelman dismissed the legitimacy of the Letter of Intent, arguing that any documents Pierce said he possessed had not been ratified by the trustee. Pierce's response was to claim that Kelman was Karpelès' 'partner who has secretly been representing his interests the last five years', a claim that Kelman called '100% libel'.

There were further dissenting voices, too; Kim Nilsson posted on his personal blog that 'Despite its laudable promises, there are plenty of reasons to fundamentally distrust the underlying motivations and actions of the people involved [in Gox Rising].' With the kind of examination that MtGox creditors already had reason to be thankful for, Nilsson pulled apart the motivations that McCormack had found so hard to discern, claiming that Pierce's promise that of the stolen 647,000 bitcoins 'some of it can be found, a lot can be recovered' was bluster with no basis in reality; that the Coinlab lawsuit was already being fought; that the claims were already at 100%; that the repayment plan to creditors was directly comparable to that offered as part of the civil rehabilitation process; and there was no evidence that Pierce could do things any quicker than the Tokyo District Court, especially given that the trustee and the court would have to go through the proposal first. Nine days after interviewing Pierce, McCormack sat down with Pag, who revealed details of the strange conversations he'd had with Pierce and his team and suggested what might happen next:

> *I just can't make sense of what he is suggesting. But ultimately, I think he's been kind of narrowed down and corralled to the point where he's not really suggesting or proposing anything. I wouldn't be surprised if, in the next two or three weeks, we just quietly didn't hear any more about him.*

Pag was to be proved right, for a while at least. With Nobuaki Kobayashi seemingly giving no further consideration to Pierce's Gox Rising plans and Karpelès not playing ball, Pierce and Gox Rising slipped off the radar. This wasn't to last, however. In July 2019, New York-based private equity firm Fortress Investment Group offered to buy MtGox customers' claims for $900 per bitcoin. This was almost double the dollar value of the initial claims, which would have made it a tempting offer once upon a time, but with bitcoin payouts potentially on the table following the civil rehabilitation filing, this seemed like a mistimed offer. Clearly, Fortress was preying on fears that the civil rehabilitation might not be approved and MtGox might continue into bankruptcy. Fortress's approach, speculative though it was, gave Pierce an idea, and in May 2020, he tried the same thing, although he offered just $800 per bitcoin, $100 less than Fortress had offered ten months previously. The press release that accompanied this offer made no mention of a new MtGox exchange, stating only that Gox Rising was 'investigating potential avenues for bringing better liquidity options to claim holders'. Indeed, rather than being a legitimate offer, the communication appeared to be the limp, desperate quack of a dying duck rather than a mighty one. BitOcean Japan, which had been in the early running to take over MtGox, also failed in its bid to buy the company, although it did obtain approval to open a crypto exchange in December 2017, which it launched the following year under its own name.

Goxrising.com is still online today and is still promising to 'help drive the ongoing Mt. Gox civil rehabilitation process to a positive conclusion', but the fact that the project's Twitter account hasn't been active since October 2019 suggests that this chapter of the MtGox story is, perhaps thankfully, closed for good.

Chapter 22 – Coinlab

By mid-June 2018, creditors' nerves were jangling. It had been nearly four months since the request to move to civil rehabilitation had been handed to a bankruptcy judge, and still, there was no news. Having had the door of bitcoin payouts opened up, they couldn't bear the thought of it being slammed shut again. On 22 June, an announcement was posted to the MtGox procedure website by Nobuaki Kobayashi regarding the application, and it was good news:

> *The petition was heard, and at 5:00 p.m. on June 22, 2018, the Tokyo District Court issued an order of the commencement of civil rehabilitation proceedings for MTGOX. As a result, the previously ongoing bankruptcy proceedings were stayed. In addition, simultaneously with the order of the commencement of civil rehabilitation proceedings, an administration order was issued by the Tokyo District Court, and I have been appointed civil rehabilitation Trustee.*

Claimants were understandably over the moon that bitcoin payouts were finally back on the menu, with many expressing joy at the fact that Kobayashi could now stop selling creditors' coins:

> *Great news for the crypto market. The Tokyo whale is gone! Sorry this news made me very happy in this sea of blood so wanted to share. It gives me hope for the future of crypto because no more whale dumps.*

Despite all the positivity over the potential of getting payouts in bitcoins rather than cash, MtGox claimants knew that, while this marked the end of one battle, it was simply the beginning of another, and the end-of-level boss would still be the same: Coinlab. Back in May 2017, four months after Peter Vessenes had warned MtGox customers not to expect payouts that year, Mark Karpelès had published a now-deleted open letter to the Coinlab founder on Reddit.

Karpelès's aim was to convince Vessenes to 'settle this lawsuit for the five million USD which you owe to MtGox since four years ago', with Karpelès laying out his terms:

> *What I am hoping for today is to see both sides stop hostilities and accept the situation. Your $75 million USD against MtGox and Tibanne is clearly without merit, Coinlab never suffered any losses and never even started providing the expected service, and MtGox will never see the $5 million USD Coinlab kept.*

Karpelès signed off by saying, 'At this point, going further would only increase costs without any relief in sight, instead delaying further something that shouldn't take that long.' Other Redditors chimed in, agreeing with Karpelès and beseeching Vessenes to settle and remove the roadblock that was holding up the rehabilitation process. Vessenes, however, failed to publicly acknowledge the letter, having been advised to keep quiet by his legal counsel, given that it was the subject of an active court case. The battle, it seemed, would go on.

One downside to the move to civil rehabilitation was that the claims process had to be restarted, although the claims validations themselves would not need to be recalculated, with creditors able to simply reuse their existing claim value if they wished or have it reassessed if they preferred. The result promised to be better for everyone, especially because the exchange's Bitcoin holdings were revalued at their current rate of exchange: a much healthier ¥749,318 ($6,833) per bitcoin compared to the original valuation of $484. As with everything regarding MtGox, though, it wasn't to be that simple. As the civil rehabilitation process got underway, Kobayashi revealed that alongside verified claims, he would also be recognising certain unclaimed 'zombie' accounts (customers who hadn't made a claim), ringfencing funds in the event that these customers did so in later years. This amounted to a staggering 89,200 claimants on top of the 24,750 already verified, further diluting the amount of BTC and BCH that everyone would get.

As the civil rehabilitation claims flooded in, a keen eye was kept on what Coinlab would do. Its initial claim during the bankruptcy process had been $75 million, the amount it said MtGox owed it for breach of contract, and there was no reason to think it would alter this valuation. However, when Coinlab's civil rehabilitation claim was revealed on 1 February 2019, the MtGox community, indeed the entire Bitcoin community, was floored; Coinlab was demanding $16 *billion* from MtGox. This astounding figure, the company said, was due to losses from Karpelès reneging on the contract to give Coinlab the US business back in 2013. As a result, Coinlab said, it had lost out on significant income given the boom in the crypto sector in the years since, handing the advantage to outfits like Coinbase, which it valued at $16 billion and which it, therefore, claimed it could have been worth. Regardless of its amount, Kobayashi was legally bound to take the Coinlab claim seriously and assess its merits.

The response from the MtGox community was, naturally, one of disbelief and anger. Vessenes was accused of perpetrating an 'abuse of law', while another creditor questioned whether it was possible to counter-sue the Illinoisan for the losses incurred by the 'baseless lawsuit'. Given that the trustee couldn't exactly put $16 billion aside and pay out creditors with the remainder, the Coinlab claim took priority, potentially adding years to the repayment schedule. Andy Pag took to Twitter to try and get answers from Vessenes, suggesting that the move was 'done purposefully just to block any creditor pay outs', but he was met with silence.

Not long after this filing, Edgar Sargent, a US-based attorney representing Coinlab, published a lengthy post on Reddit in which he argued that 'Coinlab did not come to the MtGox bankruptcy seeking to 'hold up' the estate with ginned up claims' and nor was it 'using its claims to try and prevent distribution to depositors or other creditors'. He added that if the case were indeed frivolous, as many were claiming, then MtGox would have sought to get it dismissed, but instead, it had pressed ahead with defending itself, meaning the claims must have some merit. If Sargent had hoped to sway opinions, he was badly mistaken; he was asked to 'crawl back under your rock' and was told that his arguments were nothing but 'hot air being blown out your rear-end'. In an April 2019 blog post, Kim Nilsson went into great detail about the 'joke of a "calculation method"' Coinlab had used to come up with its figure, which was based on the assumption that, had MtGox not collapsed, it would have retained a 25% market share over the fifteen-year length of the contract. Whatever the reason for the lawsuit, vexatious or legitimate, it led to Kobayashi announcing a six-month delay in rehabilitation proceedings to deal with the disputed claim. This led Karpelès to call Coinlab a 'big stopping block to moving forward' in an interview with *Cointelegraph*.

While this battle was raging, a solution for retrieving up to 200,000 of the stolen bitcoins had arrived from a very unexpected source. In August 2019, Andy Pag posted a document to the Mt.Gox Legal forum entitled 'MtGox Russian Recoveries Proposal' in which he said that Russian law firm Zheleznikov and Partners (ZP Legal) was proposing 'pioneering legal action' to recover the sum by launching criminal action against individuals the law firm said it knew to have been in receipt of the MtGox bitcoins:

> *Our plan is to represent the Mt.Gox creditors and help them report to Russian law enforcement so that the investigators could establish the connection between the stolen funds from MtGox, the operations of BTC-e and WEX, using [Alexander] Vinnik's case.*

WEX (World Exchange Services) was the successor to BTC-e, launched by its co-founder Aleksey Bilyuchenko and a Belarusian associate, Dmitry Vasiliev, using an existing BTC-e database. ZP Legal went on to say that it would work on a no-win-no-fee basis, with its fee, were it successful, being between 50% and 75% of all monies recovered (all bitcoins would be converted to cash), as well as an hourly rate of $320. Managing partner Alexander Zheleznikov claimed to *Coindesk* that creditors holding claims for a combined 15,000 bitcoins had already signed up for the action, representing less than 8% of the bitcoins he claimed to be able to recover. Zheleznikov imposed a 22 September 2019 deadline, giving interested parties a month to hand over their claims. The proposal was, unsurprisingly, met with huge suspicion by creditors. Kim Nilsson stated that the fee was 'unconscionably high given that these are people's lost savings we're talking about', while Daniel Kelman was also doubtful, questioning the fee structure and the potential for it to 'spawn additional litigation for the MtGox estate' if it went wrong, among other complaints. He summarised:

> *These lawyers have treated their engagement like it's a mystery box, asking us to first gamble with a majority of our right to recovery before we can take their legal strategy out of its package.*

The legitimacy of this offer was thrown further into doubt, given the situation surrounding Alexander Vinnik at the time. Vinnik was, of course, in the middle of his extradition battle at this point, and some creditors surmised that the Russian government was using ZP Legal to try to increase the number of Russian victims of Vinnik's crimes, thus increasing the pull towards Russian extradition. Zheleznikov told *Coindesk* that, were it to aid in Vinnik's extradition to Russia, this would simply be a happy accident:

> *If Vinnik's extradition helps the case, we're glad to see any legal event helping our plans, but the extradition itself is not our goal and we don't represent Vinnik's interests.*

When it comes to Russian criminal affairs, of course, there are rarely such things as coincidences.

The ZP Legal proposal was the last straw for many as far as Andy Pag's involvement in MtGox went. Pag had already announced his intention to sell his claim and stand down as leader of Mt.Gox Legal in an interview with *Coindesk* (a claim he later denied) four months before publicising the Russian offer, which he said had first come his way that February. Pag blamed the incessant delays caused by the Coinlab lawsuit as the reason for his exit from the MtGox arena, but this hid the truth that he was simply no longer wanted. In late February 2019, a website called 'Mtgoxtransparency' was set up, which claimed that the MtGox civil rehabilitation process was being 'abused and tampered with in a way which serves individual interests' over those of creditors. These concerns, it continued, were 'known within mtgoxlegal', but it was its creators' aim to make these accusations, and the evidence behind them, more widespread. The site's author accused Pag of performing a '180-degree flip' in his opinion of Brock Pierce and his Gox Rising plans, claiming that Pag pushed acceptance of Pierce's plans to Mt.Gox Legal in return for a financial windfall, some of which it claimed Pag was set to pocket for services rendered. The author made it clear that siding with Gox Rising presented little to no upside to them in the short or long term but plenty for Pag and Pierce, and signed off its opening claims unequivocally:

> *While we greatly appreciate [Pag's] efforts up until this point, there is really no innocent way to look at this whole situation. It stinks from all angles.*

Pag responded on Reddit, saying that the criticisms were 'a little unfair' and claimed that some critics were 'too angry to read critically what's infront of you'. Pag accused those criticising his support of Gox Rising as having ignored his latest claims that Pierce and co. hadn't backed up their side of the deal, leading to him walking away from it, and denied that financial inducements had been offered either way. He also defended the fact that he was being paid by Mt.Gox Legal, saying that he had given up other jobs to front it, and so he deserved to be fairly remunerated. The following day, Pag recorded his interview with Peter McCormack in which he repeated these defences and explained the level of trust that was still being placed in him:

> *I think the best part of $300,000 over the last eighteen months has gone through that account. If I wanted to grab all that money and disappear off to Mexico...I think it'd be pretty hard for anyone to do anything about it.*

Pag added that he had no intention of doing this, but that it showed how the trust-based system had 'worked very well so far'. Regardless, the die was cast, leading to Pag supposedly selling up and shipping out that April, much to the relief of many. His return in August to promote the ZP Legal offer was the worst idea at the worst time, with the responses to his Reddit post announcing the offer summing up the lingering resentment towards him:

> *'Andy, I think I speak for all of us when I say please stop shilling your scammy products here. Youre no longer welcome at mtgoxlegal so now youre hoping to bag a few unsuspecting people on Reddit who don't know how much this has been discredited?'*
>
> ------
>
> *That guy spent years in convincing everyone to pay him to join his legal action group then just before CR [civil rehabilitation] he sold his claim and started promoting that other scammer and alleged pedo – Brock Pierce...So now Andy is promoting some Russian scammers. Awesome, way to go Andy.*

ZP Legal took the 15,000 bitcoins sent to it by desperate creditors, and potentially more, and has never publicly reported back on its progress. Meanwhile, those who didn't want to hand their claims over to dodgy Russian lawyers simply hunkered down and waited for Coinlab to see sense, something that didn't look like it was going to happen anytime soon.

Chapter 23 – Verdict

Mark Karpelès awoke on 15 March 2019, knowing that he was going to end the day either a free man or a convicted criminal. According to *Fortune*, his hopes were not high:

> ...despite what he feels is a weak case against him, he thinks the odds are he'll be found guilty, at least during this first trial; Japan, which has a more than 99% conviction rate, is also one of a few countries that allows prosecutors to appeal an acquittal twice. In a year or two, he could be sent back behind bars.

Karpelès headed to the Tokyo District Court, entering the courtroom with his legal team and sitting nervously down, fully expecting a guilty verdict and yet more legal battles ahead to clear his name. The three-judge panel entered, the formalities were observed, and the verdict was read. To his unutterable relief, the court had found that Mark Karpelès hadn't used company money illegally and also ruled that his use of Willy and Markus had indeed been conducted 'to hide the fact [MtGox] was missing a lot of bitcoin' and not for 'personal gain' or any 'ill intent'. The judgment summarised [translated]:

> We find the charge of electronic record tampering to be true and that it deserves punishment, but there's no criminal evidence re embezzlement (dominant or reserve type) or violations of company laws, resulting in a not guilty ruling.

Despite this acquittal, Karpelès was firmly admonished by the court, which blamed him for causing 'massive harm to the trust' of his customers and saying, 'There is no excuse for the defendant, who is an engineer with expert knowledge, to abuse his status and authority to perform clever criminal acts.' Karpelès was given a sentence of two years and six months for the record tampering, which would be suspended for four years. To all intents and purposes, he was a free man, the one in a thousand who managed to beat the Japanese justice system.

Karpelès left the courtroom stunned at the verdict, knowing full well that while he had gotten himself into this mess in the first place, the uniqueness of the case had worked massively to his advantage. Had MtGox been a traditional financial institution, then the prosecution would have been able to put a far stronger case together, but their lack of understanding of the Bitcoin blockchain hampered their efforts and led them to put square pegs in round holes. In fact, as *The Wall Street Journal* reported, the Karpelès case had been a public embarrassment for Japanese state prosecutors, with the outlet noting that the court 'effectively rebuke[d] prosecutors for going too far'. One of the judges on the panel even mentioned Alexander Vinnik's name during the verdict hearing, a pointed reference that would have made the state's team shift even more uncomfortably in their seats. The Japanese press attributed far fewer column inches to the verdict than they had with Karpelès's arrest; the story was buried, along with the reputations of more than one public prosecutor.

The reaction from many in the Bitcoin space over Karpelès's exoneration was a mixture of frustration and surprise, with many amazed that the Frenchman had overcome Japan's 99.9% conviction rate. A BitcoinTalk thread about the news was filled with negative comments about the light sentence, which is perhaps unsurprising given that many of its users were MtGox victims:

> *This is what I have expected they found him guilty but he will not spend even an f.....g second in prison!!! This is the justice we have today. I am really mad because I have lost a lot of BTC by Mr.Gox and was sure that Karpeles would have the pleasure to bend down for soap for several years in the prison shower surrounded by horny fellow convicts.*
>
> ------
>
> *It's pretty interesting to be rich and powerful. If you steal a couple of fruits you will go to jail and he stole a lot more than that...Of course it is a really light sentence, really really light one.*
>
> ------

I see that everybody agree that this sentence is just a joke. Literally, I know a case where a guy was sentenced two years of prison for stealing bread from the bakery. How does this apply to the judgment of Karpeles?

What these respondents, and many like them, didn't seem to factor in was the fact that Karpelès wasn't on trial for the theft of the bitcoins, presumably because, as one respondent did point out, 'no solid evidence of his direct involvement in a hack was found'. Nevertheless, it is understandable why they felt that justice hadn't been done, even if Karpelès's crime was incompetence and covering up the truth rather than the criminal activity some were still accusing him of.

Despite his victory, Karpelès knew that he wasn't out of the woods yet; prosecutors were allowed two appeals, constituting two more chances to put him before potentially stricter judges. The state deliberated for two weeks before stating that they would not appeal the decision, perhaps fearing the backlash of a further defeat. After almost four years, it was over. Karpelès may have secured a highly improbable victory, but he wasn't satisfied with one element of the verdict: the data manipulation. Desirous of clearing his name, he appealed himself, with his defence team arguing that prosecutors didn't understand how cryptocurrency exchanges worked and painting him as the victim of an ill-informed witch-hunt. This appeal was rejected in June 2020, however, with Karpelès calling the ruling 'unfortunate' before adding that he was 'reviewing its contents alongside my lawyers', with an appeal to the Supreme Court a possible next step. However, after consideration, he decided not to follow through, perhaps realising the core battle had already been won.

With the criminal trial over, Karpelès could have been forgiven for thinking that he could start to put MtGox behind him and forge a new life for himself. However, rather than being over, the truth was that his legal battles were just beginning, with two class action lawsuits to fight, either of which could financially cripple him. The first, filed by Gregory Greene in February 2014, was supposed to have been settled as part of Brock Pierce's Sunlot deal, but the collapse of Pierce's plans had brought it back to the table. It had since been bogged down by one of the defendants, Mizuho Bank, filing to have the case dismissed on jurisdictional grounds and Greene's inability to actually serve Karpelès with papers. This wasn't achieved until May 2017 when Judge Gary Feinerman ruled that Karpelès could be served via email, which he duly was. By this point, three other individuals had added their names as class action leaders: Joseph Lack, Gregory Pearce and Anthony Motto. The claims of Lack and Pearce were dismissed in December 2017 because they weren't Illinois residents where the case had been filed, while Motto dropped his claim in August 2018 after Judge Feinerman voiced doubts that Motto's funds had been trapped on MtGox at all. This left Greene to fight on by himself.

Karpelès filed a motion to dismiss the case in late August 2018, stating that the Illinois court had no jurisdiction over him given that MtGox had been located in Japan. However, as Karpelès probably knew all too well from his experience with Coinlab, the simple act of serving a customer in a US state legally makes you liable to its laws, and so it proved; in July 2019, four months after receiving his not-guilty verdict, Karpelès was told that the Illinois court *did* have jurisdiction over him and the case would advance. Mizuho was luckier: being a Japanese bank, it was found to have no presence in Illinois, and all charges against it were struck off.

While this lawsuit was playing out, another had been started. The suit, filed with the Ontario Superior Court of Justice in March 2014 by class representatives David Joyce, Sancho McCann, Alexandre Pippin and Paul Collin, had sought to represent all Canadian MtGox users. It named Karpelès, MtGox, Mizuho and Jed McCaleb as defendants and was seeking damages of CAD$500 million ($465 million). This was the second case that should have been settled as part of the Sunlot deal, but in June 2016, it was settled in a different way: a message on the website of the prosecuting law firm, Carney Lawyers PC, informed claimants that, 'On June 17, 2016, this action will be dismissed on consent of all parties' with no explanation forthcoming.

One down, one to go.

Or not.

Frustrated at being booted from the Illinois class action, Gregory Pearce filed again, this time from his home state of Pennsylvania, in January 2018, just days after his expulsion from the Illinois case. Again, Karpelès and Mizuho were the targets of his ire, and again, both claimed a lack of jurisdiction. This brought an identical result: the claim against Mizuho was dismissed due to lack of jurisdiction, but the claim against Karpelès was allowed to continue. The Japanese bank, which by now must have been ruing the day it ever agreed to let MtGox open an account, was finally free of its customer from Hell.

Karpelès was deposed at the US Embassy in Tokyo on 11 November 2019 as part of the Greene case, where he disputed the claims made by Greene and gave evidence of his innocence. As part of their evidence-gathering process, Greene's team had requested copies of various documents from Karpelès's Japanese trial to back up their claims of conversion and negligence. However, Karpelès had argued that he was unable to produce the documents for fear of criminal liability in Japan. In a stroke of luck for Karpelès, the Japanese prosecutor sided with him and prevented them from being released, leaving Karpelès an open goal; he demanded that the conversion and negligence charges be dropped due to lack of evidence, which they duly were. On the back of this, Karpelès filed for summary judgment in the entire case, but this was denied in 2020.

Karpelès adopted a different tactic in the Gregory Pearce case in Pennsylvania, shifting the blame for the failure of the platform onto Mizuho and Alexander Vinnik, despite (or perhaps because) both entities were completely divorced from any possible action in the case. Karpelès argued that while there was no evidence he had stolen any bitcoins from the exchange, there *was* evidence to suggest that Vinnik had a strong part to play in the hacks and that the trial couldn't possibly continue without the Russian present to be questioned. He also argued that he, Karpelès, shouldn't bear responsibility for Mizuho's cash withdrawal delays from mid-2013 onwards, saying it was the bank's systems and processes that caused the delays. Using this reasoning, Karpelès filed a motion to dismiss the case on 9 August 2019, and seven weeks later, on 26 September, Pearce dropped his case.

Back in Illinois, Karpelès's legal team had been busy filing oppositions to various elements of Greene's class action case, including Greene's own witness testimony. By June 2021, Judge Feinerman felt he had enough information to rule and did so, stating that the 30,000 cases which made up the class action were, in fact, not identical, based on each user's individual actions on MtGox and their understanding of what their protections were. These disparities, he said, meant that mini-trials would have to be held for each individual case, something that was clearly impossible, and so he struck out Greene's class action. He did, however, give Greene leave to appeal or file a personal case against Karpelès, but Greene chose neither, and on 17 January 2022, the last legal action against Mark Karpelès was closed for good nearly eight years after the first one had been filed. The former MtGox CEO had fought a criminal case in a country with a 99.9%

conviction rate and three lawsuits totalling billions of dollars in potential damages and had won them all. His defence cost him the small fortune he had amassed during his time as MtGox CEO, but most importantly, he had his freedom, which, as he knew from personal experience, was worth all the money in the world.

Chapter 24 – Identified

As Alexander Vinnik began his lengthy trudge through the American justice system, he may have thought that Russia was about to forsake him, but he was wrong. Frederic Belot, a member of the French legal team that had unsuccessfully defended Vinnik at the Paris trial, urged Russian Foreign Minister Sergei Lavrov to include Vinnik in a potential prisoner swap that was in the works between Moscow and Washington. This news presented very real concerns for MtGox creditors: if Vinnik was allowed to return to Russia, he would never be tried in the US and would never have to reveal anything about the MtGox hackers. In a letter to Lavrov proposing Vinnik's candidacy, Belot alleged that Vinnik had suffered stress brought on by his solitary confinement in France and, as a result, psychiatrists believed he had 'a partial loss of memory'. His memory seemed good enough for him to be confident that he had nothing to do with BTC-e or the laundering of any funds from it, however.

The prisoner swap went ahead without Vinnik, with US basketball player Brittney Griner and Russian national Viktor Bout both being repatriated on 8 December 2022. Vinnik's legal team tried the same tack when they attempted to make him part of a prisoner exchange with former Marine Paul Whelan, who had been arrested on espionage charges in 2018, and again in May 2023 following the arrest of *The Wall Street Journal* reporter Evan Gershkovich that March. These efforts, too, failed, perhaps suggesting that Vinnik had slipped down Russia's priority list.

On 23 November 2022, 10,000 bitcoins that had lain dormant in a BTC-e wallet since 2015 were moved to cryptocurrency exchanges and personal wallets, among which was a selection of the holdings taken from MtGox, representing the first time any MtGox proceeds had moved in almost nine years. The personal wallets couldn't be identified, but Chainalysis was able to reveal that the recipient exchanges were those that 'service Russia and other Eastern European countries'. This clearly strengthened the Russian link to the hack, and in 2023, this connection was solidified.

In the seven years since the US task force had started investigating the hack on MtGox, there had been no public hints that they were close to identifying those actually responsible for the act. Everything to date had been focused on the laundering of the funds, with the closest links to the hack itself coming through the suspicion that Alexander Vinnik may have been, but probably wasn't, the person who compromised the exchange. There had most certainly been no hint whatsoever that on 30 December 2019, charges against two suspects had been sealed following a New York grand jury. This revelation was made public on 9 June 2023 when the Department of Justice unsealed the charges, three and a half years after the grand jury verdict; one of the accused was twenty-nine-year-old Aleksandr Verner, who was said to have been part of the gang that infiltrated MtGox and then helped launder the proceeds, while the other was none other than Vinnik's former partner in crime, Alexey Bilyuchenko, whose escape from Crete in 2017 in the wake of Vinnik's arrest was looking even more timely. The news that the task force had been sitting on the names of two of the hackers for so long stunned those familiar with the case, although the nationalities didn't: both were Russians.

The charges, split between two US district courts, were worth waiting for despite the mammoth delay. The Southern District of New York indictment didn't beat about the bush when it came to summarising the pair's activities:

> *In or about September 2011, Aleksandr Verner and Alexey Bilyuchenko, the defendants, and their co-conspirators...gained and caused others to gain unauthorized access to the Mt. Gox server in Japan, which contained, among other things, the Mt. Gox customer and transaction database and the private keys for Mt. Gox's Bitcoin wallets.*

The Department of Justice also alleged that BTC-e's launch date, occurring between two hacks on MtGox and less than a month before the hot wallet was so spectacularly compromised, was not a coincidence, arguing that Vinnik and Bilyuchenko had launched BTC-e with the express purpose of laundering the MtGox proceeds through it. No light was shed on the 77,500-bitcoin hack or the 1Feex hack, with the charges relating solely to the crippling two-and-a-half-year theft that had started on 11 September 2011.

The Department of Justice also laid out the pattern used to launder the funds once they had been obtained, referencing a series of financial transactions 'designed to conceal and disguise the location, source, and ownership of the proceeds obtained from the Mt. Gox Hack'. The first cache of stolen coins, taken between September 2011 and July 2012, was laundered through BTC-e and Tradehill, with the proceeds then sent to bank accounts owned by the series of shell companies related to Canton Business Corporation, the shell companies that Sergey Mayzus had successfully sued in 2017. However, the indictment revealed a rather more leftfield way in which the gang laundered the rest of the funds. Around April 2012, they entered into an advertising contract with an unnamed New York-based Bitcoin broker, which supposedly allowed the broker to advertise on BTC-e's site and pay BTC-e for the privilege. However, investigators found no such adverts on BTC-e for this or any other broker, but what they did find was evidence of the owner of the brokerage being pushed to send $6.6 million to BTC-e's shell companies. This was done through the unnamed Bitcoin exchange the broker used, with the volume of the wire transfers earning them 'credit', which the gang used to launder 300,000 of the stolen bitcoins, once again sending the funds out to Canton and its shell companies through Mayzus Financial Services.

Having given MtGox a month to replenish its bitcoin wallets, the gang then embarked on the hack that would end up killing the exchange, once again using the combination of BTC-e and bitcoin-accepting US companies to launder the funds. A DHS report unsealed in the same week as the indictments revealed that $2.5 million had been sent to Canton-connected bank accounts in Latvia between April and November 2013, with two firms in particular identified as helping in the laundering of the funds through more fake internet advertising deals: Charlie Shrem's Bitinstant and Memorydealers, a computer hardware refurbishing operation run by none other than Roger Ver. This merely layered more irony on the MtGox story, with the two men who tried to help Mark Karpelès keep MtGox alive inadvertently helping to kill it by laundering some of the funds stolen from it. It wasn't clear whether the DHS was accusing the two companies of knowingly being part of the money laundering process, but both accepted bitcoin payments, and Shrem had been arrested in January 2014 for failing to report suspicious banking activity to US authorities, operating an unlicensed money-transmitting business and helping launder bitcoins for a Silk

Road seller. It isn't a stretch, then, to imagine that Shrem also laundered the MtGox hackers' bitcoins, and Bitinstant may even have been the entity referred to as the New York-based Bitcoin Broker.

While Aleksandr Verner was an unknown quantity with no public links to any hacking gangs, having been earlier identified by Andrey Zakharov as connected with a Canton shell company, Aleksey Bilyuchenko was the exact opposite. Kim Nilsson, for one, was not in the least surprised to see Bilyuchenko indicted, telling me that people had 'kept privately pointing me to Bilyuchenko for years, but there wasn't really anything I could pursue there'. Bilyuchenko had hardly kept a low profile since the collapse of BTC-e, becoming embroiled in a legal battle in Kazakhstan over the fate of WEX. WEX had started life well in 2017, thanks in the main to Bilyuchenko being able to build the site from a backup of BTC-e's database he had retained, but the crypto market crash of 2018 saw usage and profits plummet. In the summer of 2018, WEX customers experienced a fate to which many MtGox customers could relate: they began to notice withdrawal problems, leading to the exchange being taken offline six months later, with the $450 million worth of cryptocurrencies on its books vanishing without a trace.

Bilyuchenko was naturally suspected, but when customers in Russia and Kazakhstan began to file police reports, suspicion fell instead on the man that Bilyuchenko had put in the hot seat: CEO Dmitry Vasiliev. When Bilyuchenko was summoned to testify as part of the investigation into Vasiliev, he told an incredible story: in a trap set up by one of his financial backers, Konstantin Malofeyev, Russian security service operatives had coerced Bilyuchenko into handing over all the WEX holdings in April 2018 on grounds of national security. Only afterwards did Bilyuchenko apparently find out that they were imposters hired by Malofeyev.

Bilyuchenko was not arrested, with the authorities instead zeroing in on Vasiliev, who was apprehended in Italy in July 2019 on the basis of an Interpol Red Notice, served by Kazakh authorities. However, Vasiliev was released after a month due to procedural errors and returned home to St. Petersburg. He remained on the radar of Kazakh authorities and was arrested by Polish police in August 2021 on the still-active Red Notice. Kazakhstan tried again to extradite Vasiliev, but this doesn't seem to have been successful, as, nine months later, he pitched up at Zagreb Airport, Croatia, trying to enter the country. Once more,

Kazakhstan tried to grab him (the fruits of its efforts are unknown), but the entire venture was rendered moot when, in October 2024, the Kazakh case against Vasiliev was dropped due to lack of evidence. Vasiliev didn't have long to thank his lucky stars, however; just weeks later, he was picked up by Polish police again, this time on a U.S. arrest warrant as part of the money laundering case involving WEX. Vasiliev was extradited to the U.S. in June 2025, where he faces charges of fraud and money laundering.

By early 2022, Russian authorities had seemingly twigged that something about Bilyuchenko's story didn't add up, and he was arrested in March at a private airfield in Moscow on charges of misappropriating the WEX funds. Arresting officers discovered 190 million Russian roubles ($1.7 million) in cash in two suitcases in his possession while officers searching residences belonging to Bilyuchenko and his accomplices seized another 50 million roubles ($425,000), $1 million and €70,000 in cash as well as computer equipment, hardware crypto wallets, luxury goods and documents. As a result of four years' worth of cat and mouse, Bilyuchenko, who in the years since his association with WEX had changed his name to Alexey Ivanov, was, at the time of the unsealed MtGox indictments, in the middle of a trial over the stolen WEX millions in his home city of Novosibirsk in central Russia, where he was also hit with a civil claim over the loss. Bilyuchenko was found guilty of embezzlement in September 2023 and was jailed for three and a half years, having appealed to Vladimir Putin himself for clemency over the ten years he was expected to receive. Bilyuchenko's name has been added to the United States Secret Service's most wanted list in case he ever decides to take a holiday to Greece after he has served his sentence.

As to why authorities chose June 2023 to unseal the charges, the answer was found in the court filings released the same day: Alexander Vinnik's public defender, David Rizk, had pressured the US government into releasing the names in the hopes that it might take some of the pressure off Vinnik and aid in his prisoner swap efforts. In February 2025, Rizk's efforts finally paid off when Vinnik was named as one half of a prisoner swap deal that saw US schoolteacher Marc Fogel, who was arrested in August 2021 for trying to enter Russia with seventeen grams of medical cannabis, going the other way. Having instigated his arrest, chased him for two and a half years, and finally brought him to justice, US authorities allowed Vinnik to return to Russia and welcomed Fogel back into the country with a White House ceremony. Whether Russian authorities proceeded with the charges they had laid at Vinnik's door during the extradition battle is not known, although the answer can be assumed. Clearly, the US was satisfied that it had gotten all it could out of Vinnik and preferred to bring one of its citizens home rather than endure the cost of imprisoning him for decades.

Kim Nilsson tweeted about the indictments through WizSec to say that he was pleased to note that his original findings had been backed up by the authorities:

> *Reassuringly the indictment lines up with the results of our own investigation. Following those publications, numerous tips over the years pointed at Bilyuchenko's involvement, and clearly the Department of Justice followed those same leads.*

He also added, however, that the fact that the Department of Justice was seeking forfeiture of any assets traceable to the hacks was 'hardly a reason for the MtGox victims and creditors to get their hopes up'. Such a position was understandable, given that almost all the money had been squirrelled away, spent or remained otherwise untouchable, and even any funds that might eventually be recovered would remain with the US authorities.

Sadly for those looking for more insight into how the hack actually took place, the indictments provided no further information. US authorities confirmed that the MtGox servers had indeed been compromised and the hot wallet and mass of private keys taken, but that was as far as the Department of Justice was willing to go. Given that the MtGox task force was wound down after the 2019 indictments, such details will likely remain unpublished unless Bilyuchencko or Verner are brought to trial in the US. As seems to be the way with many crucial issues concerning MtGox, we can see the tip of the iceberg, but there is a lot that remains tantalisingly out of sight beneath the surface.

Chapter 25 – End in Sight

When MtGox creditors received the welcome news that the Tokyo District Court had approved the move back into civil rehabilitation in June 2018, hopes were high that things were finally about to get moving. However, in the two and a half years since this ruling, little had happened to validate any such optimism. MtGox trustee Nobuaki Kobayashi had yet to finalise the plans for the civil rehabilitation deal, with every few months seeing another delay as he cited a further area that needed more examination before he could put a deal to the court. The situation was not helped by creditor groups lobbying Kobayashi to ensure that the elements that were most important to them were contained in the draft plan he was putting forward, ideals that didn't always line up with each other. Creditors were only expecting about a fifth of their claim to be actually paid back to them, given what was left at this point, but the difference between bankruptcy and civil rehabilitation was now vast: a 100-bitcoin claim would have returned a cash payment of around $9,700 under the original bankruptcy terms, whereas a civil rehabilitation payout would see them receive BTC and BCH worth some $580,000 as of January 2021. The supply had been reduced, however, due to Kobayashi's selling, which had stopped in mid-2018 when the dollar value of the claims had been met.

The coffers had been boosted, however, by the fact that Bitcoin Cash had undergone a fork in November 2018, with a new token, BSV, being created as a result. This endeavour, which was spearheaded by none other than Craig Wright after a massive falling out with Roger Ver over the direction of Bitcoin Cash, meant that every holder of BCH got an equal number of BSV tokens, too. This landed the trustee with a further 142,846 BSV tokens to take into account, worth $28.5 million at the time of the split, augmented by a similar number of Bitcoin Gold tokens, following another fork. These were sold off, but, as of July 2025, all the BSV received from the split were still in the trustee's possession.

There was also the thorn in the side of the entire MtGox rehabilitation affair to consider: Coinlab. Despite its clearly excessive $16 billion claim, Coinlab was showing no intentions of backing down. Kobayashi had rejected the claim as part of his initial assessment, which left Coinlab needing to file an independent claim assessment with the Tokyo District Court. This it did in March 2019, with Coinlab and Kobayashi both presenting reports from experts who had assessed the validity of Coinlab's claim. The key factor in the claim was whether Coinlab was properly licensed to act on MtGox's behalf when it was supposed to launch its US operation back in 2013. Kobayashi's expert judged Coinlab to have been, in the words of Andy Pag, 'a long way shy of the mark' in terms of regulatory readiness, while Coinlab's expert claimed that the company had, in fact, exceeded the demands required to satisfy regulators at the time.

In August 2019, the court ruled on the matter, rejecting Coinlab's protestations that it was fully licensed and agreeing with Kobayashi's assessment that Coinlab's claim was worth just $4 million rather than $16 billion. This left Coinlab with one final attempt – a lawsuit – although doing so would require a deposit of 1% of the amount sought, which many believed Coinlab would not be able to afford. However, Peter Vessenes's backers were willing to stump up the cash for him to fight, with one of them, early Bitcoin investor Tim Draper, stating that he was happy to 'continue to support our entrepreneur'. Coinlab filed, reducing its claim to ¥50 million ($440 million) in the process, with observers concluding that it had only been able to obtain $4.4 million in funds for its 1% deposit. They were convinced, though, that, were Coinlab successful in this endeavour, a second lawsuit for the remaining $15.56 billion would soon follow. Kobayashi counter-sued, arguing that Coinlab wasn't procedurally allowed to reinflate its claim in the way that it had done, and the saga looked like it would drag on for years, holding the MtGox civil rehabilitation process up as it went.

The Coinlab lawsuit also had an impact on the potential distribution of the MtGox assets. Once the suit was filed, Kobayashi was duty-bound to ringfence the funds being sought by Peter Vessenes. The total amounts from approved claims sat at around 860,000 BTC/BCH and ¥8.8 billion ($78 million) in cash, while the amount allocated to unapproved claims sat at about 130,000 BTC/BCH and ¥50 billion in cash ($442 million). As a result, nearly all the unapproved cash was allocated to the Coinlab claim. The battle between

Kobayashi and Coinlab continued into 2020, with neither side giving way; Kobayashi was adamant that Coinlab would not get anything like the $16 billion it was ultimately demanding, while Coinlab dug its heels in and said its calculations were fair. Vessenes, already unpopular, became a hated figure in the MtGox community over his intransigence, with Coinlab labelled the 'biggest scammers in bitcoin' by one aggrieved claimant.

Behind the scenes, however, things were actually moving forward. Coinlab had been brought to the negotiating table by Fortress, which was willing to pay Coinlab up front to work with Kobayashi on a proposal that would suit all parties and give the green light to at least partial payouts. It was the finer points of this deal that were causing the delays in Kobayashi filing the rehabilitation plan, but creditors weren't aware of this. Kim Nilsson would later summarise the deal thus:

> *In short, Fortress/MGIF appears to have done quite some legwork behind the scenes to make this offer possible, and at first glance it seems like an attractive one: creditors who opt for early payouts get almost all of the benefit with a near-best-case payout rate, less waiting, and zero risk from Coinlab. Creditors who take the red pill and stay in the game face a significantly longer wait (although there may be interim payouts), only a slight potential upside, and a risk (however small) of an ultimately lower payout.*

Interestingly, in the intervening years, more and more creditors, fed up with the dwindling chances of seeing their coins ever coming back to them, had been selling out to the likes of Fortress. This had made Fortress one of the largest creditors around, and with voting weight on any plan heavily determined by claim size, suddenly, it was a major player in any future decision-making.

In March 2020, Kobayashi finally drafted a rehabilitation plan that would see claims for fiat currencies, BTC and BCH honoured in their requested form, with all other crypto assets 'liquidated into cash to the extent possible'. Funds were to be allocated toward the rehabilitation proceedings first, with creditors receiving a cut of what was left. Any plan would have to be submitted and approved by the Tokyo District Court before creditors could vote on it, but at last, an important step looked like it was about to be taken. However, with the filing deadline looming, Kobayashi requested an extension. This was nothing new, given that Kobayashi had been requesting and getting deadline extensions on a regular basis since April 2019. It did mean, though, that it wasn't until 15 December 2020 that Kobayashi finally filed his draft rehabilitation plan for court approval, although there was still no mention of a potential Coinlab-Fortress deal, the details of which were still being ironed out behind closed doors.

A month later, the full proposal was finally put to MtGox creditors: rather than having to wait until the Coinlab lawsuit was resolved, which could, of course, take years and might negatively impact them, creditors could receive an early lump sum payment to settle their claim ahead of time. This would equate to 21% of the value of their claim, which would be paid out in a combination of BTC, BCH and Japanese yen. The alternative was to hold on for a higher payout and hope that Coinlab lost its claim and its separate $75 million US lawsuit against MtGox, which was still in the works. Peter Vessenes released a statement announcing the offer, in which he said that Coinlab was giving up 'many billions of dollars of recoverable damage to ensure that creditors get their share shortly', adding that coming to the agreement had been 'an incredibly complex two-year negotiation process'. Vessenes then further tested the patience of creditors when he claimed that 'Coinlab has closely listened to the concerns expressed by Mt.Gox creditors since the beginning' and added that the deal 'allows Coinlab to pursue its valid and legitimate claims without holding up payments for the rest of the estate'. A rather premature Tim Draper gushed to Bloomberg that he was 'thrilled that people are finally getting paid by Mt. Gox', adding, 'I look forward to getting my Bitcoin as do the tens of thousands of people that have claims'. Of course, if Draper had been that desperate for his bitcoins, he wouldn't have helped front the very lawsuit that had caused the delays.

News of the offer was greeted with cautious optimism by MtGox creditors. In his analysis of the plan, Kim Nilsson said that overall, it 'should be positive news for MtGox creditors', saying that the early lump-sum payment offered at least 90% of what claimants could realistically hope to get by staying the course, with the added bonus that they got paid much sooner. Others were a little more circumspect, with one Redditor opining that 'both options offered to us are like [a] lottery'. Many, too, were concerned over the low percentage of return, but a rejection of the plan would have meant a return to bankruptcy, which would have been worse for everyone. It was no surprise, therefore, that the major creditors and creditor groups were advocating a 'yes' vote.

The draft rehabilitation plan, with Coinlab's offer as its key constituent, was put to the Tokyo District Court, which approved it on 22 February 2021. Now, it was over to the creditors. Claimants were given until 8 October to cast their votes on the plan, with the final results to be given at a creditor meeting on 20 October. As the 8th approached, prominent MtGox creditors and members of the Bitcoin community, including Mark Karpelès himself, begged other creditors to get their votes in, as an abstained vote counted as a 'no'. This was a legitimate concern given the number of zombie claimants whose numbers would need to be overcome. The creditor meeting twelve days later was the most eagerly anticipated for quite some time. At the meeting, Kobayashi revealed that, although less than 50% of the creditors had voted, approximately 83% of the total amount of claim value had voted to approve the plan. The Tokyo District Court made the plan official later that day, meaning that, more than six years on from that first feisty creditor meeting, and after interminable delays, the MtGox creditors were finally on the verge of getting back at least a portion of what had been taken from them all those years ago. A clearly relieved Nobuaki Kobayashi made his feelings known in the official notice:

> *The Rehabilitation Trustee would like to express sincere gratitude to all involved parties for their understanding and support, which led to the approval of the Draft Rehabilitation Plan by a large majority of rehabilitation creditors and the confirmation order of the Rehabilitation Plan.*

The news was greeted with an outpouring of joy from creditors, although some were quick to warn that payouts shouldn't be expected imminently, with the Tokyo District Court still needing to rubber stamp the plan. On 16 November, this rubber stamp was duly applied, allowing Kobayashi to announce that the civil rehabilitation plan was now final and binding, representing the last step in the process.

This done, attention naturally turned to the critical question of when creditors could expect their payouts. Some analysts predicted that these could come as soon as Q1 of 2022, but having been kept waiting for over seven years, creditors weren't getting carried away. Kobayashi had asked all creditors to add their bank details through the online portal, warning that failure to do so could delay payouts for all, but this had proved problematic for a number of reasons, not least because the portal was buggy and made the completion of the form impossible for some. Then, there were the concerns over creditors who had abandoned their claims midway through the process or even passed away in the intervening years. It was no surprise, therefore, when nothing appeared during the first half of 2022, although Kobayashi released an update in July in which he said he was 'currently preparing to make repayments' and repeated his request for bank details to avoid further delays. In response, creditors repeated their request for a working portal. Kobayashi also presented claimants with two options for repayment: they could either receive their funds in the existing mix of BTC, BCH and Japanese yen, or they could opt for the trustee to liquidate the entirety of their claim into cash. Crucially, no timeframe was given for payouts in this update.

A Reddit post two weeks later drew the ire of claimants once again, this time over expenses. According to the post, the stated expenses up to that point had amounted to an average of ¥241 million ($1.7 million) per year, with the net expenses up to July 2022 amounting to almost ¥2 billion ($13.6 million). However, the final status report in July 2022 showed that Kobayashi had spent eight years' worth of expenses in the past sixteen months alone, with some ¥2.1 billion ($14.3 million) being spent between March 2021 and July 2022. This included a ¥1.4 billion ($10 million) payout to the trustee himself for reasons that were not disclosed. This news prompted an outcry from creditors, many of whom felt that they were getting robbed all over again. One respondent on the MtGox Insolvency Reddit forum had 'absolutely no doubt that the trustee is bleeding the carcass for as much as he can for as long as possible', a theory that was echoed by another:

> *As if somebody acting within the bounds of the law can't also be acting corruptly. I'm not saying there would be a chance of recovering anything, but any casual observer can see he's been extracting as much as he legally can while delivering the bare minimum. Now he's ramping up the spending because the end is in sight.*

Some were more understanding of the hike, however, believing that the costs were associated with preparations for the rollout of the repayments, which suggested that payouts were imminent.

In June 2020, it seemed like another windfall might be coming the way of creditors when the Asset Recovery Unit of the New Zealand Police froze NZ$140 million ($78 million) from the Canton Business Corporation, the largest restraint of funds in New Zealand Police history. The funds, the police said, were owned by a Canton subsidiary, namely BTC-e, and were 'likely to reflect the profit gained from the victimisation of thousands, if not hundreds of thousands, of people globally as a result of cyber-crime and organised crime.' New Zealand police tried for nearly three years to get their hands on the frozen funds, with the delay partly down to the fact that some of it was in the form of bitcoins held in BTC-e wallets. They eventually issued a restraining order on 2 March 2023, and later that month, a New Zealand High Court judge ruled that the proceeds were indeed funds that had been laundered after being illicitly obtained, further aiding the recovery process. When it came to MtGox's association with the funds, a post by the trustee on 3 March highlighted his stance but suggested that creditors shouldn't hold their breath:

> *The Rehabilitation Trustee intends to participate in the proceedings in the New Zealand court regarding the return of the aforementioned funds. However, the possibility, estimated amount, timing, etc., of the return is unknown at this time.*

In October 2022, cryptocurrency exchange BitGo was announced as a supplementary exchange where MtGox creditors could get their payouts sent, which was followed two months later by a notice from Kobayashi imposing a deadline of 10 January 2023 for the submission of bank details and a warning that anyone who hadn't submitted their details by that point would lose their claim. Claimants took to social media to warn those who hadn't started the process yet or had somehow missed the whole thing to submit their details or risk defaulting to a fiat-only final payment after the Coinlab dispute had been settled. Worse, any money eventually awarded in this manner would have to be picked up in person from the trustee's office in Tokyo, and any that wasn't claimed within ten years would end up in the coffers of the Japanese government. This led to repeated complaints that the portal still wasn't accepting bank details or failed to function properly in other respects, with some comparing the support they were receiving from the trustee's office to that of MtGox in its final days. A payout deadline of 31 July 2023 was set, although few expected this to be adhered to. These doubters were proved right just weeks later when, in December 2022, Kobayashi extended the submission and payout deadlines by two months after Kraken announced that it was pulling out of Japan in a cost-saving measure, meaning that it could no longer facilitate MtGox payouts for Japanese claimants.

With the new registration deadline of 10 March 2023 approaching, creditors' patience was tested again when the process was once more delayed, this time by three and a half weeks to 6 April. In the notice outlining this extension, Kobayashi offered a thinly veiled criticism of the creditors, saying that 'various circumstances such as the progress by rehabilitation creditors' were behind the need to push the deadline back. In return, creditors once again pointed to the continuing issues with the registration process, with some at their wits' end over how to resolve them, while others took a more cynical view:

> *For f*ck's sake. This is never going to end. Not until these legal criminals have stolen it all. They should never have been allowed to take an hourly rate and be the ones to decide on time.*

The delay was naturally met with relief from those still unable to register and anger from those who had already been approved. Kobayashi again threatened that the boat couldn't wait forever and that anyone who missed it would be in a much more difficult situation, still seemingly unaware that those he was appealing to were stuck on the quayside, trying to alert his attention to the broken gangway. Nevertheless, the gangway was pulled up and the ship set sail on 6 April 2023, with those yet to register told that their applications would now only be considered at the discretion of the trustee. All was not lost, however: in a tacit admission that the system hadn't been fit for purpose, a new webpage had been created where those who were yet to register could do so without adding their bank details, with the full registration to be completed at some point in the future. When these early payouts might arrive was, however, still a mystery; an announcement on 7 April 2023 suggested that payouts were scheduled for 31 October, but this was far from certain:

> *Going forward, the Rehabilitation Trustee will carry out the necessary preparations to make the repayment, which include the confirmation of the Selection and Registration made by the rehabilitation creditors, as well as engaging in discussions and sharing information with banks, fund transfer providers and cryptocurrency exchanges or custodians involved in*

the repayment. In light of this, it is expected to take some time before the repayment is commenced.

Creditors were also warned that 'in consideration of various circumstances, the above deadline might be extended with the permission of the Tokyo District Court, or a different deadline might be set for some of the repayments with the permission of the Tokyo District Court'. By now, of course, such occurrences were second nature to the beleaguered creditors.

Despite the potential for further delays, the news that payouts were closer than ever raised fears that had been lingering in the backs of the minds of the wider crypto space ever since the move to civil rehabilitation was confirmed in June 2018. The spectre of mass distribution of hundreds of thousands of bitcoins led to concerns from some (mainly mainstream media outlets who conducted little actual research and enjoyed stoking the fires) that a huge Bitcoin selloff would ensue, crashing the price. However, most in the space knew this wasn't a concern for several reasons, most importantly because the payouts would be staggered by the exchanges receiving them as they required processing, and also because MtGox customers were early Bitcoin adopters and were therefore unlikely to quickly shed the coins they had waited over nine years to get back. Naturally, there would be some sales as people took healthy profits, but, as a UBS report of 2 March 2023 noted, the Bitcoin market may have already priced in such an event, meaning that the market was prepared for it, and so Bitcoin was already at a price that reflected any such inflows.

As 2023 rumbled on, reports of registration issues persisted, with frustrated claimants waiting up to three months to find out that they had been rejected, with some tearing their hair out over the fact that the system was not accepting simple information such as their full name. Faith in a 31 October payout was dwindling, and on 21 September, this was confirmed when Kobayashi posted an update in which he stated that the deadline had been shifted by a whole year to 31 October 2024. This caused consternation among creditors, with many plumbing new depths of despair they didn't know they possessed over the situation. The news prompted theories that the trustee had lost access to the Bitcoin wallets just as Mark Karpelès had done, while others maintained that Kobayashi was stringing the process out in order to bring in more money for his firm. They were mollified a little by the claim that the payments would begin 'as early as the end of this year' for those who had successfully registered their details, but this prospect was treated with scorn by most creditors who had seen too many deadlines come and go over the past ten years to believe that this one would actually be adhered to.

The delay ensured that creditors experienced the tenth anniversary of the collapse of MtGox without seeing a penny of their holdings returned to them, something that was inconceivable when MtGox went offline in 2014. However, four months and seven days later, members of the MtGox insolvency subreddit woke to see the news they'd been praying for ever since Mark Karpelès pulled the plug on MtGox's servers:

Coins credited into my account

The BTC/BCC coins are already under my control! I received exactly the amount displayed in the Mt Gox table. I'm using Bitbank as the exchange.

Other Bitbank customers reported on social media that they, too, had received their BTC and BCH following the torturous decade-long wait, as did customers of another exchange, SBI. They may have only been getting about 20% of their MtGox holdings, but getting anything back represented a victory, especially given Bitcoin's 5,000% rise in price during the same period; those who had held just thirty bitcoins on MtGox were getting the dollar equivalent of the average US house price returned to them. As a marker of how far Bitcoin had come in that time, the US Securities and Exchange Commission had bowed to pressure and allowed several US financial giants to operate Bitcoin ETFs, an event that secured Bitcoin's position as a legitimately investable asset. What these individuals had bought on a whim was being returned to them as a much sought-after commodity.

While creditors revelled in the 'surreal' and 'momentous' occasion, the market braced for impact. As blockchain observers began posting about coins from MtGox wallets heading towards exchanges, the price of Bitcoin dropped sharply from $62,000 on 1 July to as low as $53,600 on the day the first bitcoin payouts were received, a decline of roughly 10%. The fact that this drop took place before the payouts even arrived proved that the fear of the event was worse than the event itself, a thesis which played out when the price rebounded to $70,000 within three weeks. The doom-mongers had been proved wrong, with most MtGox creditors understandably holding the coins they had fought so hard to get back.

The ten-year journey, which had begun with denials, protests and placards, was finally coming to an end, and while some nursed the loss of tens of millions of dollars, the realisation that they had weathered the most unique of storms and come out with anything at all was not lost on creditors. Mark Karpelès shared in the joy:

> *MtGox customers have finally started receiving Bitcoins! After over 10 years I wasn't sure anymore if it'd finally happen, but here we are finally!! This has been a long journey and I'm happy to see we're finally getting there, only a bit more...*

Charlie Shrem responded to reminisce about the 'Good times' of the pair's IRC chats when they 'held the weigh[t] of the bitcoin world on our shoulders', while others reminded Karpelès of his missteps, bringing up the transaction malleability farrago and accusing Karpelès of not apologising for the gargantuan losses he oversaw. Even in the midst of what should have been a time of celebration, the shadow of his mistakes still followed Mark Karpelès, representing a microcosm of his past, present and, almost certainly, his future.

Chapter 26 – Legacy

The collapse of MtGox acted as a huge wake-up call to authorities around the world when it was realised that real money was at risk through Bitcoin enterprises, and lots of it. Of course, the FSA had known that MtGox was handling fiat currencies and that it was commingling these funds in further breach of financial laws, but had chosen to ignore this. However, following the collapse of MtGox, it could no longer bury its head in the sand despite the loss of face it would have to endure. Japanese authorities began looking immediately into how they would handle cryptocurrencies as an asset class as well as the exchanges that acted as custodians for users, but the US was fastest out of the traps; the New York BitLicense was launched in July 2014, just five months after MtGox's collapse, a license that all crypto-handling entities who wanted to serve users in the state needed to obtain. Those who continued to operate without one faced legal repercussions.

Japan's first crypto regulations followed two and a half years later when the Payment Services Act was amended to include cryptocurrencies, meaning that all crypto facilitators who wanted to continue to serve Japanese citizens needed to register with the FSA. Five months later, the agency approved its first eleven cryptocurrency exchanges, but the new guidelines were criticised for giving the whole crypto sector a 'stamp of approval' as one Japanese banker put it, something that many believed it didn't deserve and that might lead to problems down the line. The FSA denied this, saying that the new regulations were 'imposed on the exchanges so that they can take appropriate measures for money laundering and protection of users'. However forward-thinking these regulations might have been, there was a loophole: exchanges could keep operating while seeking a license, and it didn't take long for this provision to be exploited. While working on its second filing, having already been rejected once, crypto exchange Coincheck was hacked on 26 January 2018, and coins worth

$523 million were stolen, exceeding the value stolen in the MtGox hacks at the time of their theft. The hack was a huge embarrassment for the FSA, showing as it did that its new guidelines were still ineffective in preventing gargantuan losses. This time, it couldn't escape criticism and hit back by ordering swift reviews of all other exchanges operating in the country.

While the collapse of MtGox was the biggest threat to Bitcoin at the time, its impact has proven to be thankfully minimal, with only those who either didn't understand Bitcoin or were already ideologically against it using MtGox as a stick to beat it with. In truth, much of the criticism and doom-mongering following the exchange's collapse came from the mainstream press, which had little understanding of the intricacies of Bitcoin and whose only exposure to it at the time was through the collapse itself. It was inevitable, then, that they had a warped view of the nascent sector, having only ever witnessed it through the lens of Silk Road's illegal activities and now a catastrophe that cost tens of thousands of people a total of half a billion dollars. These people had no interest in understanding Bitcoin and never would, so the collapse of MtGox was like catnip to them.

While MtGox did set Bitcoin adoption back many years, it's also important to remember how it helped grow the Bitcoin ecosystem in the first place. It can't be forgotten that MtGox onboarded more than a million people into Bitcoin and provided them with the first chance to actually trade bitcoins for money in a relatively safe, structured way compared to the alternatives at the time. The fact that Mark Karpelès actively sought to be regulated in multiple countries and implemented AML/KYC procedures proved that he wanted to do things in the right way. In this respect, MtGox was way ahead of its time. MtGox also, ironically, helped Bitcoin to grow to the point where, in Kim Nilsson's words, it was no longer needed by the time it went under:

> *Bitcoin has not collapsed as a result of MtGox collapsing, so while MtGox was in many ways a trailblazer, at the time of the collapse of MtGox the ecosystem was no longer dependant on MtGox itself.*

In short, Bitcoin was not MtGox, and MtGox was not Bitcoin. Many have argued that the collapse of MtGox was the reason Bitcoin endured a bear market from 2014 to 2015, but this isn't the case; Bitcoin's price peaked at $1,200 in December 2013 and had been in a downward trend for some three months by the time MtGox collapsed. Willy and Markus undoubtedly helped push the Bitcoin price up with their relentless buying and pulled it down on the other side with its huge selloffs, but it wasn't the reason the market had begun to reverse the prior December; any asset that caps a two-year bull market by going over 10x in a matter of weeks is primed for a reversal. Pundits, critics and mainstream media outlets predicted the death of Bitcoin in the wake of the exchange's collapse and have done so continuously with each scandal that has followed in the decade since, but Bitcoin continues to defy them. On 28 May 2016, the Bitcoin price returned to $484 for the first time since MtGox's implosion, and it hasn't looked back since; on 5 December 2024, it stunned critics by crossing $100,000. Bitcoin's popularity continues to grow, along with the 'hash rate', the amount of mining power dedicated to protecting the network. The Bitcoin network is, therefore, more used, utilised and better protected than ever before.

Much is still unknown about how MtGox operated and how it was ultimately compromised, information that will never be known unless Mark Karpelès chooses to volunteer it or the hackers are compelled to reveal their secrets. I tried to obtain an interview with Mark for this book, but he failed to reply to my communications, which also goes for some of the other major players in the story, although it's highly unlikely that he would have confided in me any more than he has in others. Kim Nilsson's tireless reporting in the years since MtGox's collapse has allowed us to build up a picture of many aspects of its operations, such as the completely inefficient way it handled its customer assets, the manipulation that Karpelès conducted to try and balance the books and the fact that it was almost certainly operating in a fractional reserve capacity from around August 2013. What Karpelès knew and what he didn't know remain matters of conjecture. Many argue that he simply *had* to know that the exchange was running on empty, but his mismanagement of other areas of the exchange was so bad that the notion he at all times had a firm grasp on the company's financial position is by no means a foregone conclusion.

Despite all the intricacies and rabbit holes associated with the MtGox story, all that people tend to remember is the huge losses, which is unsurprising. When Kim Nilsson presented his research into the MtGox affair at the Breaking Bitcoin meetup in Paris in 2017, there were audible gasps in the audience as he revealed how the exchange had been brought to its knees, mistake by mistake, hack by hack. When he got to the final slide, which summarised the total losses suffered by MtGox, he was greeted with stunned silence as the audience tried to take in what they were seeing: through three years' worth of theft, mistakes and poor investments, MtGox lost or surrendered more than three-quarters of a million bitcoins and $60 million in cash. These figures were enough to stun a room full of experienced Bitcoiners, most of whom thought they already knew the story, and, despite having now crossed the 10th anniversary of its demise, it's no surprise that the tale of MtGox keeps shocking new entrants to the space, especially when the value of the loss is translated to contemporary prices. It's also important to remember that while the coins the hackers stole are long gone, the pain caused by the collapse of MtGox is still very much felt by the creditors who had to wait more than ten years to get back just a fifth of what they lost, never knowing if they ever actually would.

As the Bitcoin and crypto space has evolved, the security measures implemented by exchanges have dramatically improved to the point where another disaster on the scale of MtGox is almost unthinkable. This is also partly because, while there are still giants in the crypto exchange world, there is no entity as dominant as MtGox was between 2011 and 2014, and there will never be again. The landscape has changed in a myriad of ways since the days of MtGox, with state-sponsored North Korean groups such as Lazarus having taken over from Russians as the primary agents of attack, often targeting decentralised exchanges rather than centralised ones like MtGox, which are now recognised as much tougher targets. The collapse of MtGox also ushered in the concept of self-custody, and there is a greater emphasis today on keeping one's assets off exchanges and on secure devices under the sole control of the owner, something that many exchanges advocate.

Despite ten years having passed since the last bitcoin was swiped from the exchange, the 2011-2014 hack on MtGox still places in or near the top five biggest-ever crypto hacks by dollar value, a fact that puts the scale of the loss into perspective: Bitcoin's price has increased more than two hundred times since the event, and yet the theft was so huge that it still figures highly in such charts. The collapse of crypto exchange FTX in 2022 carried a tab some sixteen times higher in value than that of MtGox and was the highest-profile incident since MtGox went under, leading to instant comparisons between the pair. There are more than a few similarities between the paths that both exchanges took, including the activities of those at the helm, but there are crucial differences in the way the operations were handled that set them apart. Most notably, in November 2023, FTX's CEO, Sam Bankman-Fried, was found guilty of seven fraud-related charges connected to how FTX operated, something that firmly differentiates him from Mark Karpelès. Nevertheless, people will talk about MtGox and FTX in the same breath whenever the subject of catastrophic crypto collapses arises, and if history is any guide, we will have a third name to add to the list in another ten years or so.

Assets may change, but people don't.

Chapter 27 – Blame

When it comes to apportioning blame for the collapse of MtGox, there is a large cast of characters to consider.

Can we blame Jed McCaleb, the man who built the exchange with shoddy code, got it into debt and then scarpered? The evidence surrounding the sale indeed suggests that McCaleb was desperate to rid himself of MtGox, hence why he all but gave it to Mark Karpelès. And then there's the fact that he advocated keeping the 1Feex hack secret and using the Gox Bot to fill the hole. McCaleb touched on the subject of his complicity in a 2019 interview where he said that he 'definitely could have found someone other than Mark to take it over' but that he had 'zero control over what he was doing' after this point. Many still point the finger of blame firmly at Jed McCaleb for the problems at MtGox, however, and with good reason.

Can we blame U.S. authorities? Mark Karpelès certainly does, claiming that the $5 million seized by corrupt officials from MtGox was the match that lit the fire, all because they felt that he wasn't being helpful enough with their Silk Road investigation. Can we blame Mizuho Bank, which created the bottleneck in the cash withdrawals and deposits system in 2013 that many perceive as the start of MtGox's downfall? Can we blame the hackers, who perpetually plundered the exchange for almost three years and eventually brought it to its knees? Can we blame the FSA, which staunchly ignored what MtGox and Mark Karpelès were doing and failed to protect the customers over whom it had a duty of care?

All these people and institutions are partially responsible for the failure of MtGox to varying degrees, but one man, of course, stands at the centre of the Venn diagram of blame: Mark Karpelès. The man who didn't do any due diligence before taking the exchange off Jed McCaleb's hands in March 2011. The man who knew MtGox was in debt to itself even before he became CEO. The man who used trading bots on his own site to try and buy back massive losses, artificially manipulating the price of Bitcoin in both directions as he did so. The man who either didn't notice that his company was rinsed clean over a two-and-a-half-year period or knew and didn't say anything. The man who was seemingly more concerned with the quality of the pastries in the Bitcoin Café than with the quality of the security procedures within his company. The man who fiddled with gadgets while Rome burned.

In September 2017, blockchain critic David Gerard summarised that 'In security terms, Mt. Gox fell down the stairs and hit its head on every step', and, indeed, given the level of control he exerted, it is easy to label Karpelès the sole agent of MtGox's destruction. While Karpelès is cognisant of his role in the catastrophe, he's also keen to remind people that this wasn't a one-man shitshow. In an interview in February 2019, a month before his verdict in the Japanese trial, he told Peter McCormack that no one realised how big Bitcoin would get or that its growth would make MtGox such a prime target:

> *I could think today of many ways this could have been done better, but I don't think at the time anyone had any idea of how things would go or what specifically could be done to prevent this.*

Karpelès added that making the cold wallets auditable would have been a priority had he known of their importance at the time. This, in hindsight, is obvious and should have been so back then. In the interview, Karpelès also took issue with those who said he wasn't present enough when things were going south and that he hadn't taken enough responsibility:

> *I don't know actually what enough is, and I guess it is different for everyone. My goal is to just not stop doing what I can do as long as there is something I can do. When I was running MtGox I always tried to make sure everything was running smoothly. Obviously, it was not enough and MtGox went to bankruptcy, so I did my best to make sure the bankruptcy would run smoothly and as fast as possible.*

This version of events is at odds with what almost all those who worked at MtGox have said, however, including Ashley Barr:

> *I felt Mt.Gox was an RPG to Mark, as he didn't quite grasp the reality that the money being...deposited into his bank account meant more to other people than just numbers on his screen.*

Sentiment towards Karpelès has changed dramatically since the collapse of MtGox, and even more so since his exoneration by the Japanese court in 2019. For years, he was the face of the exchange's implosion, the man that many believed had lost or potentially even stolen almost a million bitcoins, most of them belonging to customers who trusted him when he said the site was secure and the company was solvent. To some, he was Edward John Smith or Dick Fuld, ignoring the risks and mismanaging the entity under his control so spectacularly that it was always doomed to fail. Others equate him to Charles Ponzi or Bernie Madoff, a sociopathic fraud looking to manipulate his customers' implicit trust and profit from them. Karpelès has not deviated from his story that he was guilty of nothing more than mismanagement of the exchange, with his innocence in the matter of the thefts backed up by various means: the research from Kim Nilsson and others; the arrest of Alexander Vinnik and the charges against Alexandr Verner and Alexsey Bilyuchenko; his refusal to buckle under the ceaseless interrogation of Japanese prosecutors; and the fact that he has not, seemingly, come out of the MtGox affair sitting on a pile of hundreds of millions of dollars. There remain, of course, many questions to be answered over what Mark Karpelès knew about MtGox's financial situation and when he knew it, but we will almost certainly never get the answers to these, given that Karpelès has no wish to risk seeing the inside of the Tokyo detention centre again.

In his AMA, Ashley Barr revealed how he had come to believe that Karpelès wasn't malicious at heart:

> *My honestly feeling is I liked Mark, as just...a geek. I'm a geek, I get other geeks. We're all wired differently but similarly and I enjoyed that about him. I think most others had the same experience, and i think it reflects in his media personality (harmless, but awkward and untrustworthy).*

Likewise, Thomas Glucksmann was forgiving when thinking back to his time working for Karpelès:

> *I don't consider him to be a 'bad' guy and genuinely believe he was trying to solve the [banking] issue.*

Kim Nilsson, too, believes Karpelès was simply the wrong person in the wrong job at the wrong time:

In the years I've known him I've never seen a malicious act or word from him. He just seems to want to be nice to everybody, and gets uncomfortable when it's not possible to get along. He's like Ferdinand the Bull, with all this madness going down centered around him while he just wants to sit and smell the flowers.

These opinions are typical of those who worked at MtGox or spent any time with Karpelès; he was simply the wrong man at the wrong time, someone who almost accidentally became the driver of a fast-moving financial juggernaut and had no idea how to control it. Karpelès has also gone on record to state that the amount of time he spent working on the Bitcoin Café has been overblown, taking issue with Glucksmann's appearance on a BBC podcast about the collapse of MtGox when the Englishman referenced the doomed project.

In his Reddit AMA in April 2018, a few exchanges between Mark Karpelès and MtGox victims illustrated this shift in sentiment towards the former CEO over the years:

I have no question. I lost an INSANE amount of bitcoins on Mt. Gox. I was so mad for the longest [time] and it really wasn't justifiable. At the end of the day shit happens, we all knew the risk and greed prevails over all. I hope you are able to forgive yourself for what happened. I hold no grudge and wish no ill upon you mate.

For what it's worth, I hold no grudge against you anymore and your behavior recently has been exemplary. I sincerely hope that the time you served in jail already will cover your possible sentence. When I put myself in your shoes, I don't think that I could have coped with the extraordinary amount of pressure and doubt you've had to live with for so long. I'd probably be a depressed recluse or a fugitive.

These conciliations are symbolic of how many feel about Karpelès now. Time has certainly helped heal the pain, along with the realisation that Karpelès was the victim of a police stitch-up in Japan. Most believe now that he was negligent rather than malicious, a man who quickly got out of his depth and never got his head back above water. Anyone with any knowledge or experience of neurodiversity will recognise certain familiar traits in Mark Karpelès; the eye-contact issues in his youth, the lack of impulse control, the inability to focus on boring tasks and the need for perpetual stimulation all point towards attention-deficit/hyperactivity disorder (ADHD) or a similar condition. As someone who suffers from ADHD myself, some of the stories about Mark Karpelès chime with my own experiences, and such a diagnosis would explain a great deal about his childhood and actions when running MtGox. Ashley Barr is also a subscriber to this theory, saying in his 2015 AMA that Karpelès is likely 'somewhere on the autism spectrum' and that employees were also aware of his traits and learned to work around them. It would not be a surprise, therefore, if Karpelès receives such a diagnosis in the future. This does not excuse his behaviour, of course, but it might help explain some of it.

In his AMA, Karpelès was asked if he could change one thing about how he'd run MtGox, what would it be? Karpelès's answer was perhaps obvious:

> *When buying MtGox I should have had people around me to advise me and help with the management, starting with the MtGox transfer contract. I'm a tech guy, and Bitcoin was a tech thing at the time. In April 2011 there was an article in Forbes which changed Bitcoin forever, and I found myself managing emergencies every day without any time to do the work that needed to be actually done.*

MtGox and Mark Karpelès found themselves back in the news in November 2022 when FTX collapsed, losing a staggering $8 billion worth of customer funds. As I have noted, comparisons were instantly made between the collapses of MtGox and FTX, but the situation regarding the latter was very different, with evidence immediately coming to light that Sam Bankman-Fried and some of his executives had engaged in a staggering amount of criminal activity while running the $30 billion empire. In his 2023 book on the collapse of FTX, *Going Infinite: The Rise and Fall of a New Tycoon*, author Michael Lewis paints a picture of Bankman-Fried that sounds somewhat familiar: he was a child prodigy with a mind more suited to dealing with machines and mathematical computations than with people; he found 'normal' to be boring in his adolescent years and sought ways to stimulate his intellect, stimulation which, in adult life, led to disastrous results; and he had grand visions of what he wanted to achieve but made fatal errors that undermined his plans. There is also a certain irony in the fact that Bankman-Fried was an avid Magic: The Gathering player.

On 12 November 2022, the day after FTX fell into bankruptcy, Mark Karpelès offered some advice to Bankman-Fried, who had started an odd virtual apology tour:

> Tips when your company goes bankrupt (actually applies to everything legal in my experience): don't talk about it on social networks. Any lawyer will tell you to stfu about this kind of shit because anything you say is a liability to yourself and others.

This statement, coming from someone who had been in a uniquely similar position to Bankman-Fried eight and a half years prior, was pregnant with meaning, not least because it was the act of not saying anything that had caused Karpelès to become a figure of suspicion back in 2014. And yet, here he was, telling Bankman-Fried, correctly, to do exactly as he himself had done. This irony, and the fact that the advice attracted no ill will from readers, showed that Karpelès's redemption arc seemed to have come full circle.

Karpelès was ever present on Twitter in the days and weeks following the collapse of FTX, offering support and advice to those affected by it and breaking down the ramifications of the bankruptcy filing for creditors with no experience in the matter. He created a public FTX balance sheet, which he updated as information came out, to make sure customers remained fully informed. He also bristled, understandably, when mainstream media outlets decided to profile some of the major culprits in the FTX scandal in a positive light, asking, 'How do you get this kind of coverage in this kind of situation?' Given the type of coverage he had received for almost four years relating to charges on which he was never tried, this was a very fair question.

As we have already seen, the Mark Karpelès redemption arc does not extend to everyone associated with the collapse of MtGox. Some creditors still can't get over how Karpelès abandoned his duty of care while dealing with what to some represented their life savings, how he covered up the problems at the exchange with press releases that masked the truth and how his words of contrition didn't match up with his actions following its collapse. Kolin Burges, for one, feels that Karpelès has been given almost a free pass over his actions, believing the Frenchman to be a master manipulator who has been able to elicit sympathy he doesn't deserve. This is understandable given everything that creditors have been through and the fact that some of them could have retired years ago had MtGox not gone under. If they haven't made their peace by now, it's unlikely they ever will.

Were the story of MtGox a work of fiction, it's hard to tell what the overarching message would be. There is no all-encompassing lesson to be learnt from it; instead, there are several equally important ones we can consider, all of which differ in importance depending on one's perspective. First, Mark Karpelès should never have bought MtGox without being 100% sure what he was buying and what condition it was in. This, he says, is his biggest regret, and it goes hand in hand with a famous saying in the Bitcoin community: trust but verify.

Second, Karpelès should have come clean over the state of the exchange when he found out about the early hacks and the financial deficit. His first responsibility was to his customers, and any such message could have been worded in a way that didn't send users fleeing for the exit. At least the situation would have been known about, and customers could have made informed decisions.

Third, Karpelès should, as he later admitted, have sought help right from the outset of his tenure and then delegated as the company grew. His need to be involved in everything, from laptop repairs to coffee bean sourcing, was hugely restrictive for MtGox at the start and even more damaging at its untimely conclusion. Part of Karpelès's desire to be across everything was almost certainly born from the necessity of preventing anyone from finding out the parlous state of the exchange's finances, but this doesn't excuse involving himself so much with the technical side. Trust, it seems, was in short supply at MtGox, and this lack of it in the people he had hired was critical in precipitating its downfall. Asking for help is not a sign of weakness. In fact, as Mark Karpelès can testify, the opposite is true.

Finally, many outside observers have mocked and chided MtGox customers for leaving their funds on the exchange, asking what they expected from a platform that had been hacked more times than a centre forward on a pub football team. The truth is that during the last seven months of MtGox's life, it became increasingly hard for customers to get bitcoins or US dollars off the exchange even if they had wanted to, while those who believed what they were told by the company and its leadership should not be held responsible for being lied to. Some were naïve, perhaps, but there were mitigating circumstances, as Jesse Powell pointed out following MtGox's implosion:

...there are plenty of people new to Bitcoin who have no clue about Gox's past. They just see Gox come up over and over when they search for Bitcoin, and as the market leader on charting sites, etc. There are not warnings plastered all over the internet telling people not to trust Gox. People continued to prop Gox up as the premier exchange, and they drove a lot of naive traffic who signed up and deposited funds.

I know from bitter personal experience that victims of scams always look back and see times when they should have twigged that something wasn't right, and the same is certainly true of many MtGox customers. In this respect, a healthy dose of scepticism and a reduction of risk where possible is the lesson that many creditors will have taken from their experience.

It's important to remember that while Mark Karpelès was heavily complicit in the downfall of MtGox, he did not hack the exchange or steal any coins. His crime was to leave the door open for burglars to walk through, and for being too busy polishing the ornaments to realise they were stealing the carpet from under him. We will never know what MtGox could have achieved had it not been repeatedly hacked or so badly mismanaged. These two elements were crucial in bringing MtGox down, but they weren't alone; MtGox was crippled by a perfect storm of criminal endeavour, spectacular mismanagement and once-in-a-blue-moon timing. There will probably never be an asset that experiences the stunning growth that Bitcoin enjoyed during those early years, and MtGox just happened to be in the right place at the right time, but with the wrong man at the helm.

In April 2018, Mark Karpelès secured his first job following the collapse of MtGox when he was hired as Chief Technology Officer for tech company London Trust Media. The appointment caused such a stir that his new boss, Andrew Lee, was forced to pen a blog post to defend his decision. In the piece, Lee opined, 'If we, as a society, do not give second chances to those who fall, then we as a society will cease to progress. It will have a detrimental chilling effect.' He also alluded to Karpelès's 'many great successes and mistakes', which he said had made him 'strong and wise, and we can only learn from his experience'. Karpelès stayed in this role for a year before launching a new software development company, Karpelès Lab Inc. In November 2020, he joined cloud computing company Shells.com as Chief Technology Officer, which garnered no headlines whatsoever, and split his time between the two organisations. On 7 October 2024, Karpelès celebrated the opening of the cryptocurrency exchange EllipX, for which he was also Chief Technology Officer, marking his first involvement with a crypto exchange in the ten and a half years since the death of MtGox.

Karpelès is still active within the crypto community, helping MtGox creditors and advising FTX claimants on what to expect from the bankruptcy process. His suspended sentence ended in March 2023.

He still bakes.

Acknowledgements

This book would not have been possible without the assistance of those who took time out of their busy schedules to offer their invaluable insight into their experiences of working on MtGox and working with Mark Karpelès. Some of those I interviewed requested to stay anonymous, but many will recognise their contributions throughout the book, and I offer a huge thank you to them. Others were willing to forego their privacy and go on record, for which I am eternally grateful, particularly Kolin Burges, Kim Nilsson and Thomas Glucksmann.

I would also like to thank my proofreaders, especially within the creditor community, who helped me get to grips with the complexities involved in their battle.

As I have alluded to, some of the key players in the MtGox story either rejected or ignored my interview requests for this book. I remain hopeful that these individuals will come forward in time and that future editions will include their testimonies.

References

Given the nature of the source material, providing a traditionally presented list of references would have resulted in over thirty printed pages consisting of highly impractical and often long-winded web links.

As a result, this web link will take the visitor to the full list of references online, including tweets, blog posts and other internet-specific sources: www.drbitcoinpod.com/ultimate-catastrophe-references.

www.ingramcontent.com/pod-product-compliance
Lightning Source LLC
LaVergne TN
LVHW011816060526
838200LV00053B/3801